h
11|7|06

How to Get a 2:1 in Media, Communication and Cultural Studies

How to Get a 2:1 in Media, Communication and Cultural Studies

NOEL WILLIAMS

SAGE Publications
London • Thousand Oaks • New Delhi

First published 2004

SAGE Publications Ltd
1 Olivers Yard
55 City Road
London EC1Y 1SP

SAGE Publications Inc
2455 Teller Road
Thousand Oaks, California 91320

SAGE Publications India Pvt Ltd
B-42, Panchsheel Enclave
Post Box 4109
New Delhi 100 017

British Library Cataloguing in Publication data

A catalogue record for this book is
available from the British Library

ISBN 0 7619 4911 9
ISBN 0 7619 4912 7

Library of Congress Control Number: 2003109253

Typeset by M Rules
Printed in Great Britain by The Cromwell Press Ltd,
Trowbridge, Wiltshire

For Owen, and his 2:1 in Communications

CONTENTS

LIST OF TABLES AND FIGURES

Tables

Figures

ACKNOWLEDGEMENTS

This book owes much to my family and my colleagues, though all its flaws are, of course, my own. Without my armchair editors, Natasha and Carrol, Taran, my technical support, and Owen, my man on the other side of the lecture theatre, half the pages would be blank and the other half typos trapped in the printer.

It's hard to say how much of the advice in this book I owe ultimately to my colleagues. But many years working with Peter Hartley, together with his excellent books, have given me much of what I know on the personal side of communication, whilst Anne-Florence Dujardin continues to show me how little of writing and its teaching I really know. And to all my colleagues at Hallam, past and present, I owe both ideas and inspiration.

PREFACE

It has always seemed to me that people studying media, communications and culture would benefit from a book that links the business of studying to the subjects being studied. After all, studying communications is also practising communications. So that's what I've attempted here, in an introductory way.

By outlining brief first steps towards a wide range of relevant topics, I hope I'll help many students find a way into the richness of these subjects. By attaching those topics to each other, wherever it makes sense, I hope students will gain a better sense of the intellectual interrelationships that weave around cultural and media debates. And by embedding the conceptual in detailed practical advice on communication and learning, I hope I have offered pointers which help prove some of the concepts. 'Prove', of course, has two meanings: to test the concept, and to show that the concept works. Both meanings apply.

One theme runs through the book: connection. The good student makes the links. The better student makes more and better links. Through the structure of the book as well as some of the ideas it advocates, I'm trying to encourage readers to look across subject boundaries and explore the connections between ideas. One such connection is of theory to practice. Another is between communicator as learner and communicator as professional. Others thread between many concepts in the sprawling disciplines of media, communications and cultural theory, and their contributing disciplines. Some links are historical, some are conceptual, some come from application, some from theorizing. My hope is that students reading this book are intrigued and energized by the possibilities of their subjects, so they'll find new connections.

That, I think, is the way to an upper second degree, and even a first-class degree: being able to see beyond what is said to what might also be said. Diligent application of my book's ideas, will go a long way. But the readers who can apply all the practical ideas, and use them to find a new road into their subjects, they are the ones who will get the most from their learning.

Noel Williams
September 2003

I

What is the study of media, communications and culture?

I.I How to do well in media, communications and culture

Read widely. Think critically. Write appropriately. That's all you need to do to get your 2:1.

Of course, this begs a few questions, notably of the 'what?' and 'how?' kind. What do I read? How do I write? What should I be thinking critically about? How do I think critically?

Those are the sorts of questions I'm addressing in this book. No-one can give you the 'answers' in communication, media or cultural studies, because there are no fixed answers in the way that there are in maths, chemistry or French. But I can tell you where to look for your own answers, and how to recognize them when you've found them. I can't tell you how to know more, but I can tell you how to find the knowledge you need. And, whilst I can't guarantee to make you a better communicator, I can tell you what you should be doing, so you can tell for yourself where you're improving and where you need to improve.

Some academics will object to the title of this book. And I'm one of them. It seems to encourage what is called an 'instrumental' approach to study: getting students to do the minimum needed to get through their course, and that's all. If you're inclined to do this, you'll do it with or without my book.

But that isn't my aim at all. You can't create a 'crib' full of all the answers on media, communication and cultural studies (which I'll refer to as 'MCCS' from now on, to save time). You can use this book like a crib, and no doubt it will help some students get through their course with less work than they might otherwise have done. I'm not sure whether that's a good thing or a bad thing. But I do know that a good MCCS student has to do more than this. Getting a 2:1 is about more than knowing a few facts.

My book is about making you into a 2:1 student, not about tricks that make you seem like a 2:1 student when you're not really. From my point of view, this book

I

is about making better students, better learners and so better communicators. The title is just a way to sell the book.

In this chapter I will:

- tell you something about what media, communication and cultural studies consist of;
- outline what you need to learn in order to do well at those studies;
- describe the structure of the book, and how you should be able to use it to guide your learning.

I.2 What are you studying?

Communication is a process, carried out through different media, made meaningful by the cultural context in which it takes place. This means that the same activities can be looked at from three different perspectives. Each of these perspectives emphasizes part of the activity, giving us three different disciplines with overlapping concerns:

- communication studies, which tends to focus on the process of communication;
- media studies, which tends to focus on the media used for communication, especially the mass media;
- cultural studies, which tends to look at the whole social and cultural context in which meanings are made.

So these three disciplines necessarily overlap, which is why this book is relevant to students of all three. Much of the same knowledge is needed by students in all three areas; many of the same concerns arise and the same skills are needed.

But all three disciplines also have their own histories and politics and strive for their own identities. People only ever study communication or culture in a particular context. This context might be very specific and applied, focused perhaps on a specific set of problems in a particular area: business communications would be an example of this. Businesses have a limited set of difficulties, a restricted set of issues in their organizational context – and study of the relevant communications processes can help address these issues. Business communication offers a very clear applied context in which particular processes can be examined. So any course which concerns itself with business communication tends to look at particular processes, especially with a view to improving practice – processes like group communication, report writing, interpersonal communication and oral presentation. (For an example, see Hartley and Bruckmann 2002.)

A rather different context would be to explore the whole nature of meaning-making in human activity, looking perhaps at myth-making, language systems, the social construction of meaning or cultural change over time. In this much grander conception of communication issues, people are less concerned with the application of knowledge to practice, or with particular processes, solutions or skills. Instead they are interested in global aspects of human meaning-making. Here the behaviour of an individual or small group in a concrete situation is of little relevance: what we are interested in is social processes, the nature of culture, the interactions of people in the mass.

Because the media studied in media studies courses tend to be the mass media (television, film, radio, newspapers), media students tend to look at the social and cultural end of communication. Because the processes examined in communication studies tends to be those of particular people in particular concrete situations, communication students tend to look at the personal and psychological end of communication. But there is ultimately no separation of communication studies, media studies and cultural studies; and areas such as sociology and discourse analysis, which have both social and applied dimensions, can equally be found in courses of all three kinds.

So, in this book, it's not part of my purpose to try to tease these three disciplines apart. I'm coming from a communications perspective, so I tend to see media studies and cultural studies as centrally concerned with human communication. But another writer will point out that media are essential to communication, and argue that the study of communications is centrally about the media used. And a third writer will say, of course, communication is a process and it takes place through media, but that it is the history, social context and whole cultural code which determines what is possible with such a medium, what 'counts' as communication, and so how meaning is made.

Any course in one of these areas will have a particular flavour, a particular feel to it which results from the way it deals with some of these tensions. It may, for example, offer you learning which is more 'media-oriented' or 'culturally-oriented' than 'communications-oriented'. Or it may offer you a suite of choices, perhaps through optional units, that allows you to construct in some way the kind of course you would prefer to see. You might be looking for a strongly intellectual review of the range of current thinking on society and culture, in the same way that you might be interested in philosophy or politics. At the other extreme you might be interested in developing a set of skills which you feel will help you in the real world of effective communication and jobs – interviewing, writing, communications technology. Or, of course, you might want a combination of these which lets you look at particular areas you are interested in, such as language, or, perhaps, non-verbal communication or the history of print.

There are so many areas that you might find in your course that no one book can cover them all. But that's not what this book aims to do. Instead I'll offer you two things:

- key skills and knowledge that you will almost certainly need, no matter what flavour or choices your course offers;
- more general skills, sources and strategies that enable you to develop yourself in those areas I have not room to address in detail.

I.3 Multidisciplinarity and interdisciplinarity

MCCS is multidisciplinary. That is to say, none of the three main areas has its own, clearly defined discipline of study, unlike mathematics, say, or history, which have reasonably clear boundaries and a long tradition of studying phenomena in particular ways.

But the approaches used by MCCS come from many different disciplines, and the traditions of study in each of these areas can be traced back only a few decades (mainly to the 1970s). In a very simplified way, you can say that several disciplines existed more or less independently until the 1970s, but at about this time researchers and teachers saw that there were as many links between these disciplines as there were differences between them, especially where the focus was on the things people do with information. Elements of disciplines such as sociology, cognitive psychology, social psychology, linguistics, information science and anthropology were brought together to illuminate the way people communicate and the cultures they create. (Chapter 5 will help you understand some of the many different disciplines that interrelate in this way.)

For a student this is both good news and bad news. It's bad news because it means, in principle, that you need to understand at least the basics of several different disciplines in order to understand the breadth of your own subject. It also means that the potential field of study is immense, because the boundaries between, say, sociology relevant to cultural studies and sociology not relevant to cultural studies cannot easily be drawn. In fact one of the things that continually exercises the intellects of many academics in these disciplines is the attempt to draw these boundaries.

Debates about the distinction between cultural studies and communication studies, or the proper province of media studies, or the relevance of cognitive psychology to mass culture, are generally interesting, and can often lead the reader into new, even exciting areas. However, ultimately such debates do not mean very much, because the boundaries of these studies are pragmatically defined in two ways:

- *By what needs studying.* Often MCCS is responsive to current issues in contemporary life. If MCCS has a value to society in general, then that will largely be in helping us understand the way we live now, how we can improve understanding of the cultures we interact with and the communicative webs we find ourselves in. So the three studies within MCCS almost always have a contemporary edge. They look at contemporary issues, such as the latest moral panic, the impact of innovative information technology, the wider cultural significance of a music sub-culture, or the ways news reporting on the latest war has been constructed.
- *By what people actually research.* This, of course, is something of a circular definition: the object of study of MCCS research is what MCCS researchers choose to research. You might object that, in principle, this would allow academic MCCS researchers to examine anything they liked, anything at all. And you would be right: academics jealously guard the rights of academic freedom, which include the right to nominate anything as worthy of academic investigation.

To prevent pointless research, academia is threaded with various mechanisms for testing and assuring quality. I might be allowed, in principle, to research anything I feel like, but the outputs of that research will be judged in many different ways. Was it published? Was it well received by others in the community? Was the world changed? Do people now understand the phenomenon better? Have other people taken up the issues as something worth pursuing? Will research funders offer money on the work to help it develop and grow? All of these tests, and others, make sure that if someone does engage in a stupid or irrelevant piece of research, they are unlikely to continue in it.

In other words the academic community as a whole, and that includes you as a student, test the value of every individual's work. Although there are a few particular individuals who have a major impact on MCCS research, it is generally not individuals but the whole community who determine what is worth researching and what ideas are worth developing and perpetuating. If no-one thinks it was worth doing; if no-one can understand it; if no-one can apply it to the real world; if no-one will publish it – then the area sinks without trace.

Students may have a relatively small voice in such matters, but they do have a voice. One of your responsibilities, in developing your academic skills, is to do as good a job as you can of evaluating the work put in front of you: whether it's in a book, in a classroom, on the web or in a conference presentation [2.3]. By evaluating, that is, judging the value of all the research and ideas put in front of you, you contribute to collective opinions about the worthiness, or relevance, or appropriateness of that work in general. If students don't sign up for my course on Psychic Communication with Plants, I won't be allowed to teach it any more. If more students want to attend my workshop on New Trends in Interactive Web Design than can fit in the classroom, the chances are that I'll run it twice. If students voluntarily come along to our conference on the History of Radio Advertising, we might think about a class or a publication on the subject. And so on.

So, for a good student, multidisciplinarity has an up-side too. It means you, like everyone else in the field, are an arbiter of the value of particular approaches, particular studies, particular purposes and particular research. There are no limits to what MCCS could study, or to how those studies could be pursued, so the boundaries are set by what people in the field collectively judge to be worthwhile. Part of the trick of being a good MCCS student is to establish criteria for judging what is 'worthwhile', and applying those judgements to the information and activities that come your way.

Through this book I aim to build your power to make such judgements.

A final up-side to the multidisciplinary nature of MCCS for a student is that it can allow you to go in almost any direction you wish. Of course, within the course you're studying there will be limits: the tutors will not have expertise in everything, the library only stocks books in a finite set of areas. So you may find that an occasional interest is too specialist to be pursued. But if you look for interests that connect with what is said in class you should find many things that feel motivating, are relevant to your world, and yet still can be examined within your MCCS perspective.

Some theorists prefer to see the three overlapping areas of 'communication', 'media' and 'cultural studies' as one single, interdisciplinary study uniting all three. As you work through this book, you'll find your view of these three areas is a bit like approaching a crossroads in the centre of a busy city: all roads lead to the same point and connect with each other, but your view of the city and the crossroads itself depends on the road you are taking. A truly interdisciplinary approach to these three areas would not make a distinction between them, and it would see all the relevant theoretical perspectives as capable of integration. Such connectivity would be especially important in terms of the object of study.

However, as you will also see, the many different disciplines and theoretical perspectives that might come together to give a study of 'cultural communication' often do not readily reinforce each other. Sometimes this is for purely historical reasons, but sometimes it is due to more fundamental problems. There is, for example, a big divide between largely 'scientific' or 'positivist' approaches to studying MCCS, and those which take a more cultural perspective. It is not just a matter of emphasis; it can be a fundamental disagreement about the nature of the enterprize, about the worthwhile elements in the object of study.

To put this in an extreme way, a scientific approach may seek to uncover the underlying systematic structure of meaning in language, attempt to describe all its rules, and aim to be in a position to measure effective use of those rules (although no real approach has ever claimed to do this). At the opposite extreme, however, cultural theorists might say that every communication is different, because of the particular unique context in which it occurs, the special relations it holds to all other related communications, and the variation and ambiguity that may be involved.

The first group would suggest that the second group are not really 'studying' anything: they are simply restating or translating one text (that being analysed) into a different text (the analyst's description) and nothing is being learned or gained: it's 'pseudo-science'; it's 'subjective nonsense'. The second group would say that the first is being misled if it believes there can be any objectivity or certainty in studying media, communications and culture; that they only appear to be able to make systematic statements by ignoring critical components of the communication, and that the statements they make are simply artefacts derived from taking a distorted view of what is really going on. These two groups are never going to be happy sitting in the same room.

But you, as a student, have to live with both of them, and all sorts of shades in between. Being a good student means being able to weave your way through these dilemmas and, effectively, deciding for yourself what works best and what doesn't. Chapters 4 and 5, covering many concepts and contributing thinkers in MCCS, lay out the ground you have to navigate.

I.4 What can your course give you?

This question can be approached in three ways: by looking at what it 'should give', 'could give' and 'must give'. But expecting the course to give you things lets you off the hook. Your learning is your responsibility, as well as your university's. So let's turn these three on their heads, and examine what you should try to get from your course.

I.4.I Approach I: what *should* you get from the course?

Any university degree is, pretty obviously, an opportunity to learn. But the learning it offers is not merely facts, information and skills. It aims to develop you as a human being, so that your understanding of the world and of other people, and the way you interact with it and them, is deeper, better, more insightful and more beneficial to everyone concerned. It is about *understanding*: understanding key aspects of the human condition, understanding how you communicate with others, and how culture constrains and enables everything you do. A student with a 2:1 degree should find that out of this understanding comes a wide knowledge of human affairs which can be effectively applied in many contexts, but which can also enrich your experience of many aspects of your future life.

So this suggests that the good student should take on, with serious intent, every aspect of the course, every requirement and every criterion, to ensure that maximum learning takes place, and that understanding is as wide and as rich as the course can offer him or her.

I.4.2 Approach 2: what *could* you get from the course?

Essentially Approach 1 is a passive approach to your course. If it is well designed and the tutors have got it right, the student does his or her best to make sure that all the relevant tasks are performed as thoroughly and meaningfully as possible. Students adopting Approach 1 do everything required, and do it faithfully and responsibly, to the best of their abilities.

However, Approach 2 suggests a more proactive, or interactive relationship with the course. As well as just accepting everything that is offered, and carrying out all tasks seriously and as closely as possible to the stated requirements, the student also aims to develop beyond what the course lays out in its specification. The good student does not merely want to achieve the best results and the richest experiences of what the course offers, he or she also wants to push the boundaries a little, to go beyond what is being offered, to explore new areas, test new ideas, challenge some of the established views, experiment with different approaches, find creative solutions, and look for new routes through the material.

I.4.3 Approach 3: what *must* you get from the course?

This is the instrumental question, asked by students who simply want to pass, to get their degree and get on with their lives. By working out what you must learn, the skills you have to show and the knowledge you have to have, you can carve a path through your degree which aims at satisfying examiners, without worrying too much about what the actual value of that learning is.

This book is not really intended for students who take Approach 3. For a start, they are unlikely to be interested in getting the best possible degree: they simply want to get a degree of some kind, so they are unlikely to read the book. It has not been written to enable a student to take the easiest road to satisfying assessment criteria, although parts of it could probably be used in this way, as it gives many checklists and guidelines which, if applied mechanically, ought to lead to reasonable results. However, I've written it for students adopting one of the first two approaches: who desire to get the best educational experience they can, or to give the best educational performance they can.

Both Approaches 1 and 2, if followed seriously, are likely to lead to a 2:1 qualification. Approach 1 is simplest, because it accepts that everything the course says is the case, and simply aims through application and intelligence to deliver the best responses in each case. It requires hard work, but it may not throw up many difficulties beyond the detailed ones of how and when to do things.

Approach 2 is harder, and more risky, because the student is implicitly challenging some aspects of the course: 'Surely it can be more than this? Why isn't that topic in the course? Isn't there some way that multimedia technologies and content analysis can be combined?' The student is looking for creative approaches to work, exploring the edges of the conventional course.

Sometimes this more adventurous approach can create problems, such as:

- irritating or upsetting tutors by apparently being critical of their teaching;
- getting distracted by irrelevant ideas;
- being seduced by apparently creative novelty which is actually nonsensical.

So students who use this sort of approach typically get more variable marks: sometimes the risks pay off and they get first-class marks; sometimes they fall foul of their own cleverness, and end up with a poor mark. Overall, the variation tends to cancel out, so that a high 2:2 or a good 2:1 tends to be the result. And, of course, the student who gets it consistently right may well end up with a first.

Only you can decide whether hard work and application are enough, or whether a little creative risk should be attempted with the aim of getting a fuller challenge from your course, and possibly boosting your marks as a result. Tutors like to see creativity, such as attempts to bring unusual approaches to bear, or to explore an innovative solution to a problem, or practical work which does not simply follow the mainstream. But tutors also have to assess work against clear marking schemes, and if your work goes too far from the requirements laid down, it may be so 'off the wall' that reasonable marks can't be had. For these reasons, it is perhaps best to combine Approaches 1 and 2: follow the rules, apply yourself diligently, carry out each task thoroughly on every occasion, but keep your eye open for the creative moment, when the small risk that might pay off. Don't hang everything in one assignment or course unit on a single novel approach, but look for small ways that you can explore creative, slightly novel, elements in your work.

You will find some examples of these kinds of creative approaches in Chapter 6.

I.5 Communication skills

MCCS courses are somewhat unusual in that the topics you can learn about may also be the means you use to express that learning. You might, for example, write an essay about writing, or design a multimedia application on communications technology. You might take part in a group presentation on giving a talk, or find yourself analysing texts about text analysis.

This means that much of the time the subjects you are learning about may also help you be a better student: learning about the psychology of information processing might help you understand and improve your own information processing. So there is a special 'meta-skill' that it's useful for MCCS students to acquire – the skill of recognizing when something you are learning about may help you in the practise of your course.

Students sometimes tend to compartmentalize their learning. They may separate what they think their tutors want them to know from the real world they are learning in. For example, you may think that 'persuasive communication' is a topic you would learn about, and perhaps write an essay on, and maybe put into practise in a practical assignment such as designing an advertizement. But anything you learn on that topic might also be useful to you if you have to convince an Examinations Board to approve your dissertation proposal, or give a presentation to get you elected as student representative, or develop an argument in an essay for which you have little supporting evidence.

Good students recognize the value of what they learn in enabling them to learn better, and do not compartmentalize their learning. They see the connections between things, within and across the different parts of their course; they apply theories to their practice; and they use aspects of their practice as examples in their accounts of theory.

Apart from this 'meta-skill', of recognizing communications information that can be useful to you in practice, what are the key skills a MCCS student might require? Pretty obviously these skills fall into two groups – skills needed as a student, and skills needed as a communicator. The first group is often referred to as 'study skills', and the second as 'communication skills'.

I think 'study skills' is something of a misnomer. It suggests, on the one hand, that there are some skills which are only used when studying, and, on the other hand, that being a good student is just about being able to study. In fact, the skills needed to be a good student can apply in many contexts apart from studying. And you may well be able to study effectively, yet still have some difficulties as a student. So we might be better off regarding these as 'learning skills' rather than 'study skills' – ways of being a better learner, no matter what the context you have to learn in. These are the subject of Chapter 2.

Your view of communication skills will depend on your view of MCCS. But, clearly, some people can talk better, write better, interact more effectively or be more persuasive, and these skills are important not only when you leave university, but also throughout your academic career. So, from the word go, you need to hone your voice and be heard. Chapter 3 examines communication skills.

1.6 Using this book

The multidisciplinary nature of MCCS makes my job difficult, as this book needs to be relevant to a wide range of different students. If this was a much bigger book, it might have been possible to address all the needs of everybody who might be studying MCCS. But if it was a much bigger book it would probably be too expensive for most people who might want to use it.

So the way I've designed it is largely as a series of short sections, each addressing a particular topic or area. Generally, you should pick and choose only the sections that apply to you. Although you will find that almost everything in the book connects to your study in some sense, some parts of it will be more important than others, because of the particular way you are studying, or the particular topics you are exploring.

Different students also have different approaches to learning, so I designed this book to be used in any or all of four ways. My four uses are as follows:

- *Structured learning.* Start from the list of Contents and read a chapter or a section as particular needs arise. For example, if you have just begun your course, you are unlikely to want to read the section on dissertations, but you might want to read all of Chapter 2 'What makes a good learner?'.
- *Reference.* Use this book like a dictionary, encyclopedia or bibliography, starting from Chapter 7. Chapter 7 is a trouble-shooting guide. It is an index to all the main topics in the book, a glossary of many important concepts, and also a list of possible problems and questions you might have, for which it offers advice, references to relevant sections of the text, and references to other helpful sources.
- *Browsing.* Use the book a bit like a website, jumping from topic to topic and section to section as you discover subtopics that interest you. You will see that, throughout the book, all the main sections are numbered with a chapter number followed by a section number, like this: 1.6. Cross-references between sections of the book are shown in square brackets like this: [1.6], enabling you to move backwards and forwards through it, taking excursions into topics along the way as you need them.
- *A logical read.* Read it from cover to cover, like most other books, learning as you go. You might perhaps skip-read the whole book early in your course, to develop a good idea of what it covers, then re-read the relevant chapters later, when you need specific support.

You can, of course, read different parts of the book in different ways. My suggestion for how to start is to read Chapters 3 and 4, which give you key guidance on how you can be effective as a learner, and how to develop your skills as a communicator, and then use the rest of the book as reference when you need it.

You may be able to think of other uses for my book. However, I'd probably prefer not to know about them!

HELPFUL TEXTS RELATED TO CHAPTER 1

The following books will get you a long way into the fundamental issues of studying MCCS:

- Corner, John and Hawthorn, Jeremy (eds) (1989) *Communication Studies: an Introductory Reader*
- Durham, Meenakshi Gigi and Kellner, Douglas M. (eds) (2001) *Media and Cultural Studies: Keyworks*
- Fiske, John (1990) *Introduction to Communication Studies*
- O'Sullivan, Tim, Hartley, John, Saunders, Danny, Montgomery, Martin and Fiske, John (1994) *Key Concepts in Communication and Cultural Studies*
- Rosengren, K.E. (1999) *Communication: an Introduction*
- Storey, John (1997) *An Introduction to Cultural Theory and Popular Culture*

2

What makes a good learner?

Introduction to the chapter

This chapter gives you practical help on studying media, communication and cultural studies. It is divided into four main sections:

- an outline of general factors that will help you be an effective learner [2.1];
- how to learn from sources [2.2];
- how to analyse your sources [2.3];
- how to learn in classes [2.4].

2.1 How to be a good learner

Motivation is the key to being an effective learner. One skill of a good learner is to know what is good for you, and how to identify it. An easy but dull class may be of less worth to you than one which is more challenging, but intrinsically interesting. And if you find yourself in sessions which seem dull, pointless or unmotivating (and most of us have had this experience), ask yourself two questions:

- Why does this class seem valueless?
- What can I do about it?

Often the answer to the first question is that you cannot see the point or, if you can see the point, it does not seem to be a point of any importance. And often the measure of importance is that it does not seem to have any immediate impact on the real world of day-to-day living and work. Some students, the moment they hear words like 'theory', 'philosophy', 'concept' or 'ideology', immediately switch off, because they feel that the abstract world of ideas is not 'real' and so of no 'relevance' to the 'real world'. I put all these words in inverted commas because, of course, they are all words which have a huge range of possible interpretations, and will mean different things to different people. Some ideas are always in some sense relevant to some views of the real world. But if we can immediately perceive that relevance, we tend not to think of them as concepts or ideas or abstractions, but as something that is inherent in that real world (as we see it). These are the kinds of things which we tend to judge as 'obvious' or 'common sense'.

The task of the good learner is to turn information which seems abstract and unconnected into something which seems obvious and common sense. It is obvious, for example, that the earth is flat and that the sun goes round the earth. These are common-sense observations, which, it turns out, are completely wrong. But to understand why they are wrong, we have to grasp some ideas which are more abstract than the immediate evidence of our senses.

Or, to take a communications example: it is obvious that, when you talk, you choose the words you are going to use. Obviously, you have a thought and you put it into words. That's common sense. That's obvious. So, if two people meet, they may choose to start their conversation like this:

'Hi. How are you?'
'Great. And you?'
'Oh – you know what they say – mustn't grumble.'

But how much choice are these speakers really exerting in this conversation? You might argue that they make absolutely *no* choices at all in such a conversation: the initial greeting is dictated by the situation, the response is conditioned by receiving a greeting; the answers given correspond to a formula based on the context of the questions; even the phrasing is completely formulaic – no thinking is involved in formulating any part of this conversation.

So, are our conversations controlled by our own choices? Or are they entirely predetermined by a set of social and contextual rules and conventions, with even the form of our language already determined for us by those rules? (For conversation analysis, see [4.12].)

The good communication student is interested in questions like these not merely because they might be of practical value in the real world (people can learn to be better at conversation by recognizing some of these rules and making more conscious use of some conventions), but for their own sake. Once you become aware of such ideas, you suddenly notice that they operate in all sorts of ways in our everyday lives, controlling and enabling various aspects of the way we interact: the whole world of human interaction changes as you perceive how much open choice we truly have.

The good learner will be interested in issues like these and always seeking to fit MCCS ideas not merely to his or her own immediate context, but also to a wide range of other situations, to communications and culture in general.

Of course, if you see yourself as a communication practitioner, an interviewer, a script writer, a speech therapist, such information will also be vital to your work. And, as a student, you will necessarily be practising what is preached – students must communicate effectively. But to learn well in MCCS you also need to try to open yourself up to the belief that very little in human culture of communications is as straightforward or obvious as it might seem to be. The very fact that we are all embedded in our own cultures and communication practices, which seem so natural, makes it hard to learn about others, about MCCS in general, because this seems remote from 'everyday' MCCS.

2.1.1 Make your learning work

Different people learn best in different ways, so knowing what works for you is sensible if you want to succeed. But there are also some processes which contribute to good learning in general, and all good learners try to pay as much attention to these as they can:

- *Recognize that you need to learn.* Identify what it is that you need to know about, and why, and be clear in your own mind about what knowledge, skill or understanding you need to acquire or improve. Recognize your weaknesses and the barriers to learning that you need to overcome.
- *Motivate yourself about those needs.* The more you want to satisfy your learning needs, the more likely you are to succeed in doing so. But if you do not see those needs as a priority in your life, you are much less likely to satisfy them.
- *Monitor how well you are doing,* against the needs that you have recognized. Keep records of how well you are progressing, and take serious notice of the comments and feedback you get from others, particularly from your tutors and lecturers. Feedback may tell you that you have achieved your aims, or it may identify new learning needs or things you still need to do.
- *Fit it all together.* Don't see each part of your learning as totally separate from all the others. Instead, look for connections that help you make sense of each part of it. As we'll see elsewhere in this book [2.3.2], 'making sense' is often about the jigsaw task of relating new knowledge to old.

2.1.2 Remember and relate

A good student tends to have a good memory, especially for assignments such as exams, but in MCCS merely being able to memorize a series of facts is unlikely to get you a good degree by itself. Students with poorer memory, but a more flexible and creative handling of what they can remember, are likely to do better. The real trick is to make good use of what you do remember.

However, you need good factual information to offer good arguments (e.g. to produce good, concrete examples of particular processes or theories). Mnemonics (memory aids) can help in some cases, but a better aid to memory in general is to know the connections between the different facts or points that you want to remember. For example, you might remember that Saussure [5.32] was the first structural linguist, and Lévi-Strauss [5.24] the first structural anthropologist. But if you remember that Lévi-Strauss developed his concepts of structural anthropology from Saussure's linguistic ideas, you know something about the relationship between these two separate facts. Saussure came first, Lévi-Strauss's ideas were a 'development' of earlier ones; structuralism [4.48] did not really exist with Saussure, but with the later generalization of his ideas – and so on.

The more connections between elements of knowledge you acquire, the more that knowledge is likely to stick. So, whenever you come into a new area, try to decide how it connects to what you already know and look for different kinds of relationships. The connections may be obvious or they may depend on an interpretation: one idea may be the opposite of another, or a development from it, or an example of it; or connected by time, by the people involved or by the practical aspects of communication or culture they impact on.

2.1.3 Develop your organizational skills

Good learners tend to be organized, but organization does not necessarily make a good learner. You need to know where to find information of many different kinds. You need to know how to record the results of your research and other learning, so they can be used later on, perhaps in circumstances you have not anticipated [2.4.3]. You need to be able to see the connections between things, and know how to explore them, and how to discover those connections where they are not immediately apparent. You need to be able to create lecture notes, revision notes, reading notes, summaries, web links and bookmarks, files on paper and on disk, working drafts, prototypes and rough cuts, and perhaps backup copies of all of these, and to find them all at need.

MCCS courses tend to contain a lot of information, and to demand that you keep a lot yourself. So a working filing system of some kind will almost certainly make your life easier. This doesn't mean that you need a brand-new filing cabinet, with multicoloured files all containing typed labels arranged in alphabetical order! All you need is a place to store each kind of information you need, and, most importantly, the will to put all information of that kind in that place. The biggest cause of disorganization is not the lack of a system, but the inability to stick to that system. It's too easy to simply place the next paper on the nearest pile, thinking 'I'll sort that out later', and simply build bigger and bigger piles.

The same goes for note-taking [2.4.3]. If your notebook or folder simply records all the notes from all sources in the order you found them, then it's not organized. You might have notes from a lecture on media followed by those from a book on language followed by a series of website URLs on non-verbal communication, then some ideas you had for an essay on social control: your only organizing principle here is 'the order in which I found the information'. Unless you are able later on to remember exactly the order in which you gathered all your information, this only looks organized because it is all in one notebook, but it is really no more than a long list.

There are different ways you can organize things and, unfortunately, the same information can usually be stored in several possible categories. That's why information retrieval is a science, and why you need a single system which you understand and stick to. Common organizing principles are as follows:

- *By information source* (lecture handouts and notes in the same place, web URLs and printouts in another place, notes from the library and books you own in another place). Some people, for example, keep the notes on their own books inside the books themselves, keep all material from digital sources on disks, and all lecture material in a single folder.

- *By information type* (all notes in the same place, all essays in the same place, all handouts in the same place). This is helpful for retrieval when you have a clear sense of the type of record you are looking for – 'I knew there was a lecture on that topic . . .' – but not much use when you are trying to gather all you have on a given topic, irrespective of the type of information it is.
- *By topic.* This is the most common type of system. The difficulty comes with trying to define what counts as a topic – when do you have a new topic? When do you have a subtopic? The easiest solution to this is to say that everything within a particular unit or series of lectures is the same topic (relying on the coherence of the course design). This makes a lot of sense, because you should be able to find all you have for a particular assignment or research task in the same place.

The main problem with all of these approaches is that of cross-linking. Although your course will have been designed as a series of separate units each with its own topic or theme, tasks, coherence and assignment, the reality you are studying isn't like that. Material in one unit is almost certainly going to be connected to, and relevant to, material in other units. It would be an odd degree if this wasn't so: we can divide up the different elements of human communication in order to study them, but 'human communication' is still one large and complex, interrelated topic.

Weaker students tend to stick entirely to the artificial boundaries established by the course design, but better students are aware of the relationships between different modules, and organize their material appropriately. Just as the good student looks for relationships in order to make sense of the subject, so that student's organization of information is likely to reflect that understanding. When this book looks at assessment (Chapter 6), we will see that these relationships can be a major factor in the 'good answer'.

The easiest way to deal with this problem is to include in your notes a few notes about the notes, telling you what other topics you think are related, where those related topics are and perhaps also something about the nature of the link, such as 'Note: "Register" is distinct from "Style" – see lecture notes, week 2'.

2.2 Learning from MCCS sources

This section focuses on research skills:

- finding information:
  - using this book;
  - using libraries;
  - using other sources;

- reading effectively:
- how to choose the right texts for the job;
- how to analyse MCCS texts;
- making notes from texts.

As well as researching information from sources, there may also be a point in your course where you need to obtain primary data for yourself: for example, to carry out research on the general public or on a particular community. These skills are usually needed late in your course, typically when writing a dissertation, so they are discussed alongside assessment, in section [6.7].

2.2.1 Finding information

Good research for a student requires a three-way balancing act. Simultaneously you have to balance:

- the time it takes to find information;
- the importance of the information;
- the time available to read the information.

In other words, you want to spend as little time as possible looking for the information, in order to give yourself as much time as possible to read it thoroughly. Yet you have to bear in mind the importance of the information: the more important it is, the more time you may need to devote to searching for it, to ensure you get the best information sources you can. So the more familiar you are with the pros and cons of different sources, and the means of getting information from them, the more efficient you are likely to be.

Within your university:

- Know the location of the main subject sections in the library, for all relevant material.
- Be aware of all the different media that might hold relevant information.
- Locate information in advance of the need. Don't wait until the last minute, as most of your colleagues will be doing the same.
- Set up good working relations with other students so that you can share resources, and help each other track down resources when they're missing or scarce.

More generally, wherever possible, bear four key skills in mind:

- Identify the right sources for the job.
- Search with a clear focus.
- Use a variety of sources.
- Use information critically.

2.2.2 Identify the right sources for the job

Make sure you consider all possible sources. Not all sources will be suitable for every task, so you need to be familiar with them all to make the best choice for each task that arises.

Libraries Libraries are sources of both long-term and short-term reference information. If you don't know where to start your information search, then you may as well start with the library. Library information may be indexed in various ways:

- by author/editor;
- by topic area;
- by title;
- by accession (i.e. the order in which the library acquired the material).

Become familiar with the cataloguing systems in the libraries you have access to. Usually there is one main university library, but there may be others belonging to particular colleges or departments. The most common cataloguing system is the Dewey decimal (DD) system, which is now almost a universal system among libraries in the UK because of its comprehensiveness. However, remember that even this system isn't absolutely complete (there are provisions for libraries to add their own sub-categories) and it is also open to interpretation: for instance, when books might belong under more than one heading. Communication topics may be filed under writing, psychology, business, computing or sociology, for example.

Here are some of the main DD codes you may wish to remember:

- 020 Library and information sciences; the latter sometimes includes texts on communication.
- 028 Reading, use of information media.
- 071–9 News media, journalism.
- 121 Epistemology (theory of knowledge): although relevant texts may be found almost anywhere in philosophy (120–9), this is the most likely area for theories relevant to MCCS.
- 126 The self, 127 The unconscious and the subconscious, 128 Humankind: these three numbers may be used by libraries in quite different ways. However, the social nature of communication and culture means that they often contain relevant texts.
- 150–8 Psychology.
- 190–9 Modern Western philosophy.
- 300–7 Social science and culture.
- 390–9 Customs, etiquette and folklore.
- 400 Language: again, almost any category here may be relevant, but numbers after 430 are specific to individual languages, so the earlier numbers are likely to be the most used, especially 410 Linguistics, 419 Verbal language, 425 English grammar, 427 English language variations.
- 700 The Arts and 800 Literature: there may be some relevant items here depending

on how your course is tailored. Of possible use are: 729 Design and decoration, 770 Photography and photographs, 808 Rhetoric.

Make sure you examine the exact system in the library you use. If a book isn't under the decimal category you expect it to be, check other related categories or cross-check by title or author.

Remember also that libraries don't simply hold books. You can find a great deal of other kinds of information in the typical academic libraries, such as:

- journals and periodicals, both current and archived;
- reference works, such as dictionaries, organizational directories and encyclopedias;
- abstracts, which are essentially collections of summaries of other articles and books, essential for tracking down all that is currently known on a particular topic;
- catalogues of other libraries.

Don't forget the most useful resource, however: the librarian. Librarians have esoteric expertise which few lay people are able to acquire. Many university libraries dedicate particular librarians to particular subject areas, so get to know who yours is. Don't bother them with trivial queries that you can easily address yourself, but don't be afraid to broach complex or difficult tasks with the librarian before you attempt them. Often the librarian will simply suggest a topic area or an abstract to look at; but sometimes he or she is willing to go to great lengths to track down the relevant material for you.

Online resources   Any library resource may be held in paper or electronic form. In addition, you may find online databases, search engines and reference resources which help you track down bibliographical and other information. You may be able to use these yourself, if you have access and the skills, or you may have to rely on a librarian to use the resource for you.

Online sources can be quick, easy and flexible and can offer quite complex searches. However, they may require some technical expertise to use well, and creating helpful queries can sometimes be difficult: for example, when there are many texts on your topic, or when the keywords are used in different fields. A search for all articles on 'communication', for example, will throw up thousands of possible resources, and will include material from such fields as engineering (telecommunications), computer science, military research, artificial intelligence and literature.

The key to using online resources effectively is to identify keywords which will yield the references you want and only the references you want. This may mean that you need to make several attempts at your search as you try to identify the best combination of keywords to do the job you want.

Using websites for research   As with any other resource, you have to use websites critically and with care to get the best out of them. However, websites have some problems less obvious in other information sources.

Firstly, they vary widely in the quality of information, because anyone can make a website. Although this is a big strength of the medium, it is a weakness from the point of view of someone trying to evaluate the quality of information. The authority of an academic source can usually be determined from that source: an article in an internationally circulating journal or a chapter from a book published by a reputed academic publisher (such as Sage) is likely to be more authoritative than, say, a booklet available free in a Sunday paper. But there is no equivalent for a website.

If it is not clear from the website what the authority of the site's author is, be careful in relying too heavily on what is said. Authority, of course, can come from a number of different sources: the writer's qualifications, experience, current role and responsibilities or other credentials; the extent to which other people cite the writer as an expert; or other publications by the writer. If you can't get any of this information, this does not mean that the writer has no authority, merely that you should be very careful in interpreting the information.

Even if the author appears to have authority, it might not be authority in the subject addressed by the text: having credentials in communication doesn't mean someone is a good source for information on Shakespearian tragedy or the history of film.

Secondly, websites often have unclear purposes. Whilst many do declare what they are supposed to be there for, more do not. Some may even be unclear to their originators. Some websites are simply collections of personal accretions, like the junk collected in a drawer: people create them because they like creating them, not because they have any particular directions or intent. Other websites combine several functions, without distinguishing between them all that clearly. For example, a site giving information on a country, may also be persuading the readers that it is a good place, and its ideology [4.23] and government are to be supported – in other words, what can in part be descriptive information can readily turn into persuasive political propaganda. Many websites are essentially promotional, either simple advertising or more subtle persuaders: what purports to be helpful information on examination turns out to be self-promotion (e.g. where 'the key features of our services' are listed, this often turns out to mean 'look how much better we are than our competitors').

These persuasive and promotional functions can be found as much in academic (or pseudo-academic) websites as elsewhere. So be careful how you read any web document. Do not just take it at face value: look for indicators of its true purposes, and watch out for any 'hidden persuaders' which incline you to accept the document at face value rather than taking a critical stance towards it.

Human sources As well as librarians, other people may be useful sources of information and ideas. Other students, including those on other courses and in other years; tutors and lecturers on the course, but also, perhaps, elsewhere; administrators, who may help you track down places or people who hold particular information; and even friends and relatives, who may have relevant knowledge and experience – all should be considered as possible sources of information.

More formally, organizations and groups of particular kinds may hold information or opinions that can help you. Much communication is organized in nature, facilitated, maintained or carried out by people in particular groups. Culture, of course, is a social phenomenon. This means that there will nearly always be groups constituted with an interest in the area of communication or culture that you are researching. Of course, their interests are likely to be partial, biased by particular perspectives, history or expertise, so you need to treat what they offer with critical care; but for any contemporary investigation they can be very important sources of data and secondary information.

Audio-visual sources   Communication and culture also involve artefacts, of course, so these may be of use to you in information gathering, either as sources, or as objects of study. Audio-video sources such as film, video, DVD, CD-ROM, slides, photographs, radio and audio-tape may all hold information you need to investigate. Don't neglect these alternative sources.

2.2.3 Use a variety of sources

Your job is to find not only relevant sources but also a *range* of them, tailored and combined for the purpose. The good student does not merely locate lots of information, but uses information of different kinds, synthesized from different sources. When you are exploring a new topic, it can be particularly useful to select a variety of sources, as:

- browsing or scanning many different sources can give you an overview of the area, and tell you something about the different kinds and quality of information available;
- comparing different sources allows you to practise your critical skills and helps you evaluate the complexities of the field and the way it is handled by others (i.e. the process of making sense by finding relationships [2.1.2]);
- trying to establish the range of different ideas in the field tells you something about how much consensus or disagreement there is in it, and whether you can simplify it for your own purposes.

Using a range of information from different sources almost certainly means you will find contradictions and conflicts in that information. Your own accounts will need to reconcile these conflicts in some way. Literature reviews can be very important in social studies like media, communication and culture, as the strength of your own argument depends very heavily on that of your sources and how you handle them [6.5.5]. In order to give a balanced and critical account, you need to bear in mind the various principles of critical analysis (discussed in [2.3]), and to use the following approaches in your note-taking [2.4.3] and essay writing [3.2.2]:

- *Summarize all the different viewpoints you have found.* This shows the range and depth of your understanding.

- *Show how and where different views differ, and coincide,* and explain why. This shows your command of the field, and of the historical, theoretical or conceptual difficulties which led to the various competing views.
- *Look for ways of combining different viewpoints.* For example, are apparent contradictions really different examples of a more general truth? Would the different viewpoints make sense in different contexts? Are the different ideas developed from different purposes of the analysis? This can show your logical skills and creativity.
- *Don't force different ideas together if they really cannot be reconciled.* Sometimes there are simply several contradictory ideas, theories or beliefs, and they all exist (religious faiths offer good examples of this). Your task in such cases is to try to explain why different viewpoints exist, and to evaluate their adequacy in respect of the particular topic you are exploring.

From a student's viewpoint a comprehensive source can often be most useful. Everything will be contained in one source, saving a great deal of search time. That source may also do much of the job of synthesizing and reconciling different views. If you do decide to use such a source, try to get hold of the best and most up-to-date one in the field. (You will find some advice on possible sources in Chapter 7.)

However, you should beware of the key flaws such sources may have. They tend to summarize other people's views, rather than present them directly, so what you are getting is watered-down extracts, not the thing itself. Consequently you are getting the editors' interpretations of those ideas, which may mean that they are more superficial than in the original, or simplified in order to make them fit within the constraints of the book. Editors also may have their own agenda and their own viewpoints.

2.2.4 Search with a clear goal

The best rule for getting good information is to be clear about what you are looking for. Why do you need this information? What is it going to be used for? The clearer the goal you are trying to achieve, the easier the search is likely to be, and the more obvious will be the solution when it arrives. Examples of clear searches might be:

- A factual search: How long was the telephone in use before mobile phones became popular?
- A search for opinions to support an argument: I need three different writers who believe that communications technology leads to changes in social interaction.
- A search to generate a hypothesis about a problem: 'Moral panics' occur when a particular moral issue is foregrounded by popular media. What theoretical perspectives might explain why this occurs?

Sometimes an assignment task will make the goal of your search clear. If it doesn't, then seek clarity by getting further advice.

Where you have a complex information need, such as trying to compare and contrast [2.3.3] competing theories of audience (see [3.1], [4.2], [4.31]), you can clarify your goals by breaking the more complex search down into a series of smaller ones: What are the main competing theories of the audience? Within each, who are the main authorities? What is the key text in each case? What are the three key ideas in each text? By trying to answer specific questions that are useful to you (without losing sight of the overall purpose), you are likely to find your search easier to handle and complete.

If for some reason, after much searching, you have not found what you need, making your goals clear at the very least identifies the gaps that need filling. If you really feel you don't know where else to go to satisfy them, you may need to take these goals to someone else for advice: a librarian, a tutor, or perhaps another student, who may be able to suggest either ways of changing the goals, or ways of getting a different kind of relevant information. Sometimes, for example, there simply isn't any information on the topic you are looking for. You may need an expert to tell you this, and this will then help you formulate a strategy for generating that information, through primary research.

2.3 How to analyse MCCS texts

Much academic work, both for students and lecturers, involves critical analysis of the work of other people. You'll find that this phrase 'critical analysis' is often used to set apart academic activities from more mundane ones (like the difference between listening to a conversation and studying a conversation, for example). The same phrase is often used to distinguish the work of the better students from those who are seen as less capable: if you want to get the best degree you can, developing the skills of 'critical analysis' can be one of the most useful activities you can engage in.

In this chapter we'll briefly look at why academics value this set of skills, including a glance at their practical value, then we'll spend a little more time on a breakdown of the skills and how you might develop them.

2.3.1 Why do it?

Critical analysis is valuable at two levels. At the more abstract level, such skills are needed in order to develop an objective, disciplined, fair and balanced judgement of the information you are studying. In other words, they are at the heart of the academic claim to objective judgement in the appraisal of phenomena. At a more concrete level, and probably more meaningfully to most people, they are the skills you need in order to ensure that you get a well-argued, properly-balanced study, whether it's in writing an academic essay, conducting an original piece of research or assembling information for a presentation.

Remember, your aim as a student is to assemble and present the best information for the job in the most appropriate way, which means not merely getting information [2.2.1] and not merely re-presenting or describing it, but also selecting from everything available a balanced and representative collection of the most suitable material.

This means, for example, that if you are writing an essay entirely based on desk research (e.g. material you have gathered in the library), your aim is to extract from the collection of readings that you've made exactly those observations and conclusions which are most worthwhile. This word 'worthwhile' tells you that you have two key problems:

- How can you judge the worth of an observation, or a collection of observations? (This is a problem of deciding *value*.)
- How can you fit the observations to the outside world? (This is a problem of deciding *relevance*.)

You need to be able to do these tasks in as controlled and as critical a way as you can manage. Otherwise you run the danger of simply taking for granted everything that any writer says, which means you may be misled by poor argument, or find yourself simultaneously agreeing with two contradictory conclusions. If you are to use the findings of other people's writing in your own work, or you are to recommend to other people how they should employ findings (e.g. the outcomes of two different surveys), you need to be skilled in evaluating those findings.

If you aren't able to develop these skills, then you run the following risks:

- *Descriptiveness*. If you don't analyse the information you get in any way, you'll find yourself merely reporting what other people say. At its worst, this kind of writing becomes mere lists of other people's observations, and generally suggests that the writer has no real understanding of how the different views fit together. It also suggests that the writer lacks opinions of his or her own, merely recording the collected opinions of other people.
- *Confusion*. If you don't select appropriate material from your sources, and somehow link it together in effective ways, then your presentation may appear arbitrary, and disconnected, with apparently odd selections of text linked in incoherent ways.
- *Trivialization*. If you are unable to assess the value of the material you are using, you may miss the most important points and simply report the simplest, most superficial aspects (especially as these are often the easiest to find out about and the easiest to understand).
- *Disorganization*. Even if you have selected appropriate material, if you do not have a logical way of connecting and accounting for those selections, your presentation may appear badly organized. A reader will not be able to understand why the particular texts or ideas you have chosen are supposed to connect with each other.
- *Inappropriateness*. Without reasonable judgement, you cannot know whether what you are writing about is suitable or not. Often a student asked to defend a particular choice of source, or a particular quotation, will say it seemed 'relevant'. But a choice has to be relevant *to something*; a choice cannot be relevant by itself, it has to fit with a particular context or perspective. Understanding, in this sense, is about knowing how things fit together: what selection of what text or idea is appropriate to a particular argument or discussion [2.1.1].

2.3.2 How can I do it?

All these abstract claims sometimes make 'critical analysis' seem a rather difficult area for students to address. It sounds rather too much like philosophical debate and rather a long way from the everyday common-sense processes of human communication or cultural practice. However, it's not really a very difficult idea at all. Critical analysis boils down to two essentials:

- *Analyse.* Don't merely describe, report, or receive information. Analyse it. Look at its parts, look where it's coming from, look how it's made up, look at its purpose and context.
- *Be critical.* Stand back from the information or idea. Don't wholeheartedly subscribe to it, or reject it, the moment you come across it. Does it have some validity? Does it imply some difficulties or problems? What is behind it? Under what circumstances would it be true – but also what would make it false? If it seems 'self-evident' or 'common sense', why is this the case? What are the preconceptions which make it appear to be inevitably true? Remember that many such statements appear true to those who make them because they are unable to take a critical standpoint. So look at the implications of those statements, the 'taken for granteds' that were necessary to make such statements seems inevitably true [2.1]. Also, bear in mind that many MCCS perspectives developed precisely to do this sort of job (e.g. deconstruction [4.16], critical linguistics [4.13]).

MCCS students need to develop a healthily critical attitude to every idea they come across. Everything you hear and read is based on certain attitudes, conventions [4.11] and traditions. Much of it is based on vested interest, misperceptions, ideological bias, research limitations, cultural prejudice, and so on. Even a text like the one you are reading now is not a 'neutral' guide on how to be the best student you could be. It is written by a particular author, with particular expertise, a particular cultural and personal background, a particular set of views on what is good and bad in MCCS, and so on. All of my perceptions and preconceptions mean that this text will probably have a particular slant, particular strengths and weaknesses, which I am (by definition) unlikely to recognize. It's up to someone else, you, the reader, to take a critical attitude to this text; to decide what is worthwhile and what less so; to determine what can be used, and what should be regarded with a slightly sceptical air.

So, how do you apply the skills of critical analysis to a source? There is not really a 'best way' to critique a document. (In what follows, we'll assume a standard written document, such as an academic article or chapter. But, as we've seen in section [2.2], it could be any other similar source: a speech, a website, a film, a broadcast, a lecture.)

The way you approach the task of critiquing your text depends on factors such as:

- your experience of the area discussed in the document;
- the time you have to do the task;

- the reasons for making the critique;
- the people you are writing the critique for;
- the overall context in which you are working.

You can use this as a checklist so that you can work out what approach you should take each time you are expected to develop a clear critical analysis.

Whatever the specific context, the questions and issues in this section will guide you as you assess any discussion or academic paper. The first step is usually to extract the key points from each paper. Key points include information such as the following:

- What are the main *theories* on which the paper is based?
- What are the main stages of the *argument*?
- What *evidence* is being offered to support the argument?
- What *conclusions* are being reached?

You can usually reduce a paper to an abstract – a series of sentences which contain these key points. They might be actual sentences taken from the paper, or they might be your own summarizing sentences. Most people, in reading a paper, are effectively making such a 'list' in their heads, as a means of understanding what the paper is saying.

If you want to prove this, read an academic chapter or article today and then write everything you can remember about it tomorrow. You'll find that certain 'main ideas' are all you can remember, though you might also remember one or two clever phrases which summarized one or more of those ideas.

The list you produce gives you something to evaluate. You can then begin to judge the worth, or value, of the individual points you have identified. To write a good critique, you want to be as explicit as possible about the criteria you are using to make your judgements.

Let's take each in turn:

Theory   There will always be some sort of theory behind any discussion, even if this is not mentioned.

For example, much survey work is based on the theory that studying a sample of a population will tell you something about the whole population. You might say that such a theory is obviously true, but it is not necessarily so. Suppose there is a bias in the sample. Suppose the questions are answered arbitrarily by the respondents. Suppose the whole theory is invalid. (For example, we might be able to prove that every different sample of a given population gives you different results for that population. Would this suggest a flaw in the basic theory?)

So almost always you need to look for the underlying theory, and reflect on it. What sort of assumptions are built into the paper? How valid are they? What possible problems relate to that theory? Is it being applied appropriately?

Are the theories stated explicitly, or are they implicit? If the authors do not say what theories they are using as the background to their work, why do you think this is? Are they trying to disguise the basis of their work? Are there some potential problems with the theory in this particular case?

How well accepted is the theoretical basis of the paper? Is it a 'standard' theory within MCCS, or is it new and untested? Is it contradicted by someone else's work? Think of other theorists you've read about: Are there different theories which would wreck the argument offered in this paper? Can you think of other theories which would explain the same phenomena?

For all these questions, you might get an idea, a note or a comment. Sometimes, of course, such questions lead you nowhere, and sometime they are unanswerable. But much of the time they will lead you to some sort of comment or follow-up which can be a hook you can use when discussing the paper in your essay, or when you come to link this piece of reading with another one.

Argument   Academic writing (and much other writing, such as much report writing [3.2.3] and speech writing) invariably presents an argument. This argument will be the gradual development of a case that is being made, something like a legal argument being advanced in court, one point at a time. However, the argument will not necessarily be a clear one, it might not be given explicitly, and there is no particular reason why it will be perfectly logical. You might expect that academic writers aim for an explicit, coherent and logically argued case, but you'd be surprised how often this ideal is not achieved.

So ask yourself questions about the nature of the argument. Is it clear? Are all its stages worked out? Do they follow logically from each other, or are there some stages which seem unclear, or which are mere assertions rather than logical implications?

For example, if the article uses a word like 'therefore', this suggests that the author thinks two statements are logically connected. But this is not necessarily true. Suppose I say 'Clapton used a Fender. Therefore he was a great guitarist.' Both statements could be true, but they do not necessarily follow from each other. I might just as easily have said 'Clapton used a fish finger. Therefore he was a great guitarist.' What appears logical may not be.

You need to recognize that language and logical thought are not the same thing. It is quite easy to construct perfectly acceptable English sentences which are nonsense or meaningless. Use of words like 'because', 'therefore', 'consequently', 'however', and so on, suggest logical relationships between sentences or parts of sentences, but it is up to you to test the logic of those apparent relationships. (We will see how you can use these keywords in [3.1.7].) Each time you see a connection like this in the words in front of you, examine the link to see if that connection is as logical as the author seems to think it is.

Evidence   The heart of any academic discussion is the kind of evidence being offered.

An example: in the play *Othello* the main character (surprisingly enough, called 'Othello') concludes that his wife is unfaithful, and so murders her, because he sees a handkerchief. Most people would regard possession of a handkerchief as insufficient evidence of unfaithfulness. Some people can be persuaded to believe things on very slim evidence.

In the case of Othello many factors combined to make the evidence seem persuasive. Similar factors may be operating on you. Othello was predisposed to be jealous, because of the beauty of his wife. You may be predisposed to believe the article because you want to agree with the conclusions. He reacted emotionally to situations. You might rely on apparent gut feelings without thinking things through. He was in a social and cultural context which made his marriage a source of tension (he was black, she was white). You might be prejudiced according to the culture you belong to or the socialization you have experienced.

An academic (at least, a good one) wants clear, objective, reliable evidence. Ask yourself what information is being used to support the argument. Are you being given facts or opinions? Are statements that look like facts actually really opinions?

For example, if I say 'the BBC is clearly an anti-establishment broadcaster', I have merely asserted a belief. It may not, in fact, be clear at all, and I've offered absolutely no factual information to support my assertion. If, however, I say 'the BBC produce more programmes that criticize government policy than does any other channel, as the data in Table 1 show', I've tied my statement to some actual hard evidence.

Merely referring to evidence does not mean that the argument is correct, however. The evidence could be poor, or subjective. For example, it is common academic practice to quote other authors in support of the writer's viewpoint (as your tutors will expect you to do in your writing). Quotes are evidence of a kind (they show that someone else has a similar opinion), but they are only really evidence of what someone else says, and you'd be perfectly within your rights to say 'How do they know?', that is, to question the evidence on which the quoted statement is based.

Where any appeal is made to an authority (e.g. a key figure in the field), you, as reader, are entitled to judge the value of that authority. Just because the person referred to is well respected and a key figure in his or her field does not mean that everything he or she says and does is right. Why is this person an authority? Does this mean that the quoted statement must be true? Suppose the Pope was to say that he knew the Australian Prime Minister was an alien. Does the respect and authority due to him make this statement true?

Be aware also that you are likely to be influenced by the status or nature of the person or group quoted. This is most obviously seen in politics and popular culture. Whose 'definitive judgement' on rock music would you rather trust: George W. Bush, Mick Jagger or Princess Anne? Would you trust the same person's opinion on legalizing cannabis? On fox hunting?

Ask yourself questions like: How accurate is this information? How reliable is it? How up to date is it? Are the statements made actually supported by the evidence, or are they inferences, subjectively 'reading in' to the data?

Objective evidence will be 'hard facts': numeric data, survey results, actual statements by interviewees, the results of experiments, first-hand ethnographic observations. You need to assess the sources of these data to judge how good or appropriate they are. How up to date are the sources? Are they appropriate sources for the purpose? Are there many mutually supporting sources, or is the author relying solely on a single source? Is the research or analysis that led to the data presented for you, or is it not mentioned? What sort of use is made of the references? Does the author maintain a critical and balanced attitude, or simply accept them lock, stock and barrel? (For example, does he or she apply the kind of analyses that your own critique applies?)

If the information is derived from a study of some kind, you need to consider how good the study was. Was it properly constructed? Did it ask the right questions? Did it look at the right phenomena? Were there any problems with the data collection?

Where evidence is not objective, it may still be useful, but it has to be used carefully, with constant provisional statement. Try to judge how true the evidence might be. Does it fit with your own experience? Does it fit with the information available from other sources? Does it link to the information given by other articles?

Conclusions   Do the conclusions follow from the argument and the evidence? Or are there some hidden assumptions or some omitted stages?

For example, suppose an article says: 'We've shown that more people watch soaps than the news. We've also shown that the news is less violent than soaps. So we conclude that the reason people watch soaps is because they are more violent.'

Does this conclusion necessarily follow from the evidence? No, it does not *necessarily* follow. All we can actually conclude is that there may be some relation between TV violence and people's viewing habits. But they could be watching soaps for completely different reasons (e.g. perhaps soaps contain more humour, or more escapism).

How generalizable are the conclusions? Okay, so they work for the material given in the paper, but will they work in other contexts? Which kind of contexts? Can you think of contexts where they might not apply? The more generalizable the conclusions are, the more useful they are likely to be, the more relevant to a range of situations, rather than merely to the example, or the sample, that is discussed, and the more likely they are to suggest a workable theory of the phenomenon they apply to.

Are there exceptions to the conclusions, or to generalizations from these conclusions? How important are these exceptions? What do they say about the argument that has led to these conclusions?

In much applied work, conclusions will be used to justify recommendations. If a paper contains recommendations, you may need to consider other questions. Do the recommendations follow from the conclusions? Could any other recommendations have been made? Why have these particular recommendations been made rather than any others? Is there any hidden agenda (e.g. do the authors have something to gain by focusing on one recommendation rather than any other?).

2.3.3 Compare and contrast

When you have an analysis of a series of articles on your topic, you need to consider the relationships between the different articles. As we saw when examining possible sources, almost certainly you will have mixed judgements about each one. There will be some aspects you are convinced are accurate and well argued, whilst others will seem weaker. Now you must pit each article against the others.

What are the similarities between different articles? And what are the differences between them? Do they support each other, contrast with each other, or perhaps contradict each other? Where they support each other, does this mean that they strengthen each other's arguments? Where they contradict each other, which is the best of the competing arguments? Why do you judge it the best (remembering your judgement of the quality, worth and relevance of the points within that paper)?

What are the good points in each paper and what are the bad points? You should try to synthesize the good points from each paper, and prune away the bad ones. Remember, however, that in your synthesis it may not be possible to fit every opinion and piece of evidence together. If, for example, you have two excellent but contradictory studies, your job is to point out precisely how and why they contradict each other, to assess the validity of the contrasting points of view, to suggest reasons for the differences of opinion, and suggest how they might be reconciled.

For example, you may find that that one study suggests that people prefer watching DVDs rather than videos, whilst another study finds the opposite. What is it about these studies that allows them to come to opposite conclusions? Did they study different groups of people, perhaps? If they did, can you identify the difference between these groups which might correlate with their different preferences?

Your own conclusions need to be a balanced appraisal of all that you have found. Don't simply emphasize one set of views at the expense of all the others. Instead, examine alternative views and show why they are problematic. Then establish what it is about your preferred view which makes it better than those you have dismissed.

2.3.4 A summary of critical analysis

If you want a few watchwords to guide you in creating your critique, remember these:

- Be as objective as possible.
- Be as critical as you can.
- Evaluate everything.
- Always test the evidence.
- Always judge the validity of the argument.
- Look for contrasts in the information.
- Look for interrelationships in the information.
- Keep asking yourself 'How do they know?'
- Find connections between different papers.
- Test conclusions by applying them outside the study.
- Use your own experience and knowledge as a testbed.

Here's an example, a draft of an essay, for you to think about. Read the text, and as you do, make some notes on it using the criteria and sorts of questions outlined above. Then look at Table 2.1 which follows, in which I've raised some issues you could have thought about.

'Computer games aid literacy'

Literacy simply means being able to read and write. Computer games aid literacy because children have to read instructions from a screen, so they need a large vocabulary.

Games will be good for boys, who, research shows, are less likely to read than girls are. More boys play computer games than girls do. So boys are likely to become more literate from games than girls are. Consequently there will be more literate boys than girls.

Some games, such as Discworld, use language in a creative way and set problems for the player. They will learn new words and have to use language in unusual ways. Therefore the player will be more literate after playing the game than before.

Furthermore, Delilah Morris says that computer games can be read in the classroom like fiction. They can be studied in the same way that Shakespeare, for example, might be studied. This means that players of computer games will actually be better at reading certain kinds of discourse than people who do not play such games.

In conclusion, although computer games may make some people less literate, there are many ways that they make players, especially boys, more literate.

Table 2.1 *Critical comments on 'Computer games aid literacy'*

Sentence	Comment
Literacy simply means being able to read and write.	Possibly okay, but who says this is what it means? Are there any different views? Why say 'simply' – is this a way of trying to pretend that it is less complex than it really is?
Computer games aid literacy because children have to read instructions from a screen, so they need a large vocabulary.	Okay as far as it goes, but is it the case that *all*, or even most, computer games require people to read screen instructions. Perhaps an example or two would be good here. What is meant by 'large'? Obviously to read some instructions a sufficient vocabulary is needed, but what is the evidence that this vocabulary is large, or that these instructions cannot be understood from 'everyday' vocabulary. What if someone were to say that the vocabulary required is actually very small? There is no counter-argument built in here – it's just the author's word against that of the objector.
Games will be good for boys, who, research shows, are less likely to read than girls are.	This absolute assertion is rather stark. It might be better if qualified by 'probably'. Better, however, would be to leave this conclusion until after the argument which is about to be given. In any case, this statement does not follow in any logical way from the previous paragraph. 'research shows' – it's a good idea to support your viewpoint with research, but much better would be to say exactly what that research is, and give a reference so it can be checked. Even better would be to quote the research, so that the authority for this statement lies with the source and not with the current writer.

Table 2.1 *cont.*

Sentence	Comment
	Furthermore, even if the research says this, how effective and accurate is it? Is this conclusion reasonable from that research (e.g. perhaps it was only conducted on a certain age group).
More boys play computer games than girls do.	A commonly held belief. But is it true? How does the writer know? What's the evidence?
Consequently there will be more literate boys than girls.	This statement does not follow logically from the previous one. Even if computer games do make more boys literate than girls, it does not follow that more boys will be literate than girls are: for example, girls may be literate for many other reasons that don't affect boys. This may *appear* logical because of the connecting word 'consequently' and because the comparison seems very similar to the previous one. But it is false logic.
Some games, such as Discworld, use language in a creative way and set problems for the player.	Here we have a vague phrase 'some games', but immediately backed up with an example. The reader will want to know what is meant by 'creative use of language', and also 'set problems'. So more detailed examples would be helpful.
They will learn new words and have to use language in unusual ways.	This seems a reasonable implication following from the previous assertion, except that there is no guarantee that someone encountering new words will *necessarily* learn them. A better version of this argument would illustrate each of the assertions (a new word and an unusual use of language) and explain why solving a problem in a game might lead to learning the word. For example, it may be that the player has to learn a 'password' in order to progress in the game, in which case the assertion that new words are learned may be a reasonable one.
Therefore the player will be more literate after playing the game than before.	This is a highly simplistic conclusion. However, if we accept the initial simple definition of 'literacy' and the argument above, then we could accept this as a logical conclusion.
Furthermore, Delilah Morris says that computer games can be read in the classroom like fiction.	It's a good idea to use a specific authority, though the reference should be given. The writer also attributes the opinion to the authority. However, the word 'furthermore' seems inappropriately used here, as there appears to be no connection between what has gone before and this point. The reader would expect this to be a developing point, something which builds on the previous argument, not a completely new topic.
They can be studied in the same way that Shakespeare, for example, might be studied.	It's not clear if this is the writer's opinion or Morris's. This would need further investigation, e.g. by reading Morris's original article.

Table 2.1 *cont.*

Sentence	Comment
This means that players of computer games will actually be better at reading certain kinds of discourse than people who do not play such games.	A very complex statement. Firstly, we might not be sure what 'this' refers to – is it the fact that computer games can be 'read' like fiction or studied like Shakespeare?
	Secondly, the phrase 'actually be better' suggests that the opposite position has at some point been proposed, either explicitly or implicitly. The only plausible way of interpreting this is that the author believes that her/his readers will believe this opposite position through 'common sense'.
	Thirdly, the phrase 'certain kinds' is vague. We want to know what the particular discourses are. (Note that the writer has implicitly included the concept 'computer game' in the notion of discourse, though this has not been introduced anywhere in the essay. Is this reasonable? Does it perhaps imply a particular theoretical position is being adopted?)
	Finally, why does this point follow from the previous assertions? The fact that computer games can be read like Shakespeare does not mean that they will be, or that the reading is of any value, or that it will have any impact on the reader. Nor does it follow that those who only read Shakespeare are going to be in any way inferior (or, indeed, superior).
	In other words there is no evidence for this interpretation or conclusion.
In conclusion, although computer games may make some people less literate, there are many ways that they make players, especially boys, more literate.	This is a conclusion, in the sense that it ends the essay, but it actually introduces a new idea, that games may make some people less literate, and this is inappropriate for a conclusion. The conclusion should really be a restatement of the key points in the main body, and a summary clarification of the assertions that result from these. It should not introduce new material.
	In fact, this points to a big weakness of the whole essay. There is no counter-evidence offered to any of the points made. This is weak in many ways. It means that no objections to the points made have been forestalled. It means that the overall argument is simplistic, incorporating no differences in viewpoint. It means that there has been no attempt to review all the available evidence, arguments and sources.

As you can see, the critical perspectives you take on other people's writing could also be applied to your own. We'll look at this in Chapter 3.

2.3.5 How to use references in other people's work

When you are reading the work of others, whether it is with a specific purpose in mind (e.g. preparing for an essay) or more generally (e.g. background 'reading around' a topic), you should be doing more than simply trying to understand and assimilate the information in front of you. Everything you read, or come across, that might be relevant to your course needs to be treated as potential source material. Whilst this is obviously true for things like set books and course readers, and the references tutors give you as part of their classes, it's also true for absolutely any source at all that you may, potentially, use in your work. So, for example, items such as journal articles, newspaper and magazine articles, websites, CD-ROMs, professional information sources (e.g. information on professional standards and practices), cultural artefacts (e.g. films, adverts, TV programmes), may all be either sources of information or objects of study.

A good discipline is to keep notes [2.4.3] on everything you read and all potential sources with each item annotated with full bibliographical information. One way to do this is to begin your notes on any topic on a fresh page (in case it subsequently wants filing in a different place from your last lot of notes), with the top of the page being a complete and correct bibliographical reference for the source. This can be helpful to you in several ways:

- It helps when creating and completing bibliographical references.
- It gives you a detailed and concrete heading for your notes for when you return to them in the distant future, making them easy to find and easier to remember.
- It saves you effort when you come to use the notes for a future practical purpose – e.g. when you use them in writing an essay. It can be really frustrating for an essay writer to complete the wonderfully argued piece of writing and 'only' have the bibliography left to finish the work, merely to find that you don't have good bibliographical information for your sources. You're then faced with a dilemma – either submit the essay with poor, incomplete or inadequate references, and inevitably lose marks as a result, or else go through the same research process that you've already once completed, in order to recover your sources and complete the referencing.

So you'll be a better note-taker, a better writer and less annoyed by the bibliographical aspects of writing if you keep full bibliographical information with your actual notes on sources. This need not be difficult to compile either, as a photocopy of the title page of your source book can often give you nearly all the information you need; and you can always annotate this with any information it does not contain.

References within other people's writing can have several uses for you, so don't ignore them. For a start, they can be helpful examples of how referencing can be done, and how it can be used to support writing. More helpfully, the list of references in a text, and the associated bibliography, can be a chain of evidence leading you deeper into the understanding of your subject. There's a long list of potential uses of references. Here are a few of the most common:

- *To lead you to other sources of information.* By locating one central (key, seminal) text, and using that as a starting point (working through the most used references, checking out the most interesting items in the bibliography), you can locate sources which are most focused on your specific topic.
- *To verify and assess the quality of the information you have discovered.* By following up references, you can test how adequate the source is, checking that it has used its information in an appropriate way. You can get some understanding of the worth of the argument, or potential holes in it. You can assess the extent to which the piece is original or derivative.

- *To 'cross-validate' information.* This is a researcher's term: it means 'to check one source of information against another'. By chasing up the references in your reading, you can see if the sources they are based on are actually saying the same thing, or perhaps in conflict in some sense.
- *To understand, and to evaluate, the strength of an argument*, the validity of a point of view, the relevance of a judgement, the quality of an interpretation. Often you will find in the pieces you read statements like '*x* argues that' or '*y* seems to suggest' or 'the data in *z* study clearly indicate . . .'. These are all interpretative statements, interpretations of other sources. How do you know if these interpretations are reasonable ones? Well, you can either take the statements on trust, or you can check the sources.

You will need to use references yourself in your own writing. When you do, bear all the above points in mind, from your reader's point of view. We'll look at this in more detail in [3.2.5].

2.3.6 Some common abbreviations in academic texts

Academic texts use their own conventions, which sometimes includes abbreviations derived from Latin. Table 2.2 lists the most common ones.

Table 2.2 Common academic abbreviations

Abbreviation	Meaning
ed., eds	editor(s)
edn	edition
e.g.	(exempli gratia) for example
et al.	(et alia) 'and others' (used when a book has several authors, as in 'P. March et al.')
et seq.	(et sequentia) 'and following'
f., ff.	'and the following' (to refer to page numbers as in 'pp. 30 ff.')
Ibid.	(ibidem) 'in the same work' (as previously cited)
i.e.	(id est) that is/that is to say
loc. cit.	(loco citato) 'in the passage already cited' (that is, in the same passage referred to in a recent reference note)
op. cit.	(opere citato) in the work already cited
p., pp.	page(s)
passim	here and there throughout a text
sic	exactly like this (usually where a quotation seems unusual)
trans.	translator, translation, translated
viz.	(videlicet) 'namely', 'in other words' (usually after words or statements, about to be elaborated)

2.4 Learning from MCCS classes

The fourth part of this chapter focuses on class activity, from the point of view of effective learning and self-organization. In particular, we will look at:

- efficient use of study time;
- meeting deadlines;
- effective note-taking;
- effective project work;
- working in seminars;
- working alone and working in groups;
- using practical tools for learning.

2.4.1 Efficient use of study time

It is generally true that the more time you spend in study, the higher marks you are likely to get. However, you can study too much, just as you can study too little. Whilst not studying enough may leave you unprepared, spending too much time studying may harm your performance through exhaustion. And the mere fact of sitting with an open book on the desk in front of you does not mean that you are studying. You need to assign quality study time, protect it, use it as well as possible – and then the rest of your time should be less troubled with pressure or guilt of work undone.

In particular, bear in mind the attention curve (Figure 2.1), derived from cognitive research [4.7]. This graph shows the amount of typical attention (hence learning) over time. You'll see that attention is high to start with, and rises a little early on, then, after about a third of the session, falls off quite rapidly, and continues falling until it gets very low, before picking up a little again towards the

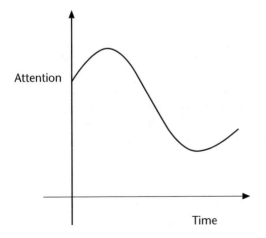

Figure 2.1 *The attention curve*

end. You'll also notice that it doesn't say how much time this takes: there are no units or scale given. This is deliberate, because the timescale for this curve is largely irrelevant, as long as the learner knows roughly how long the whole period is going to be.

For example, in an hour's lecture, the learner usually arrives reasonably keen, wanting to know what the session is going to be about, wanting to learn something interesting from it. Early on in the lecture the learner takes quite a few notes, and feels that he/she can really get to grips with this topic and get something out of it. But between ten and twenty minutes in, this enthusiasm fades away, and continues to fade for the bulk of the session, until it reaches a low of 'very little learning' about ten minutes from the end. At this point the learner realizes that (a) the session will soon be over and (b) she'll therefore get a break, whilst (c) she hasn't been paying attention very much for the last half hour so (d) she's not really understood most of what's been said, and so (e) she had better get a few notes down so the whole session hasn't been wasted: so her attention lifts again for a short period.

What can you learn from this?

- Recognize that it is natural for attention to wander and learning to fade over time.
- Recognize that the best learning is done at the beginning and, to a lesser extent, the ends of sessions, so make the best use of these times.
- Be aware that anything you can do to lift attention locally at any time within a learning session will also lift attention globally (i.e. if you pay attention more at a particular moment, it will take longer for your attention to sink back to its previous low) – so varying the learning process can be a good idea.
- Don't set learning sessions which are too long. The longer they are, the greater the middle period of low attention will be. Better to have several, different shorter learning sessions, because the beginning of each session is likely to lead to better learning than the middle of a longer session using the same time slot (i.e. three different hour learning slots will give better learning than one three-hour slot).

So this means, when working out how to make the best use of your time and study well, bear the following in mind:

- *In each study period, focus on a clear task.* If you simply sit down to 'read something', you won't know why you are reading, what the relevance of particular parts of that reading are, how you can select the most useful information, what you should be learning, and so on. Unless you are merely reading for entertainment or to scope a particular area (e.g. to check out if mass communication [4.29] is an interesting area to study), you should study with a particular goal in mind: to answer a question, to find support for a discussion point, to understand the main claims of a particular author, and so on.
- *Use short periods of learning, broken by shorter breaks.* A study session of about an hour, followed by a break of ten minutes, makes good sense: an hour is not too long to get bored, long enough to learn something new, and not so far away from the 'break' that you don't feel motivated to complete the work in time.

- *If it doesn't work, stop.* Often students feel they have to read a book cover to cover in order to know 'everything' on the topic. This is frequently a mistake. In the first place, one book won't tell you everything, no matter what its claims. On the other hand, it will probably contain too much for your particular purposes, so you will end up with too much information you can't use. This is one reason why studying with a clear goal makes sense: you can judge pretty accurately when the book has served its purpose.
- *Variety will probably help.* Study in different ways, using different media, in different environments, for different periods.
- *Take seriously any course recommendations on the amount of time needed for a particular piece of work.* Most courses will suggest how much work you are expected to spend on a particular task. For example, it may be the expectation that every hour in the classroom is to be matched by two hours reading relevant material, or that ten hours should be spent writing a particular essay. Take these guidelines seriously, but treat them only as guidelines.
- *Don't copy the habits of other students, unless they happen to work for you.* Different people learn in different ways, but the bad habits of other people won't help you work better.

2.4.2 Meeting deadlines

Deadlines are irritating, but necessary. Without a deadline some students would never stop writing, and a few would never start. The communication professional has to meet deadlines, sometimes very tight ones: journalists may have twenty-four hours to file a story; civil servants may have to write advice to government at one hour's notice. In these contexts, three weeks to write an essay would seem luxurious.

When working with a deadline, the first task is to be certain of when the deadline actually is, and the second to know the consequences of missing it. If '4 p.m. on Friday' means that delivery at 4.05 p.m. on Friday results in a mark of zero, this is an important deadline that you must meet. But if the deadline really means 'some time before Monday morning', and the penalty is merely that your tutor will be a little miffed, you could probably deliver by lunchtime on Monday and suffer no more than a lecturer's irony. So be certain where you stand with deadlines. Usually, ignorance is no excuse.

Of course, meeting deadlines is also courteous and in your interests: if you are persistently late, tutors will begin to look on your work negatively; and the later you are, the more serious the consequences you might have to face.

Four rules can help you to meet difficult deadlines:

- Do important work first (that which is essential, or pressing).
- Do difficult work first (as this will take the most time).
- Construct a schedule for each task, with a timetable of subtasks.
- Stick to the schedule. But if priorities change, don't be a slave to them. And don't be tempted to put problems off.

If the worst comes to the worst, and you're going to be late unavoidably:

- Contact relevant parties (tutors, administrators, other students).
- Be clear about why you are late – don't deceive yourself. Try to be honest with others, too.
- Secure a clear date and time for an extension, and stick to that. An organized student should never need to renegotiate additional extensions.

The most common reasons for failing to hit a deadline are:

1   You start the work too late.
2   You do not realize how much work is needed.
3   You do not realize how difficult the work is.
4   You can't find usable resources.
5   You have personal difficulties, such as illness or family problems.

Problems 1 to 3 are largely in your control, and so are your responsibility and unlikely to be seen by tutors as good reasons for delay. The solutions are obvious: start early, analyse the amount of work involved and work to a plan.

Sometimes problem 3 comes out of the blue, where even the best-laid plan proves unhelpful. Here you should immediately seek help, probably from a tutor. Usually unanticipated problems occur because the task is unclear, because you have missed or misunderstood the task or context, or because the tutor has not realized there are potential issues of the kind you have come across. In all three cases the tutor should be the most appropriate source of help and, even if not, seeing him or her early may help you solve your problem by yourself. At the very least, it will alert him or her to your difficulties if, later on, you feel the need for the extension.

Problem 4 may be partly down to you: for example, if you've left it very late to look for resources. Or it may be a resourcing issue – the library doesn't have enough books for the students; the computers keep crashing because they're getting old; the video can't be booked because another course needs it. Such issues should be brought to the attention of the appropriate people, as it is unreasonable to ask students to carry out particular tasks if suitable resources cannot be made available.

The best way of protecting yourself against this problem is to make sure you have good resources well in advance of the need. Here the quality of your early information gathering [2.2] and note-taking [2.4.3] may be put to the test. However, if you were not sufficiently on the ball to get notes in advance, or to buy your own texts, and you can find nothing of reasonable quality on the web, and no-one you know can lend you suitable resources, think about the following possibilities:

- Do a different topic or assignment from the choices available to you.
- Negotiate a variation of the task with the tutor, one which allows you to use different resources. For example, the tutor may be willing to consider an alteration to the essay title which lets you use materials of a different kind.
- Carry out some original research, to generate your own data for the task. (For

example, if you were to produce information about how people vary their speech in different situations [4.27], you could visit those situations and record actual practice.)

Problem 5 should be treated by all reasonable universities as a valid justification for an extension. However, what counts as valid varies from place to place, even from course to course, so it is in your interests to check out the relevant regulations and procedures. You also need to be clear what your options are: sometimes an extension is not the best solution. If you've been ill, for example, you are unlikely to get a really good piece of work in for your very last deadline. But perhaps simply getting an adequate piece of work in will be good enough if, for example, it won't depress your overall mark below a critical threshold.

2.4.3 Effective note-taking

When we listen, we do not pay the same amount of attention all the time, as the attention curve [2.4.1] shows. So *effective* listening means being able to focus attention specifically on the things being said. Note-taking is the most useful way to do this. As your attention switches between hearing and writing, the shift is likely to make both activities a little more successful. As you hear things, you have to turn them into meaningful notes: you are not just hearing sounds, but trying to turn them into coherent meanings which make sense to you, and record them. In the act of writing, you are gleaning the important information from what has been said, and partly translating it into your own forms of expression.

It's unlikely that you have been taught how to take notes. Most people learn their techniques without any training or even reflection – they simply do it. So it's worth looking at your note-taking habits to see how they might be improved. Think about the following:

- What do you take notes for? (Is it record keeping? Is it for revision? Is it to give a basis for essay writing? Is it to help you understand the topic? Is it simply because everyone else does it?)
- How do you take notes? (Do you simple write virtually everything down, without much reflection? Do you only note down facts? Do you annotate your own notes with comments, ideas and issues of your own? Do you note possible relationships with other information? Do you organize your notes exactly as in the source, or do you create structures that are more useful to you?)
- How do you use your notes? (Do they simply sit in an file, never to be opened or looked at? Do you only use them when revision time arises? Do you use them in lots of different ways, depending on need and circumstances? Do you sometimes find your notes useless and have to return to sources?)

Answering questions like these should help you develop a better note-taking technique. If your notes are merely to help you focus on lectures, and you never use them outside the lecture, you might as well throw them away afterwards – but you can still examine how useful they are in helping you understand what has been said. However, if you expect them to have some use outside the session, as most people do, the better you can relate the notes to those purposes, the more use you are likely to get out of them.

For example, if you expect to use them mainly as spurs for essay writing, then annotating them with your own ideas, issues and suggestions as they come to mind may make them a much more useful resource. But if you expect to use them primarily for revision (e.g. largely as a record of the topics mentioned in a lecture), then your own annotations may interfere with later understanding.

Sometimes notes have good content, but are hard to decipher because of their physical arrangement on the page. The simplest way to improve your notes, if they are hard to read, is to use lots of white space. If you leave lots of space between and around notes, each note will be easier to read; you are likely to write in slightly larger and clearer handwriting; and you leave yourself space for future annotations, or for drawing connections between topics if needed.

Note-taking as a way of working   Outside classes, some people find they work best by writing everything down – others make few, or perhaps no, real notes, whether in class or outside. If you do make notes, you are likely to remember things better, because the act of writing requires you to consider, critique and select from the information around you. But if you turn note-taking into a slavish copying of everything you come across, without applying any judgement, you are unlikely to be engaging with the material, and all you are doing is providing yourself with copious material to use as learning material later. Revision should be a process of *re-learning*, of consolidating what you already know; not a process of learning for the first time.

If you don't like to take notes, or find them useless, it may be that you are taking the wrong sort of notes. Or it may be that your learning style is such that copious lists of words simply don't work for you. For example, you may be a strong visualizer, interested perhaps in the semiotics of advertising [4.44], in creating your own website [3.4], in non-verbal communication [4.33] – areas which are fundamentally not verbal. Such interests might be indicators that language is not your preferred form of communication or of learning. (These interests don't necessarily indicate that, of course – there is a great deal written about all these subjects.) In such a case, perhaps graphical note-taking is the way to go.

Possibly the easiest way to create an organized account of the structure and content of a talk is through a mind map (also called 'brain pattern' and 'spider diagram'). This technique is also useful for generating information, see [6.4.3]. If you want a simple, quick, yet rational and organized note on a talk, try using a mind map.

Alternatively, it may be that the easiest way for you to work is to annotate texts, interleaving post-it notes or scraps of paper left at the right page within your books. As I read, I always have a notebook or blank piece of paper to hand, and scribble on that instead. The key thing is to use conventions which are consistent and familiar (so that when you return to your notes in six months' time, you can still understand what they're about). I use the following conventions in my notes, which you are welcome to follow if they help.

- All notes have a title, author or speaker, date of publication or lecture.
- Each topic is given a heading, and subtopics are indented below it.
- Exact quotes are put in inverted commas (quotation marks): if from a book, then a page number is given; if from a talk or meeting, then the initials of the speaker are given.
- If a note makes me think of a problem, objection or query about the point, I write a comment in square brackets next to or under the note, with a question mark at the beginning of it (this shows me that it's my query, not a question asked by the lecturer).
- If I have a bright idea of my own, I put this in square brackets, and place an arrow in the margin pointing to it.

Be honest with yourself about your notes. Know what works for you, and don't sucker yourself into working practices which some clever academic has told you will improve your learning, if you actually find them an irritating distraction.

2.4.4 Effective project work

Almost certainly in a MCCS course, you'll be expected to do some practical work. The requirements might be quite extensive, although usually there are choices to be made so you do not engage with all the possible practical activities that are on offer. Possibilities include:

- practical research, such as conducting surveys or interviews;
- applied writing tasks (such as business reports, copy writing, proposals);
- applied graphics tasks, probably combined with writing (such as advertisement design, or a visual presentation);
- use of specific software packages (e.g. spreadsheet, database or presentational software);
- web page or multimedia design;
- radio, video, film or TV work.

Clearly these all demand very different skills, though there are many overlaps between them. One book cannot cover them all, especially the technical specifics of such tasks as using a video camera or multimedia authoring software. However, at various points in this book I give you advice on many of these tasks, and much of the general communications advice can be applied across the board. For example, this book's advice on audience analysis [3.1.1] applies to just about any medium and any purpose.

So what are the general skills that might apply in *any* project work?

Firstly, you need to acquire the relevant technical skills. This might be how to white balance a camera, how to add graphics to a web page, or how to analyse survey data: a long list of possible skills could apply here. The more you acquire, the more versatile you will be, and also you'll find it easier to promote yourself when you eventually step into the full-time job market.

However, the best students recognize that technical skills are only a means to an end, and do not get distracted by the fascination of the tools and choices made available by the technology or medium. The best possible lesson to learn when faced with a new technical area is that you will never learn everything there is to know about that system: by the time you are coming close, it will have been superseded by something else.

But you do not need to know everything about that technology or skills area in order to be competent in it. Confidence in its use is much more important than comprehensiveness, especially the confidence to go about learning something new about it. When you first learn to word process, for example, you do not learn every result of every menu selection and keypress before you can type interesting, useful and well-presented work. In fact, most users of word processors never use many of the functions available to them. But almost every user produces work adequate to their needs. And the good users, the really skilled ones, are those who know how to develop additional expertise when the need arises. In particular, they learn how to:

- experiment;
- undo the mistakes their experiments make;
- use available help and support resources;
- adapt material and lessons they already have;
- use the tools efficiently;
- find out more about the tools.

These are examples of the generic skills you can develop in project work:

- *Learn how to experiment with the tools and the medium.* Don't be afraid to make mistakes. And when you do, don't be afraid to examine them. Often, the best learning comes from understanding how a particular flaw arose. Sometimes, the most creative enterprises result from earlier false starts. For example, it is not unusual for someone creating a video or a web page to return to an earlier, discarded, design in order to re-develop later ideas.
- *Be sure you can return from any experimental action to an earlier, safer version, if needed.* This means: make copies, save copies, store copies in an effective and organized way. If you keep all your earlier work, you can always retrace your steps, and always combine the good features of your first design with the good features of a later one to create something better.
- *Be aware of all available sources of help and information.* Make use of them when you need them. Different people do have different preferences here, so recognize what yours are, and try to make sure that you have what you think of as the best help available. Possibilities include: built-in help facilities; online help (e.g. the university's

intranet); relevant manuals and textbooks; helpsheets provided by the tutor or organization to go with the project resources; the tutor; other staff; other students; and external experts.

Different sources may be most useful for different needs, and therefore you should try to make the best use of *all* the resources available to you, rather than just relying on your friends, the tutor or the online help.

- *You don't have to do everything from scratch.* The good learner can adapt and build on earlier ideas, earlier designs, discarded plans, drafts, sketches, outlines, false starts, incomplete ideas, and so on, to build new projects in different areas. Often creativity comes with a leap from one domain to another.

  This does not mean 'always use the same ideas'. It means quite the opposite. Try to be creative, novel, innovative: look at everything from several different perspectives. That's one of the big advantages of studying media, communication and culture: everything around you is both a theoretical construct, something you can study from some perspective or other; and, at the same time, it's a practical illustration, an artefact which might give you ideas for your own practice.

- *Train yourself to look at every example of communication around you*, to see what you could learn and how you might use that learning in your own practice. The two obvious ways to do this are:
  - Look critically at all communications: how would you have done it better?
  - Look admiringly at all communications: how did they do that, and how could you do the same?

- *Develop a range of technical skills and understanding.* This is last in the list deliberately. Skills in using the medium and the tools are important if you are to do a creditable job. But they are seldom the most important: they are merely a means to an end. They can be a distraction, and it is rare in the professional world that any individual masters the whole range of relevant skills: they understand the nature of those skills, and they acquire the basic expertise, but they focus on specific areas of expertise and rely on others, in teams, to offer the expert-level skills that a truly professional job requires. No TV producer or video games designer carries out every element of their craft themselves. But all professionals understand the skills of their colleagues, and the needs for them, and seek to combine their different expertise in the most effective manner.

This means that one global skill for project work is generally team work. Often your project will be a group project, as this is the only practicable way some projects can be achieved in an educational context, and it is the best model of the professional context. But even where the project appears to be individual work, you may be reliant on other people for advice and input. In almost any complex (i.e. real-world) project in communication, you will be working with material that someone else has created, and, therefore, potentially, may need to interact with those people to alter or improve the nature of that resource.

So, develop your social skills. You will particularly need these when working in seminars. (Some relevant texts are: Argyle 1994 and Hartley 1999. See also [4.25], [5.1].)

2.4.5 Working in seminars

Two of the commonest complaints by lecturers about students is that they 'don't do the work for seminars' and 'don't participate in seminars' (and workshops and tutorials). Some students see lectures as the real point of learning (this is where the new information appears that they have to learn to reproduce in the exam) and seminars as something you have to attend because you have to attend. This is a very instrumental view of what learning is about, one typical of the student who is happy to get by without much involvement with his or her own education.

Of course, part of the reason for students' disinterest in seminars may be that the lecturers don't use them very well. Sometimes lecturers themselves are not very clear of the purpose of a seminar, or are somewhat nervous about the subject area, and so fall back on what are basically 'mini-lectures with opportunities for a student to say something'. If you find that you keep getting seminars of this type, which are essentially merely opportunities for the lecturer to say some more about a topic, then you need to find ways of challenging the seminar as it is presented.

Actions you might consider are as follows:

- Make efforts yourself, or with some of the other students, to move the session closer towards its supposed purpose. For example, make a point of asking questions and offer examples that enrich the learning session based on your own reading and experience. Try to get other students to respond to what you say, rather than merely sit there wondering what you are playing at.
- Have a quiet word with the tutor after the session ('I quite enjoyed that session, but parts of it didn't seem much like a seminar to me, and I know some of the others are wondering what the difference between a seminar and a lecture is . . .').
- As a last resort, make a more formal representation to someone else with responsibility for the academic success of the course. Such a representation does not need to be a complaint, as such, of course. Complaint is the best strategy in some cases, but also could be counter-productive (if, for example, it inclines the professional lecturers to close ranks 'against' the 'unfair' criticisms of students who 'don't understand what's good for them'). Usually better is a more neutral framing of a 'concern' or 'worry' or a 'lack of understanding about the function of' the area you want to complain about.
- Generalizing the problem may be one way to approach this: 'We've found that several seminars aren't really seminars at all, because there's no real student involvement. Many of us feel this is not the right way to use this time, and were wondering if some tutors could rethink their approach to use of seminar time.' Although this is a rather fuzzy and unspecific sort of 'complaint', that is precisely its virtue. No-one can say, as a result of this, which tutors are being complained about, or which students are doing the complaining. It is a general issue for all the course providers to think about, rather than a personal attack on a particular tutor by an identifiable group of students.

Getting the best out of seminars   Assuming that the tutor has got it about right, and is making her or his best efforts to deliver a worthwhile and appropriate seminar, then the value of the session as a learning experience depends very much on the students. In a lecture this is much less true: the lecturer is in charge. She or he knows what the topic and structure is. She or he has a logic, a timing, an argument, and appropriate illustrations and information designed to make optimal use of available time in presenting that topic. The primary intention in most lectures is to get information across to students' minds as effectively as the medium allows (which, in fact, is not very effectively – lectures are supposedly only about 30% efficient in transferring information; but they are a cheap way of doing it). Interruptions by students sometimes only subvert that intention, unless the lecturer has planned for student involvement at particular points.

But seminars are supposed to be about students' involvement in their learning. So student 'interruption' is not really a possibility. A well-constructed seminar does get learning points across, but it does so by enabling the students to discover these points for themselves, rather than the tutor telling them what they should think.

This is why 'guided discussion' is often the approach a tutor chooses for a seminar. The idea is quite simple. The tutor nominates a topic which all students should know something about, and which they should already share some information on, and then, by asking questions and developing responses to students' own questions, enable particular learning points to emerge from the discussion. Sometimes the objective of the discussion is very broad indeed: 'to air some of the problems in x', or 'to alert students to the conflicting viewpoints in the literature on y'. Sometimes the objectives are very narrow: such as 'to ensure that all the seven main factors in readability are known to students'; or 'to enable students to identify the three major issues that need clarifying in a political economy of the media'.

A wise tutor will have reasonably clear objectives in mind, and will have built the seminar in such a way that she or he expects those objectives to be achieved. But she or he will also suspend that version of the seminar if it takes an unexpected turn towards a different value. One of the great virtues of the seminar approach to education is that, because students have a voice, the discussion can move in unpredictable directions, which may turn out to be more valuable for learning than those originally planned by the tutor. It's the tutor's job to recognize this, and to allow it to happen where it works; but also to regulate it if it goes too far from the topic area, or prevents key learning from taking place. This can be a fine balance. (How far is 'too far'? What learning is 'key' and what can be omitted?) Students can help by recognizing what is supposed to happen (a good tutor will tell you early in the session what the aims are and how the session should work), and cooperating in that plan, regulating their own behaviour so the tutor doesn't have to.

For example, if the topic is 'violence on TV', and discussion turns to 'war reporting' and then moves to 'the USA's agenda in the Middle East', the tutor is likely to feel that discussion has strayed too far from the main purpose. But the very fact that this topic has emerged from discussion suggests that it's of interest to the students, and they want to pursue it. A good tutor will recognize this, call a halt to the discussion, summarize its key points, remind the students of what they should have been discussing, and promise to return to the interesting discussion on imperialism and the East/West divide later in the course.

But not all tutors will handle it so well, so a good student should recognize this, and do what she or he can to plug the gap. Possible actions include the following:

- Suggest to the other students that they've strayed from the topic.
- Offer the tutor an opportunity to interrupt and redirect discussion (e.g. 'Do you think US imperialism relates to the media portrayal of violence?').
- Try to move the discussion back towards the tutor's intended topic.
- Offer a suggestion to the group or the tutor on how they could go forward ('I think this is really interesting, but it's not really about TV violence, is it? Maybe we can discuss it in our student group tomorrow, or perhaps Professor Plum will incorporate something on it in his sessions on the economics of the media, if we ask him').

There are a few quite simple things to bear in mind as a student in a seminar which can help you to get the most out of it:

- Ask questions when opportunities arise. Most tutors are grateful for questions, because it makes them think students actually do want to know something!
- Don't be afraid to raise an issue or ask a question if you're not clear about some point. You may think you're the only one who doesn't understand, but the chances are that others are in the same boat. Even if you are the only one who hasn't understood the point, no tutor can help you if they're not aware that you have a problem.
- If the seminar relates to another learning session, use the opportunity to connect the two. In particular, use the seminar to clarify anything that seemed a problem in the other session.
- If the seminar calls for preparation of some kind, do it. Many seminars simply can't work if too few of the students have managed to read the chosen chapter or carry out the preliminary investigation of newspaper headlines, or whatever the task was. The consequence of failure to prepare at a personal level is that you probably won't get much out of the session, and collectively tutor and students are likely to end up wasting most of the seminar as the time is 'filled' with some sort of desultory discussion. So it's not the behaviour of a student who wants to get the best possible degree.
- Try to involve other students in the discussion. This is properly the tutor's task, of course, but some tutors are not very good at it. Your knowledge of the interests, understanding and experiences of other students may help you to direct or redirect information to bring others in at particular points, or you can simply refer a question across to someone else in a general way: 'What do you think, Kylie?' Often Kylie, who may be shy of contributing and reluctant to respond if asked a direct question by the tutor, may respond differently if asked by an equal, another student.
- When asked a question, respond fully, and try not to close the discussion down. For

example, if you are asked a closed question, don't treat it as closed, such as: 'What size is the optimum small group for decision-making?' Don't simply say 'six' and leave it at that. Instead, use your answer to open the discussion. For example: 'Research seems to suggest it's six. But it seems to me this might depend on the kind of decision-making, so this number is decontextualized. For example, shouldn't all the stakeholders in a decision be represented if the decision is to be representative? So to argue that there's an optimum number without thinking what it's for seems it might be too abstract to be useful. What do you think, Kylie?'

2.4.6 Working alone and working in groups

Some people prefer to work alone, and others work best in groups. In most professional situations, you have to do both, though the balance can be radically different for different professions. As a student, you can get advantages from both ways of working, and you need to learn how to do best in both contexts to get the best from your course and to prepare yourself for your subsequent professional life.

Key benefits of solo work can be:

- a lack of interruption and distraction;
- the opportunity to concentrate;
- the ability to follow your own interests or preferences without having to justify them;
- to test your own abilities without the aid of others;
- privacy (allowing mistakes, trial and error, etc., without risk);
- control of your own time and pace;
- the ability to learn in a manner which is particularly suited to you.

However, in order to get these benefits, you need to be very honest with yourself. You need to carry out some self-analysis to be clear in your own mind what works, and what doesn't work, for you. For example, some people prefer absolute silence for study. Any noise distracts them. But others like a background noise, which may feel comforting or familiar, making study feel more 'normal'; or they may like particular noise (e.g. a particular kind of music) because of the mood it creates.

Similarly, the environment can help or hinder your search for effective learning. Some libraries seem conducive to study, for example, being quiet, yet filled with other people engaged on similar tasks. Working alone in a library you can feel that you are one of the scholars, engaged on proper academic discovery, in a way which you might be embarrassed about sitting in your front room with your Walkman on and a packet of cheese and onion crisps propped against your textbooks.

Find out what works for you, and what doesn't, and don't deceive yourself about the truth. It's easy to pretend that what really helps you study is writing your essay whilst watching *EastEnders* with your mates playing balloon tennis over your head: this sounds like fun, and it's the sort of environment undisciplined learners claim is most 'friendly' and 'comfortable' for learning. But it's actually unlikely to be a good learning environment, and you are probably fooling yourself if you think such things.

Some people work better early in the day. If this is you, discipline yourself to get up early, and do some work before you get onto other things. For example, you might try writing in the morning, before going off to class – this can often be a much more profitable use of an hour than trying to write late at night when your body clock has slowed down and you are exhausted by the day's work.

But some people do work better in the evening, or even at night. Young people, especially, can get an intense buzz by staying up late into the dark, studying intently. Older students, of course, tend to tire more easily. But, if you are a 'night person', there is no reason at all why you should not do most of your work after 8.00 p.m., if that is *truly* the most effective way for you to learn.

Effective group work Research on group communication which looks at team work (generally in the fields of business and management) suggests that teams work best when different team members fulfil different roles. Sometimes this occurs naturally, but sometimes there are conflicts. Belbin (1981, also effectively summarized in Hartley 1997 and Hartley and Bruckmann 2002) suggests that effective teams share the following characteristics:

- There are a limited number of roles which members fulfil.
- Because of their personality [4.37] traits, particular people only tend to fill one or two roles, but they fufil the same roles in different teams and contexts.
- The overall effectiveness of the team depends on how these roles combine.

Belbin identified eight roles (named slightly differently in different stages of his work). These are shown in Table 2.3 opposite.

You can see how some of these roles might fit together in the same person (e.g. the role of Team leader and Team worker might go together, and the Monitor-evaluator and Completer might be the same person, as both imply a certain thoroughness and attention to detail). So getting an effective group does not mean that you need eight people, but it does mean that you need to address all the above in some sense within your group, and the smaller the group, the more work each member has to do.

Furthermore, some of these roles may be more attractive to some members than others, so there can be some internal conflict as members compete for particular roles (e.g. everyone might want to be Team leader or Innovator). There's no easy way to resolve this. However, you can point out to your group the following:

- If some roles remain unfilled, the group as a whole will suffer.
- No matter how attractive a particular role is in principle, it's best to accept a role that suits your personality.
- There can be good learning outcomes from attempting a role that might seem unattractive, as it means you have to think about aspects of the problem you might otherwise not have.
- By comparing your group with the roles as laid out in the table, you might be able to produce an 'overall' map of how everyone might fit, rather than try to do it on a first come, first served, competitive basis.

Table 2.3 *Belbin's group roles (adapted with permission from Hartley and Bruckmann 2002)*

Role	Typical activities within the group	Implications for group learning
Coordinator	Organizes and coordinates activities and other people Keeps the team focused on its main purposes Keeps other members involved in the activities	Person needs to help others Person needs to have clear sense of group purpose and needs Needs to have some respect or authority, and be accepted by the group as a 'leader'
Team leader	Initiates and leads from the front Challenges complacency or ineffectiveness Pushes and drives towards the goal	Needs to be able to face a challenge, and cope with unknown or unexpected situations Needs to be accepted by the group as a leader Needs to be able to motivate, interest, excite, challenge and encourage others, without causing conflict
Innovator	Offers new and creative ideas	Needs imagination and creativity May not need to work too well in other aspects of the group
Monitor-evaluator	Offers dispassionate criticism	Needs good critical and analytic skills Needs a good sense of purpose or objectives Needs to be able to offer a viewpoint without conflict or offence
Team worker	Works to enhance team spirit	Needs to be friendly, well liked by the others A sense of humour can help Should have good knowledge of other members Probably extrovert
Completer	Checks things are completed Monitors progress against deadlines	Needs good organizational skills Needs to be able to attend to detail Needs to obtain and check relevant criteria
Implementer	Practical and hardworking Focuses on the practical details	Needs relevant implementation skills, or the will to get them Needs to have a practical, applied approach to tasks
Resource investigator	Makes contacts outside the group	Needs to be outgoing, with good interpersonal skills Needs to have a good sense of what external contacts might benefit the group

In many cases, you will not need to think about these roles extensively, because people 'naturally' fall into the roles which suit them. However, if you find you have three people in the group with similar personalities, there may be some difficulty in apportioning roles.

Belbin's advice for achieving a successful team has six main elements, listed in Table 2.4 below.

Table 2.4 *Belbin's advice on effective teams (adapted with permission from Hartley and Bruckmann 2002)*

Advice	Criteria
Get the right person in the chair	Consider personality, trust and control
Have just one innovator in the group	Should be clever in relevant ways
Get a fair spread of mental abilities	It's not a good idea for all members to be very clever, as this creates conflicts; better to have a spread of abilities
Ensure a wide coverage of roles across the team	Ideally, fill all eight and ensure there's no friction about roles
Get a good match between attributes and responsibilities	The jobs people have should fit their personalities and skills
If the group seems imbalanced, adjust it	Look for gaps in performance and jobs undone, then find the right person to fill them

2.4.7 Using practical tools for learning

As universities move increasingly to student-centred and independent learning, more and more responsibility is placed on the student for his or her learning. This change partly comes because universities feel they no longer have enough money to teach students entirely in traditional ways, but also because much educational research and student feedback suggests that different students have different ways of working, and that trying to teach everybody the same way only helps some kinds of learners.

However, making you responsible for your own learning means you have to make some additional effort to find out *how* to learn. As well as having to locate all the information relevant to your course, you may also have to discover how to use it. Good learners will make maximal use of all the resources available to them, but they will also be selective in their use, according to how valuable they are for particular purposes. You should not expect to use every resource to the same extent. Nor should you simply do what you've seen other students do: what works for them might not work for you.

The key is to experiment with every available resource, and discover those that seem to you to offer the most useful information and aid. In particular, you should explore the electronic information most universities are now making available to support their courses. The quality and nature of these resources vary radically between institutions: often they are no more than electronic copies of material that you could already obtain on paper, supplemented by electronic links to other organizations' resources.

Other electronic learning tools that may be available to you, and which you should examine, are conferencing or chat facilities, email and interactive learning resources. You'll probably be already familiar with the first two of these as leisure resources: they can easily be adapted to educational ends. However, by the same token, supposedly educational conferences, fora or chat rooms can easily be subverted by personal agendas and less than academic discussion. Just as a face-to-face seminar is only worthwhile if the topic under discussion is 'properly' analysed, so with a chat room. However, you can get a lot of informal learning from chat rooms, as members are often very willing to pass on information (that's half the point, after all).

In an educational context, email tends to be used largely for administrative (and personal) tasks. Students will contact tutors to find out where the lecture is or what the deadline for the essay submission will be. However, this is to miss a trick. Email can be used by students as:

- a tutorial dialogue;
- a way of exploring problems and ideas;
- a way of sharing or developing ideas across a community;
- a repository of collective views on a topic (to be examined in a future assignment, perhaps);
- a medium for group work;
- a means of gathering information (e.g. an 'online survey').

Finally, remember that all of the learning tools you may have access to are also communications media. That means they could be regarded from a professional perspective (how could this e-learning website be better presented?) and from a theoretical perspective (what communication processes take place in this chat room?) Regarding your learning resources in this way may give you added value in the way you use them: at one and the same time you may be gathering information on a topic, learning how to do the job better, and recognizing examples of particular communication processes. If you need a topic for an essay or dissertation, there are many under-explored areas of electronic communication.

Remember also that electronic text is re-usable. So one e-learning tool is to take notes directly into a computer, either by typing or by cut and paste from other sources. This should mean that when you come to write your essay, some of the text is already there, waiting for you. You don't have to retype quotations and so on because you already have them in electronic form. This can make the process of creating your own documents quite efficient – though, of course, the bulk of your notes will never find their way into your own writing. And watch out for accidental plagiarism [6.7].

HELPFUL TEXTS RELATED TO CHAPTER 2

The following books will give you good insights into improving your learning as a MCCS student:

- Ennis, Robert H. (1996) *Critical Thinking*
- Fairbairn, G.J. and Winch, C. (1997) *Reading, Writing and Reasoning: a Guide for Students*
- Hartley, Peter (1999) *Interpersonal Communication*
- Marshall, L. and Rowland, F. (1993) *A Guide to Learning Independently*
- Race, Phil (1999) *How to Get a Good Degree*
- Rowntree, D. (1998) *Learn How to Study: a Realistic Approach*

3

What makes a good communicator?

Introduction to the chapter

Having outlined how to get good information in Chapter 2, this chapter offers help on assembling and presenting that information. Chapters 4 and 5 then give you introductions to the kind of information you'll be working with.

So the aim of this chapter is to help you become a better communicator. It starts by outlining some principles of effective communication [3.1], especially in the academic context, and then applies them to specific presentational tasks, covering:

- writing tasks [3.2]:
  - essays [3.2.2];
  - reports [3.2.3];
  - summaries [3.2.4];
  - references and bibliographies [3.2.5];
  - personal logs and reviews [3.2.6];
- talking and presenting [3.3]:
  - as an individual [3.3.1];
  - in a group [3.3.2];
  - in a seminar [3.3.3];
- using information and communication technologies for effective presentation [3.4].

3.1 Principles of good communication

3.1.1 Think of the audience

'Audience' is fundamental to communication. You can't communicate unless you have someone to communicate with. For a student of culture or communication, there are three senses in which audience research might be important. You might need to know about:

- audience research within particular theoretical perspectives (e.g. in media theory [4.2], [4.31]);

- audience in a professional context (e.g. to determine how to construct a radio broadcast for a particular market);
- audiences you'll communicate with in practice as a student.

These three concerns can overlap, of course. The difference between 'communicating as a professional' and 'communicating as a student' is not a great one, especially for any student who wants to do the best possible job. Nor should theoretical ideas of how audiences work be truly separate from actual communications practice if the theories have any value. But these three concerns represent rather different emphases: either you are considering audience in the relatively narrow and specialist context of yourself as student, or in the slightly wider, but entirely applied, context of yourself as professional communicator, or in the much wider, but also theoretically problematic, universe of 'the nature of audiences'.

Effective communication cannot take place without, in some sense, addressing the needs of the audience. If you don't provide the information readers need, or talk in the way listeners expect, or structure your website so that users can find what they want, then you have failed: little effective communication occurs. So, in an entirely practical sense, the more you know about your audience and their needs, in any given context, the more likely you are to be able to address their specific requirements and therefore to communicate effectively.

Some branches of professional communication, such as technical communication, formalize the process of 'audience analysis' quite strictly, with well-defined processes and practices intended to stipulate exactly what audience requirements are being met by a particular communication (see, e.g., Burnett 2000 and Schriver 1997). More often, however, the process is less formal, less clearly structured, more subjective, and more open to difficulty. This is because audiences are tricky beasts, and dealing with all their needs in appropriate ways can be as much an art form as a professional skill.

Understanding audiences often helps in understanding the forms and processes of communication. One way of approaching the question of genre [4.18], for example, is in terms of audience expectations: a genre can be seen as a constrained form of communication where the constraints have been established (usually through a historical process) by a sort of negotiation between audience and a series of originators.

As a practising communicator, one of the best lessons you can learn is that effectiveness depends on satisfying audience needs, which generally also means according with their expectations. Remember, though, that expectations are not necessarily tightly constrained, and can be successfully violated (usually in satisfying some 'higher order' expectation). In certain kinds of communication, it is perfectly possible to be creative, novel or different and thereby be more effective than would have been achieved by merely following the 'rules' which seem to be conventionally defined (see, e.g., [6.2.4]).

For example, films which merely follow the conventions [4.11] tend to be mediocre. The film which does something just a little different, exploiting rather than merely satisfying the conventions, often has the most powerful effect. This is because audiences generally go to films to be entertained, and part of contemporary western entertainment is surprise or shock, through novelty and variety. As we saw in [2.4.1], variety engages attention.

Compare this with a commercial report, where expectations can be quite limited (even to the point where major organizations establish 'house styles' and templates which every writer is supposed to follow). Violating the expectations here is a much riskier business, because there is no audience requirement for novelty or creativity: the primary audience requirements for a report are that it should contain useful information and that it should provide that information in the most succinct and coherent way. People do not want to read reports, but they have to. So the shorter the report the better; the less work demanded of the reader the better. Originality in the structure or presentation of a report is counter-productive.

Analysing the audience can therefore be critical to any practical work you do. But understanding audience analysis is also very important in the theoretical debates about communication in general. Are the audience merely passive receivers of information? Are they receptors, readily persuaded and influenced by propaganda and advertising? Or do they engage more actively, more critically, in more sophisticated interactions with the messages they are sent (see [4.2] and [4.31])?

3.1.2 Address audience expectations

Whatever form of communication you are using, your audience will have certain expectations and assumptions about that communication. These expectations can be of different kinds, namely:

- fundamental;
- training;
- conventional;
- personal;
- contextual.

Fundamental expectations   These are the basic expectations your audience will have about your communication, assuming that it is intended as an effective communication of a particular kind. For example, they will expect that you will make sense, that you will be using the language they speak, that you will follow the conventions of that language, and so on. Some of these are discussed by Searle [5.33].

Expectations by training   We are all trained to read and hear in particular ways. One fundamental tenet of much media, communication and cultural studies work is that there is no natural communication, but that it is all culturally determined (e.g. see Bakhtin [5.2], Derrida [5.6], Foucault [5.10]).

We learn, for example, to read bold text as more important than the text surrounding it, to hear differences in intonation across the same sentence as signifying 'statement' or 'question', and to see graphics that are close to each other on the page as linked. The good communicator recognizes the educational and cultural background of the audience, and tailors her or his communication to fit that background.

Expectations by convention   These aren't really separate from the previous ones. Rather it's a different way of looking at expectations. Every communicative form or genre [4.18] exists partly by virtue of the conventions [4.11] that it operates. As a simple example, a limerick is a limerick by virtue of the fact that it has five lines, that it has the rhyme scheme AABBA (i.e. lines 1, 2 and 5 rhyme, and lines 3 and 4 rhyme), that it has a humorous generally nonsensical intent, and that it has a particular rhythm (rather too complex to elaborate here). In fact, you only have to say 'There once was a man from Caerphilly' to bring all those expectations to the fore. In a similar way, we expect an index to be at the back of an academic textbook, a headline to summarize the story that follows it, a lecture to begin with a statement of its topic, and so on.

So the good communicator knows the conventions of the genre, and uses them appropriately. Some of these conventions can be learned quite explicitly (such as rules for clear report writing [3.2.3]). Others are more subtle, and learned by practise and experiment as much as by explicit lessons in 'rules': essay writing [3.2.2] is more like this.

Personal expectations   The first three sets of expectations I've given here are not too difficult to work with. Being a good communicator means knowing the conventions and traditions of the particular forms, and therefore the likely expectations of the audience. By developing your knowledge of these, you develop your communicative skills.

However, all individuals in your audiences will have particular experience of these forms, to a greater and lesser extent, and these experiences may be quite particular, and could affect the value of your communication quite profoundly. At one extreme, there may be members of the audience who are completely unfamiliar with the particular type of communication: quite literally, they do not know what to expect. In general, it's good practice to identify these people before you begin, so you can deal with their particular needs, perhaps separating them from the more experienced members of your audience (e.g. an information brochure may have an introductory section for complete novices on 'how to use this brochure').

At the other extreme, you may have an audience made up of many different kinds of individual with radically different experiences of the form you are using. You can see this, for example, if you try to gather people's opinions of what makes a 'good' website. Everyone's experience of the Internet is very different, often very personal, driven by their particular needs but also by their particular experiences. What they see as 'good' communication through a website will also depend very much on what they have so far experienced as bad communication.

With small audiences, dealing with personal differences in expectation is not too difficult. For example, a presentation to a small seminar group can be designed so that it begins by asking key questions of each member of the audience, or tailors itself so that specific issues known to be of interest to each member are addressed. But with a large audience, if members come from very different backgrounds, it is a major task to communicate effectively with all of them. Too low a level will patronize the experienced. Too high a level will confuse the novice.

The best advice for complex audiences is not to have them! Wherever possible, try to deal with the different subsections of the audience separately – give them what they need in the form which is most appropriate to them. This may mean different documents for different people; or perhaps structuring your talk so that you expect some people to leave half-way through. If you have no opportunity for separating a heterogeneous audience into smaller, more coherent audiences, then you have to include in the communication different elements which will satisfy the expectations of each different sub-group. This means that your communication has multiple structures, containing different information in different forms for different people at different points. In a complex discourse [4.17] such as a multimedia CD-ROM or a website, this is not too difficult to achieve. In a single written document or a talk, it's much harder.

With a written document, the best way is to provide the different kinds of information in different clearly identified places, and show each kind of sub-audience what the purpose of each of those different places is. For example, you might use boxed text to give 'additional detail for people unused to the topic', or you might have an introductory section at the start of each chapter with a general account for 'people who simply want an overview'. A talk is harder, because every member of the audience experiences all parts of it, no matter what their needs. But you can use visual aids to cover the differences in need, and you might also consider ways in which the differences in the audience can be used as a resource: for example, you might offer moments in the talk in which the experts can offer their expertise to the novice.

Contextualized expectations Within any communicative context [4.10], the communication itself can be used to create and satisfy expectations in particular ways. For example, if a document says that it is a 'Reference Guide', the reader will expect that it contains information in separable sections that are not to be read in a linear way from beginning to end. If an essay says 'firstly I will discuss the development of print as mass communication, and then I will contrast this with the development of television', then reader expectations have been created which will lead to confusion or frustration if unsatisfied (see also [3.1.7]).

But if the writer does not use such phrases in the document, the reader may not read it with the correct expectation. So guiding readers may not merely help *them* to understand what you have written, it can also help *you*. It makes the reader more likely to read your document or attend to your talk in the way you want them to. The more guidance you give them on how to read your text, the more likely it will be read in the 'right' way.

By telling readers what to expect, you can alter their expectations.

3.1.3 Prepare for a critical audience

Any audience with an academic purpose is likely to assume a critical attitude to your work. As we saw in [2.3], the heart of academic activity is reading (or listening) critically. You can be reasonably certain that *any* audience will be actively considering what you say, no matter why they have your communication. Audiences are not passive receivers of information, even if they often appear to be that way:

- They will be assessing your communication against their own purposes and against any criteria you've set up (such as: 'is what he's saying relevant to what he said he would talk about?').
- They will skip some parts of your writing if it seems familiar, redundant, uninteresting or irrelevant.
- They will slide down the attention curve [2.4.1], no matter what your presentation offers.

Good communicators know that their audience will engage in variable ways with their communication. So they learn as much as they can about the following:

- communication processes which may apply (e.g. that offering a structure to readers can reduce confusion by guiding them through your document);
- reader psychology (e.g. recognizing that variety raises attention);
- document conventions and rules (e.g. knowing which features of a document readers will expect to see, and which can be dropped).

Audiences may vary in many ways. The trick is to recognize the variations which might matter, and ignore those which won't. Market research often records demographic information, such as age, occupation, educational background, socio-economic group or class [4.5]. These can be relevant variables. For example, you must pitch your communication to the educational level of your audience, and, if it varies, find ways of communicating with people who have different kinds of understanding of your material.

However, other variables may turn out to be more important. Attitudinal variables, such as the beliefs, values and ideologies [4.23] of the audience, may seriously affect how they interpret your messages. For example, very few political speeches are heard in a neutral or objective way: they are heard by someone with a particular political background as spoken by someone with a different political background. Some audiences go to some speakers only to hear messages they want to hear (few unconverted people go to religious rallies); others go only to object to the opinions of a speaker.

In the same way, people's attitudes to the position you are taking in your writing may affect how they read it. If you are writing an essay for a tutor who you know strongly believes in Marxist [5.27] approaches to cultural theory, and you begin by asserting that Marx was clearly mistaken, you have probably started on the wrong foot. If you want to argue that Marxism has serious defects, then, for this audience, you will have to work up to it carefully, and assemble a gradual and extremely watertight case, and you will probably want to argue that 'Marxism may exhibit some weaknesses', a rather gentler case, than boldly assert that the reader's beliefs are wrong!

Environmental factors can also be important. These are external factors which might affect the way a reader reads. In the case of an examiner marking assignments, for example, the time that the marker has, and the other work he or she has marked on the same subject, will affect how your work is read. So bear the marker's situation in mind when writing if you want to get the best marks you can. If you've done the same as the other students (used roughly the same sources, not checked the grammar, roughly reproduced the lecture on the topic), and that marker has only twenty minutes to mark your five-page essay, your essay will be marked much like the other twenty.

For this reason, anything you can do to make the marker's task easier is likely to reward you and get slightly better marks. The better your presentation, the more readable it is, the better disposed will the harassed marker feel towards it. The more you set yourself apart from the average student essay, the more likely yours will be seen as better. For example, if you have not simply reproduced the information from the lecture; if you have sought out sources others have not used; if you have taken a slightly different slant on the topic; if you have organized your material in a novel way – all these can pay off in positive marks.

3.1.4 Research the audience

All the factors discussed above suggest that the better your information on the audience, the better your communication is likely to be. So part of your task as a communicator is to find out as much as you can about that audience. As a student, this is often quite easy: you know exactly who is going to read your work, your subject tutor. But are you certain of this? In my university, for example, usually the subject tutor is the marker but a sample of assignments are second marked by another tutor. Any problematic assignments may also be seen by an external examiner, a member of another university, responsible for checking the quality of the course.

And, of course, your assignment may be to write for an audience other than your tutor, for a hypothetical audience of some kind (e.g. if you are asked to write a business report, or create a curriculum vitae for future job hunting). In these cases you are supposed to be acting as a professional communicator, so information on your supposed audience may be essential for success. Indeed, finding out about, and responding to, the needs of that hypothetical audience may be a key strand of the assignment. Yet, at the same time, you are still being assessed by your academic audience. So here you would be writing for two distinct audiences, one of which is assessing the way you are writing for the other.

All of this suggests that you need some system for approaching the 'typical' writing task. Here are some key questions to ask yourself early in a writing task, to help clarify what you need to do:

- Do I have one clear audience, or several, with different needs or requirements?
- What does my audience want from my document?
- What does my audience already know, what do they need to know, and, therefore, what do I need to tell them?
- What are the benefits my audience will get from reading my document (compared with not reading it, and compared with reading other competing documents)?
- What problems, if any, can I solve for the reader in the way that I write?

The basic rule? Try to design all your communications to give the audience the information they need in a way that best meets their needs and objectives.

3.1.5 Be clear about the purpose

Any communication addresses a purpose. Usually there are several. Try to make sure that you are as clear as possible about all the purposes of your document or talk, and that you address all of them in the way you design your communication. Recognize that there are three people, or groups of people [4.19], whose purposes your communication might be addressing:

- your own purposes;
- the person who commissioned the document or talk;
- the people who will receive the document or talk.

For a typical student essay, your purpose is generally to get good marks, the 'commissioner' is your tutor, and the person receiving the document is probably also the tutor. Your tutor's purpose will primarily be to assess your knowledge of the topic and your associated academic skills, but there might also be other purposes, such as 'make the assignment easy to mark' or 'experiment with a new form of assessment'. You also may have purposes other than getting the marks: you might want seriously to learn about the topic; or it may be relevant to some practical aspect of your non-academic life (e.g. you want to get a job in public relations, so you choose an essay on that topic).

In a professional communications context, 'your own purposes' may include those of the group you belong to, such as the organization you represent or the work team you are in. The 'commissioner' will be a client or customer, and again may be either a particular individual, or a group or organization of some kind. Clients often commission documents for other people (e.g. manufacturers commission advertisers to communicate with consumers).

In all these cases, be as clear as you can about what you are trying to do through the document. Recognize also that the purposes of different interested parties may conflict. For example, your tutor's purpose may be to give you a really difficult testing assignment, but your purpose may be to spend as little time on it as possible (not good practice if you want a 2:1!). Or, professionally, a government department may commission you to report positively on consultation you feel was actually negative. Such conflicts raise ethical issues beyond the scope of this book. They will occur.

You do not have to put these observations in the piece itself (although often it helps if the introduction outlines what the communication is supposed to achieve). In some cases, you definitely do not want to make some purposes clear to other people: for example, if your purpose is to do the minimum amount of work, or to prove to your boss that you are a good employee. But it can be a useful exercise for you to write out clearly, for yourself, what you are expecting to achieve through the communication, and to use this private statement as a checklist during writing, to see how well you are doing what you set out to do.

Think about what you are trying to do in your document, that is, how you are going about the task of getting your marks. What, precisely, do you want to show in your document? What skills and knowledge do you wish to exhibit? Are you trying to:

- show how knowledgeable you are about the topic?
- prove that you have done a lot of relevant reading?
- produce a professional looking document of the highest visual quality?
- impress with your skills in argument?
- show that you are an adept writer with a good turn of phrase?

Positive answers to any of these questions would require you to do quite particular things in your work.

3.1.6 Use good information

To communicate well, you need to abstract and summarize from all the sources available to you, being selective and analytical in the information fragments you choose to include [2.2.4]. Good information has as many of the following properties as possible:

- relevant to the topic in general;
- relevant to the specific point being made;
- appropriate to audience expectations and needs;
- drawn from an authoritative source;
- objective, or drawn from objective data;
- up to date;
- precise and unambiguous;
- clearly and succinctly expressed;
- clearly connected to other points in the discussion.

3.1.7 Structure your information appropriately

Any study of communication shows that there are many different ways that information can be structured. As a practical communicator you need to decide why you might use a particular structure. Broadly speaking, there are three dimensions of choice:

- to address a writer's purpose;
- to address the reader's purpose;
- to fit with expectations (e.g. to fit the norms for a particular genre [4.18]).

Obviously this means you need to know three things when deciding how to structure your information, and we can summarize these needs as principles of good document design (see also [6.2.2]):

- Know what your document is for. (What do you want to achieve in the document?)
  - Are you promoting, persuading, informing, requesting?
  - Are you aiming for everyone, or people with particular interests?
- Think of the reader's purpose. (What do the readers want to get out of it?)
  - Why do they have your document?
  - Why will they want your information?
- Design for different tasks. (What are the normal expectations for this kind of writing? Will different readers have different expectations?)
  - Help readers find what they might want.
  - Offer different routes for different needs.
  - Address the *particular* aim(s).

When you create a structure for your document, the building blocks of your structure are not sentences, or paragraphs, but something more like 'information fragments' or 'chunks of information'. The sentences and paragraphs that you produce are representations [4.41] of these fragments in some sort of coherent order. The pieces of information that you have gathered through your sensitive and detailed research [2.2] should be turned into 'bite-sized' chunks, where each chunk is a single idea or piece of information that can be understood in one go. What counts as a single chunk of information obviously depends on your audience. If you are writing about perception for five year olds, then a sentence of four words might be a single chunk. The same topic for postgraduate researchers might be a paragraph or a page.

When you have a series of meaningful chunks, your job is to take them all and weave them together into something which can stand as a unified, coherent document. So as well as the information pieces you are presenting, you need to 'link elements' that effectively join things together. Linguists [4.28] refer to such elements as devices for 'coherence' and 'cohesion'. You achieve 'coherence' by making sure your writing connects properly, consistently and reliably to the outside world. If you cite a fact, make sure it is true. If you give a reference, make sure it is correct. If you report an opinion, make sure it is accredited and accurately reported.

You achieve 'cohesion' by fastening the different parts of your argument together sequentially in a logical way, often by using 'clue words', such as connectives. Weak student writers realize that they have to use such words, but do not always understand how to use them. Strong students realize not only that they have to use them well, but also that they are creating 'signposts' for the reader by using such words. These are contextual clues which set up expectations about structure which, as I've just suggested above, guide the reader on how to read the information you are presenting. Table 3.1 overleaf gives a few simple hints on use of some of them, but there are many other phrases you may use in your writing which serve to connect different parts of the writing together. Effectively they 'point', like a signpost, to some parts of the writing, or some relationship between those parts. If you use these phrases, as you should, check each time that you have used them appropriately. Examples include:

- 'Firstly': Writers sometimes forget to give a 'secondly'.
- 'In conclusion': Make sure it really is a conclusion, not a new argument or observation, and not followed by other new material.
- 'As I've said above/below': Make sure you really have said it, and not removed it in editing, or said something else. Also, preferably refer to the explicit page or section where it was said.
- 'To summarize': Make sure the following text briefly restates what preceded it.

More generally, you can also help readers through a document by telling them explicitly how it is constructed. For example:

- Show them the value of information.
- Explain why the information will be useful.
- Show them what the benefits might be.
- Tell them how the document works:
  - what it contains;
  - how it is organized;
  - how to use it.

3.1.8 Answer questions through your structure

There are many possible ways that you can structure a presentation, whether spoken or written. However, if no obvious structure suggests itself, a useful way of thinking is in terms of a 'question and answer' approach.

Because communication is essentially two-way, even when it appears to be only one-way (e.g. see Bakhtin [5.2]), thinking in terms of the two sides of the communication can be a useful way of getting a handle on the way to do it. Effectively you are thinking of your communication as a dialogue: the reader asks questions and you provide the answers. By recognizing that your readers will be *actively* interrogating your document and taking a critical attitude to it [3.1.3], and by anticipating the kinds of critiques and questions they will ask, you can build a structure designed to forestall their queries, and deal with them.

Questions can be used in different ways in your writing. A direct method is to question the reader, which you can find most obviously in documents like advertisements of the 'Do you suffer from dandruff?' kind. Such a question lets the audience define itself: only those who answer 'yes' will bother to read the rest of the advert.

Table 3.1 *Clue words and connectives*

Clue word or connective	Explanation	Example
and	This is a 'weak' connection. The more you use 'and', the more your writing seems like a list rather than a progression. Only use it if you really have nothing better to offer.	Weak: Gaze is a natural form of communication and everyone uses gaze. Better: Everyone uses gaze because it is a natural form of communication.
because	States causality, so make sure there is a causal relationship between the two linked statements. As we saw in Chapter 2, use of words like 'because' does not necessarily lead to logical connection. Make sure the reasoning is clear.	Weak: Myth tells us much about culture because myths are stories. [5.24] Better: Myth tells us much about culture because myths are stories created and maintained by social groups, not by individuals.
Therefore, consequently, so	States that the current clause or sentence follows *necessarily* from the previous one. The reader's automatic reaction is 'does this really follow?' If the connection is not self-evident, then there may be a case for an additional explanatory statement.	Weak: Chomsky's [5.5] theories focused on grammatical models. Therefore, they were little use in real social situations. Better: Chomsky's theories focused on grammatical models, with no consideration of social context. Therefore, they were little use in real social situations.
However	Indicates a contrast or opposition between two statements. Make sure they actually are opposed or clearly contrasted.	Weak: Email offers versatile communication. However, phones are also versatile. Better: Email offers versatile communication. However, phones are not as versatile.
On the other hand, whereas, nevertheless, however	Indicates a contrast or opposition between two statements, but the opposition between them may be more to do with the way the writer is presenting them (to make a point) than with any inherent opposition. So, make sure that it is clear to the reader how you think they contrast, what your rationale is.	Weak: On the one hand, Peirce [5.28] invented semiotics. On the other hand, it was Barthes [5.3]. Better: On the one hand, Peirce could be said to have invented semiotics, because of his account of different kinds of signs. On the other hand, Barthes could also be said to be semiotics' inventor, because he showed how semiotic analysis could be applied in a wide range of different situations.
also, moreover, in addition	Introduces additional points which are similar to that just made, probably reinforcing it.	Weak: Fairclough [5.9] uses Hallidayan [5.16] linguistics. Also, Fairclough's work is very influential. Stronger: Fairclough uses Hallidayan linguistics. Also, Fairclough's work draws on other linguists.

More subtle versions incorporate a persuasive element, such as 'Do you want to look younger?' to which few people will answer 'no'. Politicians use this approach as a rhetorical [4.42] device for controlling interviews or directing the audience in political rallies, for example 'Do we want a country where gun crime increases every year?' The answer to the question, of course, is generally the product, service or political party you are trying to advocate. If you need to write a persuasive document of some kind, this can be a useful technique.

More often, as a student, you will be providing informative rather than persuasive documents. Questions can still be used as a structuring method. In an explicitly informative document, such as a brochure or report, which seeks to answer the readers' questions, you can do this quite explicitly by using those questions as headings, and the body text as answers. For example, in an investigative report:

What was the problem?
How was it tackled?
What were the outcomes?

However, for the bulk of student writing, and for much of the subtler kind of professional writing, keeping the questions implicit can work just as well, and make structured writing a relatively simple task. In a book called *The Pyramid Principle*, Barbara Minto expands this idea into a complete method for report writing. In essence, she advocates a six-stage approach, which can work for essays and other kinds of writing as well as reports (Minto 1991).

Stage 1. Create your 'thesis statement'. This is the key point your essay or report is going to make, the 'thesis' it is advancing. It should be a single sentence that summarizes the key thrust of your argument, such as:

The account of discourse analysis given by psychologists cannot be reconciled with Foucault's account of discourse.

Stage 2. Consider what the readers' questions might be in response to such a statement. For example:

- What is the psychologists' account of discourse analysis [4.17]?
- What is Foucault's [5.10] account of discourse?
- Why can the two accounts not be reconciled?

Stage 3. For each of these questions, write an answer. For example:

Psychologists use the term 'discourse analysis' to mean the analysis of conversation.
Foucault sees all human activity as discourses.
Conversation analysis [4.12] only works for one kind of communication, but Foucault wants an approach which works for all kinds.

Stage 4. Anticipate the reader's questions for each of the answers you have provided, such as:

- Don't psychologists use 'discourse' in other ways?
- Aren't there activities that Foucault does not regard as discourse?
- Why does Foucault see all activity as discourse?
- Why does Foucault want an approach that works for all kinds of communication?

Stage 5. Continue in this way, generating answers to these questions, and then guessing the audience's response to these, until you have a 'complete' outline of your essay.

It might be difficult to know when it is complete, but indications will be as follows:

- You can't think of any more questions readers might have.
- Your audience probably already know the answers that you are generating.
- The kinds of questions and answers you are generating seem likely to be patronizing to the audience that you've identified.
- There's 'enough' material.

What you should produce by this method is a pyramid structure, something like Figure 3.1.

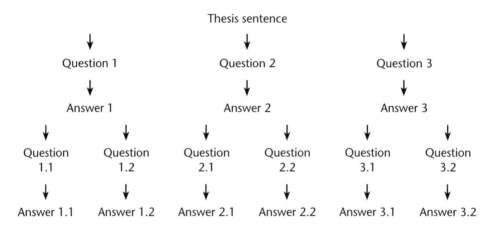

Figure 3.1 *Hierarchical structure created by questions and answers*

Stage 6. Rewrite the outline as proper prose. This generally is not too difficult if your sequence of questions and answers makes sense, because you simply trace the argument through the text you write. For example:

> In this essay I am going to argue that the account of discourse analysis given by psychologists cannot be reconciled with Foucault's account of discourse. Psychologists generally use the term 'discourse analysis' to mean the analysis of conversation, although more recent work has extended the use of the term somewhat. But in Foucault's account, all human activity, all communication, is seen as discourse. So no single approach to analysis will work.

You can perhaps see in this brief example not only how the outline can be turned into prose, but also how much of this happens by translating the structural relationships in the outline (the pyramid) into connective clue words of the kind discussed in [3.1.7]. The questions and answers are related to one another through words like 'although', 'but' and 'so', which represent the links between different parts of the structure.

In other words, the question and answer approach uses the needs of the audience to devise an argument structure, and as a result it creates prose which should use clue words appropriately, and thereby stand up to the tests of critical analysis outlined in [2.3].

3.1.9 Make appropriate stylistic choices

Stylistics is a branch of linguistics [4.28], which you may study as part of your degree. It looks at language variation [4.27], the conscious and unconscious choices we make when using language for different purposes, different audiences and different situations.

When you write or talk you are always making choices: there is *always* another way to say what you want to say. If there is not another word with the meaning you want, there'll be a phrase. If there isn't a phrase, you can construct a variant sentence. The choices you select should be appropriate to the audience and purpose, as you've identified them [3.1.4], and those choices usually mean you will be aiming to write or talk within a particular genre [4.18] or style of communication. You want to make sure that all the choices fit that overall style, and that all those choices are consistent with each other.

However, there are also general principles that you can seek to apply in choosing language, to get clear communication. These principles are generally grouped together under the heading 'Plain English' (see Collisons et al. 1992, Cutts and Maher 1986).

Usually, by 'Plain English', people mean something like 'language which can be understood easily by most people, using words and structures that the average speaker of English would be familiar with'. In other words, you shouldn't need any special education in order to be able to understand it. It does not necessarily mean informal or chatty language, as these can also have their own weaknesses and restrictions. For example, consider chatty text messages whose conventions [4.11] are by no means 'plain', in using weird spellings like 'ne1' for 'anyone' and odd abbreviations like 'CWOT' for 'complete waste of time'.

Most people's writing can be improved by applying some of the principles of Plain English. To highlight these principles, consider first the following example paragraph. It's not a real quotation, but it is based very closely on an actual document I came across. Read it for meaning, then read it again, critically, thinking about how it might be improved with clarity and the audience in mind.

> As an exciting new innovation within the University, it has been decided that selection of degree programme will be made by full-time and part-time students at the culmination of Level 1, thereby enabling deferral of informed choice, creating improved flexibility of provision and facilitating more effective employment of available resources.

You might try re-writing it to see what kinds of changes you can make which would improve it. Each of the changes you propose is a *choice*, a selection of one form of language over another. The writer of this document chose one form. You are identifying other possibilities. This is how you should always look at your own writing and speech. Ask: Is there a clearer way to say this? Is there a way of presenting which is more helpful to my readers? Is there a choice which fits the tone better? Could the writing be simpler, without patronizing people?

Before outlining some principles, let me suggest a possible way of re-writing the example paragraph which produces plainer, clearer English; language which is easier to understand:

> The University has decided that students will choose their degree programmes at the end of Level 1. This lets:
>
> - students wait to choose a degree
> - the University offer more choices
> - departments use resources more effectively

What kinds of things have I done here? Obvious ones are as follows:

- Reduce the overall number of words.
- Use words which are more familiar to the reader.
- Remove repetition and redundancy.
- Reduce the complexity of sentence structure.
- Organize the text on the page so the structure is clearer.
- Use shorter words.
- Use shorter sentences.

All of these choices made separately might improve a text, and they tend to go hand in hand. In particular, if you just apply the last two principles, you are likely to improve writing, because shorter words tend to be more familiar, and shorter sentences tend to be more straightforward. However, if you apply any of the principles mechanically, you can still end up with poor writing. After all, the shortest words in the shortest sentences would be 'I. A.', but this makes no kind of sense. Familiarity is sometimes more important than length: which would you find easiest to define, *television* or *id*?

Slightly less obvious choices, which perhaps require a little knowledge of language to recognize, are:

- Reduce the number of abstract words.
- Change the passive voice to the active voice.
- Remove nominalizations.

These three bullets use linguists' jargon (i.e. they are not Plain English!) to name three things which are easiest to understand by example. So here goes.

Most of the time we communicate in the active voice: it's the most direct form. We find it most familiar, and easiest to understand. A sentence like:

> Janet phoned Julian.

is simple, childlike, unproblematic. We know who was doing something, what they were doing, and who (or what) they were doing it to.

But we can turn such a sentence into an equivalent passive:

Julian was phoned by Janet.

The same information is here, but it has been transformed. The sentence is longer, with two extra words, and the relationship between Janet and Julian in the sentence has changed so that Julian comes first, making him seem more important in the sentence.

Noam Chomsky [5.5] suggested that passive sentences are 'transformations' of underlying active sentences, that is, that people somehow 'translate' passive sentences into underlying active ones to make sense of them. This means that understanding passive sentences takes more work: we have to do the translation. Some work by cognitive psychologists [4.7] suggests that this is actually the case: it takes us longer to process a passive sentence than the equivalent active sentence. And this makes sense, because passives generally seem less intuitive and contain more words.

But passives also allow two things: agent deletion and increased abstraction. 'Agent deletion' means 'getting rid of the agent, the person who performed the action'. We can get rid of Janet from the passive, and it still makes sense, but we can't do that for the active equivalent:

Julian was phoned.

– that makes sense.

phoned Julian.

– that doesn't make sense.

This use of the passive, where the agent is deleted, is typical of writing that wants to appear objective, such as scientific, military and government writing, which effectively hides the agent, suggesting that the person doing the thing is unimportant. 'The bunsen burner was lit and a test tube was placed over it and there was an explosion.' This sounds as if nobody was responsible. The positive aspect of agent deletion is that it focuses entirely on the process, and ignores the agent (so scientists can argue that science is true no matter who held the test tube: the positivist view [4.39]). The negative aspect is obvious. By hiding the agent, you construct actions without people in them, and raise questions which can't be answered in the sentence, about responsibility.

For example:

Communications were carried out and it was decided that all students would now pay double fees.

Whom do we protest to? The people who 'communicated' and 'decided' are hidden behind their passive sentence.

Passive sentences are often more abstract, therefore a bit vaguer, because they omit the agent, or because they obscure the relationship between agent and action, or because they lead to a *nominalization*. A nominalization occurs when a word for an action (a verb) is turned into a noun, such as turning 'separate' into 'separation' or 'communicate' into 'communication'. You'll notice that nominalizing lengthens the word, and it usually adds '-ion', making the concept more abstract.

Communication was held with Julian.

The rule of thumb is: 'if you find a nominalization, turn it back into the underlying verb'. Doing this usually makes you consider the active version of the sentence, and the agent, and whether there is a simpler way of expressing their relationship, such as:

Janet talked to Julian.

Table 3.2 below gives some things to look for in choosing clearer language, with a checklist question you can ask yourself as you review your own writing. And here are some guidelines which are likely to produce better writing:

- Choose language with the readers in mind. Avoid jargon. If you have to use technical terms, make sure your readers understand them, so give definitions or a glossary if needed.
- Be simple and direct. Avoid complexity.
- Remove unnecessary or redundant words.
- Be as specific as possible, avoid abstraction.
- Remove any emotive or imprecise words.
- Avoid abbreviations and acronyms that the readers will be unfamiliar with. Give unusual abbreviations in full on the first occasion of use, and explain them if necessary.
- Avoid ambiguous expressions and images (such as icons, which are hard to understand).

Table 3.2 *Clues to difficult language*

Long words	Are there any shorter, or more familiar words that would do the same job?
Long sentences	Can any words be cut out of the sentence? Could it be turned into two equivalent but shorter sentences?
Words ending in '-ion'	These are often verbs turned into nouns (nominalizations). Write a more direct sentence by turning it back to a verb.
Consider who is doing what	Can you tell who carried out each action? Or are they 'hidden' from you? If hidden, then consider more direct language.

3.2 Writing tasks

3.2.1 The process of writing

You will find that all sorts of people, including your lecturers, will give you advice on the 'best' way to write. Generally, they will advocate a process like the following:

- research;
- idea generation;
- structure;
- first draft;
- edit and review;
- final draft;
- printing and distribution.

Take on board such advice, but look at it critically. Will it work for you? Will it work with all the different writing tasks you have? The same goes for the advice in this chapter: it all works for many people, but not all of it is useful for everyone. If you read Sharples (1999), Kellogg (1994) or St Maur and Butman (1991), you'll see that research shows there is no one way to write well. Different writers use different processes, and may write differently depending on the kind of writing task. Learn what works best for you in particular situations.

So only take the advice in this chapter that you find useful. Apply the critical skills you honed in [2.3] to everything here, decide what works for you, and simply keep the rest in reserve in case of need. If you reflect on the way you write, you'll probably find there are many aspects of writing that you never think about. The more aware you become of these processes, the more competent you are likely to become, and the better a writer you are likely to be.

3.2.2 How do I write an essay?

MCCS typically relies on the essay for much of its assessment, because essays test many different student skills, including:

- language;
- presentation;
- research;
- academic writing;
- critical thinking;
- knowledge.

Essay writing is a complex juggling act: you have to get all these things right, all at the same time.

However, the centre of the test is your ability to make sense of disparate bits of information in trying to address a particular issue. Although this can be a rather abstract task, it represents the core intellectual activity of the good student (and the good academic): how to make sense of what is known (with all its oddities, incompleteness and variations) in trying to solve a particular problem. Even very practical, very applied work can make big demands on this kind of thinking. You need to do it well to be a good student.

This section offers a version of the essay writing process broken up into particular stages, with advice on each stage. You can follow each stage in turn, if the whole process makes sense to you, and you have nothing better to put in its place. But, more likely, you will find some of the suggestions usefully slot in to your normal practice, and others seem irrelevant, unnecessary or nightmarish. Just be aware if you reject them, of what you are rejecting.

Getting ideas: starting, and writer's block   The problem with ideas is that we tend to evaluate them before we get them. We need to close down our critical faculties for a while to let the creativity flow. Writer's block, either at the start or later on, is often due to being too critical of the ideas that want to flow. The trick is to get them flowing and suspend criticism.

Talking to other people is a good way to get over initial difficulties. A structured form of this is the group process called 'brainstorming'. Simply get together with a few others facing the same task. One person is to write down the ideas, the others to generate them.

Take the topic. Offer the first idea that comes into your head. As quickly as possible, the next person has to offer a different idea, connected to yours or not. Then the next person, responding to either of the first two ideas, or the topic. Continue like this until nobody can come up with any more ideas. Two rules should operate:

- When it's your turn, respond as quickly as you can. Don't think, generate something.
- Don't criticize, evaluate or comment on any of the ideas, yours included. If an existing suggestion makes you think of another suggestion, great, but don't make any comments that are not new suggestions.

What happens in this process? It seems a little like a party game, the random association of ideas, because it tries to create a group synergy and focus. The pressure is on you to produce an idea as quickly as possible. Everyone else is doing the same. It's a kind of competition, but you know no-one is going to shout you down, so your idea can be as silly, or pathetic, or unworkable as you like. So you shout it out. Surprisingly, this often sparks the creativity of someone else. They have a similar idea, with a twist that makes it workable. Someone else sees a different connection and throws a completely off-the-wall idea into the ring. But this makes sense to you, because it makes you think of a book you were reading yesterday. So you suggest that . . .

When everyone is exhausted, you should have a long list of ideas. Sometimes it is surprisingly long. The group can now sit down and discuss each item in the list. Some will be thrown out straight away. It doesn't really matter, because no-one has much vested interest in any of them: no energy has been invested in arguing for any of them. You can evaluate them at leisure.

Of course, brainstorming is often not possible for an essay. However, you can try a similar process on your own, but it is more difficult, as you have no-one to put the pressure on, no-one to spark ideas off, and your self-evaluation tends to assert itself. Two methods can help with this: one is mind maps [6.4.3] and the other is invisible writing.

To use invisible writing, use a computer with the monitor switched off. Start with your topic or problem. Continue typing, whatever seems to follow from that topic, and then whatever follows from that. Whatever you do, don't stop typing. Try to keep going for about five minutes.

This seems difficult, until you try it. With the monitor off, you can't see what you just wrote, so you quickly forget it, and enter a sort of 'stream of consciousness' in which ideas, words and phrases lead to others in a seemingly random sequence. When, eventually, you do stop typing and switch on the monitor, you will see, amongst the misspellings and faulty typing, some phrases and some sentences which might just be useful, because the task has forced your brain to keep coming up with things, and you've not had the chance to criticize it.

If group brainstorming is impractical, and individual idea generation doesn't work, and none of your research gives you inspiration, by far the best method to get going is to talk to someone. They do not need to know about your topic. In fact, it often helps if they don't, because they can ask the 'obvious' questions that you've missed. But lecturers are also useful, because they are experienced in homing in on key issues; and other students can be really useful just to chat to, to see what their insights or approach might be.

Planning Planning might come before or after the idea generation stage. Some people plan everything out, either on paper or in their heads, before writing a word of their essay. Others just start writing, to discover what they know or think, and that becomes the start of their plan. Others do a bit of planning, then a bit of writing, then a bit of planning.

The key thing is to do some planning at some stage. An essay is an *organized* piece of writing, which has to integrate different kinds of information and different kinds of task into one complex whole. It is not a list that you can simply start at the beginning and keep adding things to until you get 2000 words, then stop. (Although this is what many students seem to do. They do not get 2:1s.)

Probably the easiest advice to adopt is to keep the cycle of planning and writing going. If you're not the sort of person who starts with a complete plan, and then writes to that plan, then you're the sort who will alter plans as they go along. So you need to keep reviewing the different aspects of your writing to see if they suggest a variation to your plan is needed, or perhaps a new plan.

Plans can be millstones. They weigh you down with all their requirements and details. But if you break your plan down into sub-plans, smaller and smaller stages, each of which is relatively easy to achieve, the whole task becomes easier. For example, planning this book was quite difficult. A book is a big task. But, when I had an idea what some of the chapters would be, I could then break them down into their sections. And when I knew what the sections would be, I could write some of them. Writing some of them told me of some other sections I would need, so I planned them, and fitted them into the relevant chapters. In doing this, I discovered one chapter would be too long, so I split it into two chapters, which changed the sections I needed, and the structure of part of the book.

This is how I work: I'm writing part of the book as I'm planning the rest, and the writing changes the plans, just as the plans change the writing. Each part of my plan has its own parts, and when I have enough ideas, research or knowledge to satisfy one part of the plan, I write it.

Remember, also, that a plan can always be thrown away. All plans are provisional: they are aids to working, they are not commandments you are forced to live by.

Organizing material   The logic of an essay usually matches the logic of the question, surrounded by an introduction and a conclusion. The conclusion should summarize what you've said. You can put it to the test using the questions in [2.3.2]. You may find that the critical analysis questions applied to your sources also suggest possible structures, such as dealing with one set of theoretical issues, then another, then all issues around evidence.

As most essays in MCCS ask the student to debate an issue, the main part of the essay will be structured as an argument. You can use Minto's pyramid approach for this [3.1.8] or the structures suggested for reports in [3.2.3].

Drafting   You can plan without drafting, but you can't draft without a plan, even if it is only a mental plan. Your plan is a test of your draft. If you've no plan, you don't know if the draft is any good or not.

You should always write at least one draft before the version you intend to submit. Good writing is about balancing choices. It is highly unlikely that all the first choices you make will be the best ones. There may not be mistakes in your draft (though there probably will be), but there will be choices you've made that could be made differently, and possibly in a more suitable way. Is this word appropriate? Does that idea need better evidence? Is there a more up-to-date source for this idea? Could the summary be shorter? A hundred questions like these can be asked of your draft, to test it, before you re-write it for submission. A good way to test it is to use the questions for critical analysis in [2.3].

An alternative to writing a complete draft is to draft sections separately, working each section up to a final draft before proceeding to the next one. Some people find the task much less difficult this way: when they can see that one part of the work is 'complete', getting on with the next part seems less difficult.

After you have a nearly complete draft, you will still need to edit your work. See [6.2.3] for advice on this.

Writing the introduction   Only when you have written all of your essay should you write the introduction. How can you know what you are introducing until you have written it?

If you write the introduction *first*, before you write any of the main body of your essay, you are likely to write about what you *hope* to do, but, when it comes to it, may not *actually* do. It is quite difficult to write an introduction to an imaginary text, which is one reason why some people have great difficulty beginning their essays. But, once you have written the whole thing, the introduction should be very simple to write, as all you have to do is describe what you have actually written.

The essay's introduction would normally explain how the question is being interpreted, and the approach that is being taken, possibly with a theoretical rationale, and certainly with a justification of some kind. It may also give background information, to give the discussion a context, and it might discuss alternative ways the question might be understood or tackled, in order to reject these. It should also say something about how the essay is structured, what its main sections are or what the main elements of its developing argument are, and it should also indicate what it is trying to do (i.e. the kind of conclusion it is seeking to reach). None of this is difficult to write if you already have the completed essay in front of you.

3.2.3 How do I write a report?

The basic process by which you write a report might be quite similar to that which you use for an essay, as long as you bear in mind that reports tend to have different objectives. For example, a report might aim to:

- present only descriptive information;
- make recommendations or otherwise influence decisions;
- persuade readers to a particular belief or action;
- describe a process, such as an account of a group project you were involved in;
- document detail simply as a record (e.g. in minutes of a meeting).

A typical report structure is:

- Title Page;
- Summary;
- Background (including terms of reference);
- Introduction (stating the problem);
- Approach to the Task;
- Outcomes;
- Conclusions;
- Recommendations;
- References (if any sources were used);
- Appendix (if necessary).

This structure would fit a project report well, for example (except there would probably be no Recommendations) and also a report aiming to report research conducted towards making a particular decision.

Table 3.3 *Logical structures for reports or arguments*

Approach	Uses
General to particular	This is described within rhetoric [4.42] as the *deductive* approach to an argument. You start from generic principles, such as an axiom or clear truth, and show how particular detailed consequences follow from it. For example, 'All business communication depends on effective informal communication processes [*the general truth*] so in ABC Office Systems, we need good email systems and opportunities for staff to meet [*the particular details*].'
Particular to general	This is described within rhetoric [4.42] as the *inductive* approach to an argument, familiar to us from detective fiction. You start from particular observed details, such as observations or data, and show how a general truth follows from them. (This approach is also seen as 'the scientific method' and is a keystone of 'positivism' [4.39].) For example, suppose you conduct a survey that shows that 70% of students use text messaging and you observe several students using abbreviations in their email, so you conclude that 'a new form of written communication has been created'.
Spatial	Your document follows the same structure as the geography or spatial layout of the subject. This is obviously most useful when, for example, describing a place, but can also be useful when the topics you are interested in map onto some sort of spatial arrangement. For example, describing the functions of a digital video editing suite might logically be done by working across all the controls of the equipment from left to right.
Historical or narrative	Whilst 'history' and 'story' are not quite the same thing, the basic idea is the same, as far as report writing goes. Detail what happened in the order it happened. Be careful, however, not to chose this approach simply because it is easiest. You do not want to write a diary, which merely lists sequential events; you want to satisfy the report's purpose, which usually means a *causal* explanation of some kind. So your narrative will need to answer the question *why* something happened, as well as merely reporting *what* happened.
Familiar to unfamiliar	This is a useful approach when attempting to educate or persuade the audience. Begin with information they are familiar with, then gradually move towards information they know less well, by connecting it with the unfamiliar information.
Dialectic	This approach has been elevated to a precise rhetorical mechanism, and is also a foundation of Marxist [5.27] doctrine. The idea is that you state one point, then raise another in opposition to it, then produce a new point which is a synthesis of the two. In other words the process is: Thesis–antithesis–synthesis From a certain perspective, deconstruction [4.16], popular in certain branches of media theory and analysis, works along the same lines. The 'thesis' is a structuralist [4.48] account of a meaning. The deconstruction of that meaning is its 'antithesis', and the commentary which the analyst then makes is the synthesis of the two, showing how a structure contains its opposite, for example, and is therefore more complex than at first supposed.

Within the main body of the report, though, many alternative structures might be used as the logic of presentation. Table 3.3 describes six commonly used report logics. Note that these are rationales for a kind of argument or logical presentation of information, and so could be just as useful in an essay or a talk if it seemed appropriate to the audience and need. In a similar way, the question-and-answer approach or Minto's pyramid approach [3.1.8] could be used.

3.2.4 How do I write a summary?

The basic advice for writing a summary, synopsis or abstract is obvious: summarize *all* the key points of the piece you are summarizing, in the order in which they occur. However, problems occur when the following happens:

- You cannot identify the key points (e.g. everything seems as important as everything else).
- There are too many points (your summary becomes too long).
- You cannot use the original order (e.g. because you omitted points which linked other points together).

As with other writing, writing a good summary depends on knowing how it is to be used. If, for example, you expect your reader only to glance at it, and make an instant judgement (i.e. not to read the whole thing), then you may want a structure like that of a newspaper story. Here the headline is the briefest possible summary of the story, and captures attention. The first sentence of the story then expands the headline, giving a little more detail, but it is still, essentially, the entire story. The first paragraph then expands on this, giving the whole story again, but this time with much more detail. Only really interested readers will go beyond this, to read the other paragraphs, which give more background information, effectively restating the story again, but in full.

If, on the other hand, you expect your reader to read the whole of the summary in order to make an informed judgement (e.g. in deciding whether it is relevant enough to her or his needs to justify reading it all), then your summary needs to be the whole document in miniature. It does not need to follow the exact order of the original, though this is often the logical thing to do, but it should contain all the key elements of the original.

You can practise writing summaries as part of your note-taking [2.4.3], by summarizing as accurately, but as succinctly, as possible, the writings of others. Summarizing is a good way of getting to grips with the key ideas in someone else's text. In order to keep the three listed problems down to a minimum, try applying the following tests:

- If the point was omitted, would the text still make sense?
- If the point was omitted, would the reader become confused?
- If the point was omitted, would an essential part of the argument be lost?
- Is this a statement upon which many others depend?

- Are each of the different parts of the document represented in your summary?
- Is there any imbalance between different parts of your summary?
- If you missed out any parts of your summary, would it still read naturally?

3.2.5 How do I write references and bibliographies?

All academic writing, and much report writing, requires clear and complete references. A good researcher develops skills in attaching complete source information to any notes. A good academic writer annotates her or his writing with that source information.

Why use references?   The key reason for including references in your work is so that people can know where the information you are reporting came from. However, they may want to know this for many different reasons. They may want to be able to:

- distinguish between your own, original work, and work you have drawn on from elsewhere;
- decide which is primary data (i.e. raw, real, first-hand information) and which is secondary data (i.e. information which has been assembled, processed or otherwise mediated by someone else);
- be assured that the bulk of the work is your own;
- check the original sources, to make sure you have cited them or used them appropriately;
- follow up on the information or ideas you report, so they can pursue it in more detail;
- judge how much research you have actually done as part of your work (e.g. as an indicator of how much work you have actually done);
- judge the nature and quality of the research that underlies your reporting (e.g. as one indicator of your academic credibility);
- judge how appropriately you have selected and critiqued available information from all possible sources (e.g. have you simply relied on one main source; have you merely reproduced other people's ideas, or put them in a critical context; have you used up-to-date information, or relied on out-of-date sources; have you looked at all competing ideas in the topic area?);
- find an entry point for their own research in a related area;
- find a basis for constructing their own critique of your presentation (e.g. if they find themselves disagreeing with your conclusions, they might want to know if that's because of the way you have argued, or because of the use of information in your sources);
- be assured that no parts of the work have been copied, plagiarized or adapted from other sources.

Some of these reasons are standard reasons for all practising academics. Others are more to do with student work, which is being assessed (in part) for its application of academic practices.

How to use references in your own work   In Chapter 2 we saw how you can make use of the references other people give. In your own work, you must offer references to the reader to serve his or her needs.

In most writing that you engage in, which is based on information you have not gathered yourself at first-hand (i.e. where you actually have not conducted primary research in the field, but secondary research looking at other people's writings), you'll need to give sources. Almost always one or more of the reader's concerns listed above will apply. As a student, in particular, your tutors will be judging the quality of your work, and the adequacy of its referencing is a good indicator of the degree of scholarliness. So, at any point in your work where you think one or more of the above criteria apply, you should make sure you give as many good and suitable references as are appropriate to the task.

In the case of referencing, to get good marks, three criteria apply:

- Include plenty of suitable references, to show the range and depth of the literature you've read.
- Make use of those references, that is, show how they have contributed to your work by:

  - summarizing ideas;
  - placing them in context;
  - comparing and contrasting source ideas;
  - citing quotations to support your viewpoint;
  - advancing your argument;
  - showing the origins of points that you are making;
  - illustrating different viewpoints on the same issue.
- Give all references completely, in a perfectly consistent way, using an accepted academic convention.

The last of these needs a little explanation. There are many different conventions used for giving references in texts. Most boil down to two elements: complete information and clear cross-reference. 'Complete' means that every reference cited in the text must give all the information that the reader is likely to need, which usually means all the information the reader would need in order to look up the exact source of your information without difficulty. 'Clear cross-reference' means that the reader can see easily and without ambiguity which citation relates to which part of your text, which in turn means that all citations should have exactly the same format and conventions, so the reader can quickly learn how to read your citations.

Most courses will advise you on one or two conventions that they prefer you to use. It's a good idea to learn these early in your course, and stick to them throughout. Unfortunately some courses have no recommended practice in referencing conventions, and rely on individual tutors to apply them, in which case you will find that different tutors favour different conventions, and you will have to learn which is preferred by which tutor, to present your work appropriately for them.

If you have any doubt about which convention to use on any occasion, the key advice is to choose one of the most generally accepted and stick to it. Probably the most widely used is the 'Harvard convention', but even this has different forms. Using this convention, you cite a particular text in the following way in your writing:

'Texttexttexttext' (Williams 1999)

that is, you give the quotation or make your statement derived from the text and then give a short form of the author's name and the date of publication. In your Bibliography or list of references you arrange items alphabetically by authors' surname, with the data following, like this:

Widdowson, A. and Campbell, A. (eds) (2001) *Everyday Life and Everyday Things*, London: Fontana
Williams, N. (2000a) 'All You Ever Wanted to Know about Communication', in *The Answer to Everything*, London: Sage
Williams, N. (2000b) 'All You Ever Wanted to Know about Culture', in *Other Answers to Everything*, London: Sage
Xavier, P., Holt, Q. and Butler, K. (1993) 'Culture is Communication', *Journal of International Communication*, vol. 2, no. 3, pp. 34–67.

Arranging the list alphabetically means that the reader can easily move from your text to the appropriate reference without ambiguity, but you need the date immediately after the name in order to make it clear which actual text by the author you are citing. If you use more than one text of the same date by the same author, it's conventional to distinguish them by letters (e.g. 'Williams 2000a'). Note also various other conventions:

- Titles of books and journals are given in italics (or underlined if italics are not available), but titles of articles or chapters are given in inverted commas. This is because your source, in the case of a journal article, has two titles: the title of the actual article and the title of the journal it appears in. Both need to be given, so the reader needs to be clear which is which.
- Publishers are also included for books, but not usually for journals. Sometimes place of publication is also included, though this seems to be used less frequently these days (probably because of an increase in international publications).
- For a journal, the reader needs to know exactly which issue the article appeared in, so volume and issue number are given. It's also quite common to give page numbers so the article can be easily retrieved. In some circumstances you might give similar information for a book. For example, if a book was published in several volumes, and has many chapters, you might give volume number and page numbers of the chapter you have cited.
- Where there is more than one author, you cite them in the order they are given in the text itself (which may not be alphabetical order), and in your own text cite them by the same order (e.g. Windowson and Campbell, A.). However, where there are three or more authors, although you list all the authors in your bibliography, the normal form of citation in the text would be 'Xavier et al. 1993'. (For 'et al.', see [2.3.6].)

- If the originator is not the author of the text, but its editor (quite normal for collections of articles on a particular subject, for example), the bibliographical entry should have the abbreviation 'ed.' or 'eds' within it.

In many instances you may also want to refer in your text to the precise page that you are citing (e.g. if you have given a particular quotation), such as 'Williams 2000a: 37'. The Harvard convention is used throughout this book.

3.2.6 How do I write personal assignments?

You might be asked to write a self-evaluation (e.g. of a task you have carried out, such as an information search [2.2]) or complete a log of activities (e.g. logging the processes you went through in a practical project, such as producing a practical online document [3.4]) or compile a portfolio of your own work (e.g. as evidence of practical writing skills). In all three cases you will be:

- offering evidence of something you did;
- reflecting on what you did.

The evidence you provide will, if assessed, be used to evaluate your skills. Precisely which skills will depend on the nature of the task, but they will probably include research skills (see [2.2], [6.6]), writing and presentational skills (see [6.2.2]), and the practical skills associated with the activity or project (see [2.4.4], [3.4]). For a portfolio, the most important aspect is usually that it is a collection demonstrating a range of different skills and activities, probably covering different tasks, and possibly also applying your skills to examples of work in the real world.

However, often the most important learning point is your reflection. As evidence of reflection, your tutor will be expecting to see that you have:

- thought about the whole process you were engaged in;
- identified aspects which were well done or effective, and those which were less effective;
- recognized areas where additional learning or skills are needed;
- taken steps to remedy difficulties or solve problems, where appropriate;
- identified learning points which can be used in future similar activities;
- explained why you thought particular processes took place, related to suitable theories, where appropriate.

All of these show the tutor not only that you are able to do particular things, but that you can consider them objectively, and learn from them. Consequently you should be able to:

- do better at that task next time;
- reflect on and improve any other tasks in future unpredictable contexts (e.g. professional work);
- relate personal experience to more general considerations;
- develop as a learner.

3.3 Talking and presenting

3.3.1 Giving an Individual talk

The most common task you might be asked to carry out, after writing something, is to give a presentation. Presentations can take many different forms, so may make different demands of you. They may vary in formality. They may require you to perform as an individual, or as a member of a group. They may require you to present 'as yourself' (e.g. summarizing your last essay for the benefit of other members of your seminar group) or by taking some role in a presentation exercise (e.g. as a member of a 'consultancy team' engaged in a particular exercise).

In essence, however, the same principles apply as for most other forms of communication: know your purpose, address your audience's needs, know your topic, structure your communication appropriately, and choose suitable forms and media. Here is a brief review of each of these areas, from the perspective of someone giving a talk.

Purpose   As part of the opening of your talk, state its purpose. Usually you will introduce yourself, and establish your credentials in relation to that purpose, unless these are already well known to the audience.

Audience   A key difference between writing and talking is the immediate presence of the audience. In a talk you can use the audience directly in several ways, and you can vary your talk from the original plan according to how the actual audience differs from your supposed audience.

Most importantly, you can get immediate feedback from your audience. By monitoring their expressions and behaviour, you can see whether everyone understood a complex point, or whether anyone is bored or uninterested. Two small tricks can be helpful here. One is to appear to maintain eye contact with the audience, without actually doing so. The more you seem to be looking at actual people in the audience, the more likely they are to feel that you are talking to them directly. To do this, spend most of your time gazing just above the heads of the rearmost members of the audience: for everyone except those in the front rows, you will seem to be looking at them. If you are in a wide hall, and can't see everyone at once, make sure that you rotate your gaze across the whole audience.

A second trick is to watch the average height of people in the room. There are many signs that attention is falling off (nervous movements, repeated reading of notes, chatting, and so on), but one useful collective measure is how much people have slumped in their chairs. Initially, and when interested, they tend to sit upright, relatively intent; but as their attention falls off, as a group, they will tend to slide down, to slump, to lean back. By monitoring how the average height changes, you can get a measure of how interested they are.

When you notice a falling off of interest, you have to do something about it.

Remember the attention curve [2.4.1]. The audience's attention will inevitably decline, and the longer the talk, the deeper the decline is likely to be. So you need to prepare for this.

The best way to counteract falling attention is to vary the communication. We all know that 'something new' tends to 'grab our attention'. This does not need to be anything very radical: it simply needs to be different from what is currently happening. So pausing in long sections of talk, using and referring to visual aids, revealing or hiding information, raising a question and postponing the answer, changing the pace of the presentation, having a break: all these are likely to provide local (and therefore global) increases in attention.

Don't forget that having the audience there can enable you to use them to lift their own attention. You can ask them direct questions if needed (e.g. if you want to identify any differences in the audience's knowledge of the topic). You can get them involved in the presentation, if it's useful to do so (e.g. by getting them to do an illustrative exercise, or offer their own relevant experiences). You also should not feel that a presentation has to be just you talking to them: getting them to talk amongst themselves can be just as useful in many circumstances, as long as you control it properly (e.g. give them a fixed time for discussion, and then ask for brief reports back which you summarize).

Topic   Make sure you know your topic, and that the talk is properly prepared to cover the ground in the appropriate way: if it is supposed to be a brief summary, then do not include too much detail. Conversely, if it is supposed to be comprehensive, make sure that all key points are covered.

Be as knowledgeable as you can about your topic. The more you know, the easier you will find the actual presentation, because you will be more confident that if anything unplanned does happen, you can deal with it from your repository of extra knowledge.

However, it is useful also to have one or two strategies that you can use if the worst scenario occurs and you find yourself with a gap in your knowledge. Suppose someone asks you a question you can't handle? Suppose you look at your overheads and suddenly discover your mind is a blank about one of the subtopics you've written up? What do you do?

When in this unknown territory, take the advice of Douglas Adams' *Hitchhiker's Guide to the Galaxy*: Don't Panic! You are in charge, and you can remain in charge, as long as your difficulty is not communicated to the audience in the form of signals which suggest to them that you no longer know what you are doing. Several strategies can be used to fill the blanks in presentation:

- If faced by a question you can't answer, be honest about it. Say it is outside your current knowledge, but suggest a way that the questioner may find an answer.
- Alternatively, when faced by a difficult question, respond by saying that the answer to that is probably quite complex, and might be better handled outside the presentation. Ask the questioner to approach you privately afterwards (often they don't bother) or to email you with the question so that you can give a detailed and

considered response (naturally, this is a way of stalling so that you can look up or develop a decent answer).

- If neither of the above seems appropriate, another possibility is to refer the question back to the questioner ('I'm not entirely sure about that one. What do you yourself think?') or open it up to the rest of the audience ('That's a difficult one. I wonder if there's anyone here who has a response to that query').

- In situations where you have lost track, forgotten what you meant to say, or become confused by your notes, again, honesty is often the best policy, as long as you do not lose the audience's goodwill as a result. Pointing out your mistake, and making a joke out of it, can often work better than hoping that they won't notice.

- Remember that, unless you have told the audience you are going to talk about the topic you've forgotten (e.g. it's in the handout or on the overhead), they will not have a clear idea of what you were going to say. If you find yourself staring at your notes, wondering what on earth they mean, simply omit them, and find a natural movement to the next topic.

Structure   Organizing your information appropriately is as important in a talk as in a document. In fact, it can be more important, for in a document the reader can always refer backwards and forwards if need be, but audiences can only change the order of information in a talk by interfering with the speaker's plans. So you need a structure which organizes your material in a logical sequence which can easily be made explicit to the audience, and signposted as you go along.

'Signposts' in speech serve the same function as in writing: signs that help orient the listener so she or he knows where they are in the talk, according to the structure you've promised. Statements such as 'I'll firstly talk about some of the problems with small group communication, and then move on to ways of helping solve those problems'; 'now I've come to the second of the main problems people have in small groups'; 'finally, I'd just like to summarize the three problems and the six solutions I've suggested' – these kinds of signposts offered throughout the talk help people see where you've got to, and help them orient themselves if, for example, their attention has momentarily wandered, or they misunderstood what was going on.

The two most important sections of a talk are the opening and the closing. The opening sets the tone, lays out the purpose, and should make clear what the structure is, so the audience know what they will be getting, and what 'shape' it will take. You want to get the audience's attention, so start with a key statement, a quotation, a joke or a gripping visual. As with the introduction to a document, it is a good idea to design your opening last, after all the rest of the talk has been decided on.

The closing is where audience attention has momentarily lifted, and where you can make one or two summary points which might be all they take away from the talk as memorable. So it is the place where you repeat the most important observations, as succinctly as you can. (They definitely won't want you to go over the whole talk again!)

Your closing should provide a summary of the whole talk. Essentially, this should follow the same rules as for a written summary [3.2.4], but remember that it serves a slightly different purpose. In a document, the summary comes first to tell the reader what the text contains, so they can decide if they want to read it. In a talk, the summary comes last, restating the key points for the audience to remember.

One way to ensure that your audience take away something useful from the talk is to give them one or two action points they can use to apply the discussion in a real context. If your talk is largely educational or persuasive, this may not be too difficult to do: simply suggest how they might apply the lesson in a practical context. Where your purpose has largely been informative, it can be harder to offer a worthwhile action that they might carry out after the talk to reinforce its message. However, you might try ideas such as:

- looking for illustrations of the topics discussed (e.g. 'Next time you are in a café, watch the different ways people use gaze in their conversation.');
- testing some of the ideas in real contexts (e.g. 'Next time you are in a newly formed small group, speak first, and see if that ensures you end up leading the group.')
- doing some additional research or reading relevant to the topic (e.g. 'If you are interested in folktale, you might like to read Vladimir Propp's *Morphology of the Folktale.'* [5.30]).

Finally, make sure you stop. You will know from your own experience of lectures and public talks that they almost always seem to go on too long, even when they are interesting. Stage performers say: always leave them wanting more, and this isn't bad advice for most forms of communication. If your audience feel that you have used the time well, stopped at the right moment, and opened up interesting areas on which more might be said, they will feel positive about your presentation. They'll want to follow up on it – perhaps by asking you questions, perhaps by going away and doing their own research, perhaps by carrying out the action points you've outlined, or perhaps by contacting you privately. So do not make the mistake at the end of your presentation of stuffing extra information in. If people want it, they will seek it later.

Over-running is one of the worst weaknesses of a professional presenter, and one too often found in academic lectures, who somehow feel that, because they have not structured their material properly for the time available to them, they have the right to make the audience endure additional ill-structured material tagged on at the end as a form of compensation. Learn from the mistakes of those around you – if you feel a talk is too long, then it probably is too long, so cut it short.

No audience has every complained that a lecture is too short, but many have voiced the opposite complaint. If you see that you are going to over-run, or if you pick up feedback from the audience that suggests they've had enough, bring the talk to a close. This is not to say that you should instantly stop in mid-sentence. This will simply look as if you've got it wrong (which you have) and spoil the impression you've created so far. Instead, find a way of getting as quickly as possible to the end that you'd planned. This may mean skipping some material, or summarizing what you had intended to present at length. Avoid getting flustered by this problem in the following way:

- Firstly, point out to the audience that you are aware time is running out. This will tell them that you are on top of things, and about to do something about it. It is likely also to lift their attention for a short while.
- Then say what you will be doing with the time remaining to you: 'As I've only five minutes remaining, I'm going to conclude with the key facts on the Birmingham Centre' (see Hall [5.15]).
- Finally, offer those people in the audience who might want it, a way of obtaining the information you'll omit. A good way to cover this eventuality is to ensure that you have paper notes, or equivalent, for the audience – for example, you might give a summary of the talk as a handout, or offer them a website where your slides will be found.

Style and presentation   Your main stylistic choice will probably concern the level of formality of the presentation. Is it to be a chatty, informal talk, or a highly formal business-like presentation? Get clear instructions from the tutors here, as they often assume that students know what is expected, and only discover you don't when you deliver your elaborately scripted soap opera in place of the anticipated political speech.

Whatever the requirement, you do not want to give the impression that what you are giving is all style and no substance, so make sure that the stylistic choices are appropriate for the context and audience, and follow from the subject matter. It would be inappropriate, for example, to present research on police reporting of rape in a jokey manner.

Creativity   As with all personal performance, creativity is also a factor to consider. If you are looking for the best possible marks you can get, there may well be some mileage in seeking a creative angle on your presentation. This is not to say that you should go over the top in looking for some wacky or funky new way to present your information or ideas. A cleverly original presentation can still be poor communication if it misses its fundamental objectives (e.g. if it embarrasses or annoys the audience).

But if you can find a slightly different way of presenting some of your ideas, especially if you can do so in the opening or the closing (the points which generally have most impact on your audience), you may enhance your chances of success in two ways: firstly, the mere fact that you have (successfully) done something different is likely to count for you – it shows originality, thoughtfulness, consideration of fundamental rather than superficial aspects of the task, and so on. Secondly, you are likely to benefit from the halo effect: your presentation will stand out merely because it is different, and therefore it is likely to get more attention paid to it by the markers. In comparative terms it is likely to 'feel' better than the others, if they are more run of the mill.

Visual aids   Giving a talk is generally not just about talking. It is often wise to incorporate other media within the talk, if for no other reason than to maintain attention through variety. However, there are other reasons for including some form of visual in your talk:

- It is the easiest way to convey the meaning (e.g. a picture of a particular event, or an example of non-verbal communication [4.33]).
- It is the quickest way to convey some information (e.g. a graph of changes in viewing habits can be more readily understood than if you read out the data it is drawn from).
- It represents spatial or physical properties (language is often better at describing processes, but images are better at describing states).
- It is the object you are actually talking about.
- It is attractive, enticing, attention-grabbing (e.g. a cartoon to start a particular section of the talk).
- It can provide redundancy, by giving the same message as the oral content, through a different medium, so giving reinforcement of key points through repetition.
- It can provide a point for the audience that they can refer to and interpret as you are talking (e.g. a handout of examples which you refer to at different points in your discussion).

However, two words of warning when using visual aids. Firstly, do not use graphics just for the sake of using graphics. Make sure that you understand why you are choosing a particular graphic at a particular time, and not simply thinking 'I haven't put a picture in yet'. Secondly, remember that visuals can be distracting because they are attention-getting devices. If you use too many, or inappropriate, visuals, the audience may pay little attention to what you are actually saying.

Remember also that there are media you could use other than flipcharts, handouts and overheads. Computer display, audio recordings and videos can offer dynamic information (e.g. to show an interview or conduct an analysis of a dialogue).

The key word of warning with all presentational media is 'make sure they work'. The careful presenter always checks every element of the presentation before delivery, and has a backup in case the technology fails. It pays, also, to check the exact equipment you will be using in the exact setting you will be presenting. I have lost count of the number of times that I've seen presentations where the presenter had been assured that the computer was compatible, or the video had S-VHS, or the screen was large enough for five hundred people, and it wasn't.

Tips for a good performance

- Know your material well. This aids confidence.
- Rehearse the presentation. This aids timekeeping and confidence.
- Don't read a script: it's boring. Use notes from cards to jog your memory.

- Use visuals to support the talk. They can divert the audience's attention from you, act as reminders to you, and help you out if stuck.
- Speak slowly. If you can't speak slowly, take a long breath after each main point. It will seem much longer to you than the audience, give them chance to catch up with what you've said, make your overall speech pattern seem less rapid, and give you time to collect yourself for the next point.
- A little nervousness is a *good* thing. The adrenalin it releases will make you perform better.

3.3.2 Presenting as part of a group

Pros and cons of the group presentation   Group talks are popular ways of assessing presentations, as they are a more efficient use of time than individual presentations. The main advantages for a student of giving a group presentation are as follows:

- You do not have to perform for so long.
- You have other people to interact with, which can make for a more dynamic presentation.
- You probably do not need to do so much preparation for your own section.

Disadvantages of group presentations are as follows:

- They do not offer you so many opportunities to shine as when you are on your own.
- They can be harder work than individual talks when issues like dividing up the talk and managing the presentation are considered.
- They probably do not assess exactly the same skills as in individual talks (e.g. the quality of interaction becomes a factor).
- They can suffer all the weaknesses of other group activities.

The considerations that apply to a good group presentation are the same as those that apply to an individual presentation. It is the approach to, and implementation of, those considerations which is likely to differ. For example, signposting will probably need to include signposts to different speakers, not merely different sections of the talk; and cohesion becomes an issue, as people have different styles of performance and presentation.

Group identity   Usually it is sensible to consider the identity [4.22] of your group [4.19] in relation to the task you are performing. If it is a fictitious task, involving an element of roleplay (e.g. if your group is supposed to take the role of communications consultants), devising a group identity is usually easier than when addressing a real-world task, for you can construct fictional identities and roles which make sense for the task, but do not relate very closely to your real backgrounds or group roles. However, if the task is a real-world one that you have to accomplish in your real personae, you will need some self-analysis to get the best from your group, using the roles described by Belbin (1981) [2.4.6].

The identity your group devises should be appropriate to the task and coherently presented. For example, creating a business identity, with logo, mission statement, corporate uniform, business headers, and so on, makes perfect sense in the role of 'professional communicators', but not if the task is to research and present, as students, on academic theories of playground interaction.

Handling structure   In a group presentation, management of the process becomes more important than when a lone presenter. Who is going to start? You need someone who can make an impact. Who is going to conclude? You need someone with good summarizing skills. How is the handover between speakers to be managed: for example, how will the next speaker know it's their turn? Will they be introduced by the previous speaker? What will non-speakers be doing whilst others are presenting? I have many times seen presentations marred by the antics of those who are not currently centre-stage, relieved to have got their section over with. How will the visual aids be handled: by the speaker, or by someone acting as presenter's assistant? If the latter, how will they know when to move to the next visual?

3.3.3 Presenting in a seminar

It is not unusual for students to be asked to research or write on a given topic, and then to present a summary of it to class during a seminar session. The easy version of this is when the tutor simply asks you to read your essay out; but this task is relatively rare as it consumes a lot of time for relatively little learning. More likely, you will be asked to prepare a summary of your essay, or a ten-minute presentation 'related to' the topic you are writing on, such as a report of progress so far.

Such presentations should be less stressful than full-blown assessed presentations, but they can still provoke a few nerves, as you are effectively standing up to be assessed by your peers. Sometimes this leads to the presented 'playing to' the audience, giving a jokey and flippant presentation, which may please the other students, but is unlikely to be much use as a learning aid, unless the presenter is very capable. It is perfectly possible to behave like one of the lads or lasses, and still get serious learning points across, but it is not as easy as it might seem. Almost inevitably, if you seem to be treating the task as a joke, the audience are unlikely to take your observations seriously.

As this book has said repeatedly: the trick to doing this job well is to know what the job is. Know the audience, know the purpose, know the need. Almost certainly the tutor's purpose is two-fold: to test your understanding of the subject and to provoke discussion from the other students. If you're not sure about this, get a clear remit from the tutor.

Assuming the task does have these two purposes; it should not be very difficult for you to address them both. The first (your understanding) can be addressed quite explicitly by you reviewing what is known on the subject (i.e. what you know, based on what others have written), and, where you don't know or are unsure, by including quite explicit open questions: 'I'm not clear yet why there are many different definitions of information design. Is it because researchers start from different discipline areas?'.

Including such questions also addresses the tutor's second purpose: it raises issues that need exploration. You should not aim to answer, or close down, all such questions within your presentation, but to raise them as issues which can be discussed after your presentation. In a similar way, it's perfectly okay for you to point out problems, difficulties, queries, that you have come across, including difficulties with the research itself, as these are legitimate areas for discussion by learners, even if you would not normally include such discussion in the resulting essay.

3.4 Effective presentation through multimedia and web pages

In Chapter 2 we looked at the use of information and communication tools for research. However, you may also be assessed in their use, for example if you have to design a website or multimedia application. There are many good introductory books on design and building of websites and other multimedia materials (for references, see Chapter 7) so this section will not attempt to cover the whole area. Instead, I will remind you of key principles and considerations that you can refer to as guidelines when beginning a new project.

Much of the advice on good web design is essentially the same as that for many other forms of effective communication: know the purpose, address the audience, choose appropriate language, use suitable structures, and so on. If you follow good practice for writing and presenting effective documents (usually called 'document design' [6.2.2] or 'information design'), you are likely to produce attractive and usable websites. However, obviously, there are some differences between paper and electronic information.

Websites and multimedia systems typically have four characteristics that paper documents lack:

- on-screen;
- interactive;
- hyperlinked;
- dynamic.

3.4.1 On-screen presentation

Although people read screens basically as they would read a paper document (i.e. in western cultures following a rough 'Z' shape from top left corner of the screen to bottom right), they read screens more slowly than paper, yet giving them less overall attention. Screens are also harder to read than paper because both the resolution and contrast of a screen is less than that of good-quality print.

So a screen needs to have less information on than the equivalent page, and that information needs to:

- be in short lines (fewer than eleven words);
- be visibly arranged in meaningful chunks;
- be in a large readable font (at least 12 point);
- be in highly contrastive colours (preferably black and white);
- be in short phrases and sentences (e.g. bullets);
- be in lines that are broken at syntactic points;
- be conveyed in short words;
- be placed so that the most important information is in the top left (where the eye spends most of its time) and bottom right corner (where the eye comes to rest).

3.4.2 Interactivity

This concept is too complex for a detailed discussion here (see, e.g., Williams 1998). Essentially, users *can* be given more control of how they receive information than in a book, but often they are not. (For example, consider the different ways that you can access information in this book. Some educational multimedia systems simply allow you to 'turn a page' to the next lesson.) Interactivity, combined with a low attention threshold, means that users tend to browse rather than read such systems, and tend to exit a given page rapidly, compared with the equivalent paper page.

For the designer, this means following guidelines:

- Build different information access options for the user (buttons, links, navigation signposts, clues to the nature of connections to other information).
- Attract the attention very early on (but not necessarily with flashy graphics, which puts some users off; attention is more likely to remain with the page if it is clear that the page is interesting and relevant to the user's needs).
- Use dynamic presentation (animation, video, speech) rather than text, where helpful, but give the user the option of skipping it as she or he could with text.
- If the aim is to persuade or to educate, activity rather than passive reception can be helpful.

3.4.3 Hyperlinking

One of the major advantages of online information systems is the flexibility and comprehensiveness of the connections between chunks of meaning. However, this can itself lead to problems, which the designer needs to work with:

- *Semantics [4.43] of links*. When you see a hot link on a screen, you know that it connects to something, but you don't know what that something is. For example, does a link which says 'pictures' connect to some pictures, or some text about pictures, or a game called pictures, or a definition of the word 'pictures'. Better design indicates what kind of information exists 'behind' links, and indicates why users might need it.
- *Fragmentation of information*. This is one of the characteristics of electronic information system which leads theorists to talk of the 'information society' [4.24]

and 'postmodernism' [4.40]. Because a screen or a chunk of text might be accessed by users in all sorts of different ways, probably including unpredicted ways, it has to be coherent by itself. Any implied connection to another screen or chunk has to be removed, so that it is meaningful on its own. This leads to lots of independent 'byte-sized' chunks of information, but very little elaborated or developed discourse [4.17]. The information on screen consists of discourses, not discourse. Good design provides not only separate screens of discrete information, but also extended, cohesive links across screens, connecting the isolated ideas.

- *Navigation issues*. Users can get 'lost in hyperspace', which is to say, they can find themselves on a screen of information and not know how they got there, what it is, or how to return to where they came from. This problem is worsened by novice users, unfamiliar interfaces and poor navigation design. Better design offers visual clues on where people are in the system, and constant tools to enable them to return to familiar screens, connecting the isolated ideas.
- *Task-oriented systems*: people move around electronic systems with goals in mind, trying to solve particular problems or achieve particular tasks. Any help the system can give that reduces the task will be beneficial.

3.4.4 Dynamic information

Some on-screen information is dynamic when you access it, such as an animation or a video clip. Although this can be interesting, often it is irritating: for example, if a title page forces the reader to go through a whole animation before allowing access to the website. If dynamic information is offered, the user should be able to control it, including turning it off.

The information on electronic systems is itself dynamic, or transient. Web links die. Information gets out of date and is not updated. Websites promise information that is never forthcoming. If you develop an online information system, make sure either that it is not likely to go out of date quickly or that it is supported in such a way that information is regularly updated.

3.4.5 Developing your own electronic resource

If building your own website or multimedia system, bear in mind that users are more likely to suffer information anxiety using electronic resources than using paper. So it is even more important than for paper documents to keep user needs at the forefront of concerns.

In particular, your users are likely to have varying needs. Different users are likely to want different things from the system. This means that a given user will only ever want to use part of the system, and therefore some of the design will be redundant or worthless for them. Designing for multiple users means (a) tailoring the information to meet a range of different needs and (b) presenting the same information in multiple ways.

Creative design in electronic systems can come through conventional methods such as mind maps [6.4.3] or brainstorming [3.2.2], but also offers a good opportunity for collaborative ideas (as the many skills needed for good electronic communication can best be served by group skills) and by metaphorical thinking and reverse engineering.

- Metaphorical thinking is the application of a consistent metaphor to your information system, so that the user can treat it as if it was a (familiar) system of some other kind: for example, the metaphor of video controller for moving back and forth in the system, or the metaphor of book for search functions.
- Reverse engineering is simple the task of 'undesigning' an existing system, that is, analysing it to see how and why it is the way it is. This could be a technical task (examining the program code or script) but can be just as useful conducted as an exercise in critical analysis [2.3] or deconstruction [4.16]. Remember, however, that if you build a system from someone else's ideas there may be copyright, patent or plagiarism [6.7] issues, so take extreme care.

It would be a mistake, therefore, to design for one type of information as if it was for the other. Such an approach fails to make the best of the virtues of each, whilst it is also likely to build in flaws due to the inappropriateness of the design.

The strong need for audience analysis [3.1] suggests that a good plan is to involve the user in as many stages of design and evaluation as possible.

HELPFUL TEXTS RELATED TO CHAPTER 3

The following books will help you improve the quality of your communication in different contexts:
- Collinsons, D., Kirkup, G., Kyd, R. and Slocombe, L. (1992) *Plain English*
- Hargie O. (ed.) (1997) *The Handbook of Communication Skills*
- Hartley, Peter and Bruckmann, Clive G. (2002) *Business Communication*
- Marshall, Stewart and Williams, Noel (1986) *Exercises in Teaching Communication*
- Price, Jonathan and Price, Lisa (2002) *Hot Text: Web Writing That Works*
- St Maur, S. and Butman, J. (1991) *Writing Words That Sell*
- Schriver, K.A. (1997) *Dynamics in Document Design: Creating Text for Readers*
- Sharples, M. (1999) *How We Write: Writing as Creative Design*

4
Fifty key ideas

Introduction to the chapter

Chapter 2 outlined how to gather and organize information and Chapter 3 how to present it. This chapter and the next look at the kind of information you might have to deal with. Chapter 5 gives a brief overview of many of the key thinkers in MCCS, whilst this chapter offers a brief introduction to fifty of the most important ideas you will find in the field. A good student should know something about all of these, but the brief accounts here are just a starting point, so also use the references listed in Chapter 7 to follow up topics of interest. These ideas are arranged alphabetically for ease of reference, and cross-referenced so you can pursue any or all of them in ways which make sense to you.

This chapter is not a substitute for detailed reading on each of the topics themselves. However, it will give you:

- a sense of what is involved in each topic – what the main points are, so you can decide if it's likely to be relevant to your current needs;
- an insight into the key ideas, in case you simply want a glance at the area, rather than deep knowledge;
- a starting point for exploring the area in greater depth;
- reminders or hints that can spur your thinking when it comes to revision.

Although the chapter offers an overview of many key topics in the field, it may not be comprehensive for your course, because every tutor in MCCS has a different view of what the 'complete' field would look like. So also use the help given in Chapter 7, and the other references listed in Chapters 4, 5 and 7 to locate and research information on the topics I've not included.

As a general help, you will find similar lists, each with different selections, in Price (1997) (which has a strong focus on media practice, rather less on theory, and even less on cultural theory), Gill and Adams (1998) (which is a little superficial in some entries, because designed primarily for A level communication students), Watson and Hill (2000) and Edgar and Sedgwick (1999) (whose focus is cultural theory rather than communications or media).

Key concepts in MCCS fall into three groups:

- theoretical ideas, with little immediate practical application;
- practical tools, which can be used to assess and improve communication practice;
- concepts that have both theoretical mileage and practical application.

So a student has to assess the ideas she or he is presented with in different ways: there is no single measure of what makes a 'useful' or 'interesting' idea or tool in MCCS. It all depends on the situation of use or the problem being discussed. Whilst this makes the study sometimes rather difficult (you have to try to work out what contexts might make a particular idea a workable one, as well as trying to evaluate that idea on its own merits), it also offers opportunities for the clever student to be creative. It does not take much work for you to identify communication practices that have not been examined from a theoretical perspective; nor is it hard to discover cultural theories that appear to be untested in particular situations, leading you to new insights.

NOTE: *If you find a term in this chapter which is not defined, or you want some relevant reading, check Chapter 7.*

4.1 Ambiguity

One of the most important practical aspects of communication is its possible ambiguity. To make most communication effective for its purpose, we try to eliminate ambiguity as much as possible (though, in some special cases, ambiguity can be useful – see, for example, discussion of Eco's *The Name of the Rose* [5.8]). In practical situations, precise, unambiguous communication best serves the purpose. Achieving this is often half the battle in effective communication [3.1].

Ambiguity is the power of a communications signal to carry more than one meaning. Language is *systematically* ambiguous, as are many other communication codes [4.6]. That is to say, ambiguity is built into language; it is part of the system, and found throughout that system. So language can be ambiguous in several different ways. For example, in the two sentences 'Time flies like an arrow' and 'Fruit flies like a banana', the word 'flies' is a verb in the first sentence and a noun in the second, whilst 'like' means 'in the manner of' in the first and 'enjoy' in the second. So two virtually identical sentences actually have very different meanings because of the ambiguity of their different parts. Both sentences can be interpreted other ways: if you try, you can just about imagine that the second sentence could mean 'Fruit sails through the air in the same way as a banana'.

These ambiguities exist because of the continual change that language undergoes. As the world is constantly changing, we need communication codes that also evolve. If the language remained static, it would become less and less relevant to the changing world. To see this, try using the language of Shakespeare to describe the way you use your computer.

So our language must always have the potential for new uses. If it has that potential, it cannot only have a single use – each part of it must have the potential to be used in slightly different, slightly new, ways. The word 'cat' can be used to mean our pet tabby today; and when it is fashionable to dye cats' hair blue in ten years' time, then it will refer to a blue animal; and when cloning experiments produce super-intelligent blue creatures that rule the world yet still chase mice, the word 'cat' will still be useful. Those potential meanings are inherent in the word as it stands, and that means it has to be ambiguous.

Creative communication can exploit ambiguity in different communication codes, as in puns (where words are heard as having two meanings at the same time), or films such as *The Usual Suspects*, which uses visual and narrative ambiguity to make the audience interpret it one way, before bringing into play a complete set of different meanings towards its end. But effective communication often depends on eliminating ambiguity so that the message is clear to the receiver. The job of the good communicator is to know when ambiguity can be desirable and when it gets in the way.

4.2 Audiences

Audiences are receivers of signals and messages [4.32]. Usually when we talk of 'audience' we are considering mass communication [4.29]. Two prevalent models of how audiences interact with the media are media uses and gratifications [4.31] and audience effects theory. The latter is the theory that mass communications operate by having an effect on the audience (part of the assumption behind the use of phrases like 'effective communication'). Audiences are seen as mass consumers of media messages. Early mass communication research worked on this assumption, but later theories refined it in three ways:

- Some members of the audience are more important than others. They act as 'gatekeepers' to the message. They may interpret it and mediate it, modify it and reproduce it for other members of the audience.
- Mass audiences are not single entities, but break down in different ways according to particular criteria. For example, social class [4.5] may predict to some extent which newspaper people may read, but this is also affected by political affiliation.
- Audiences are not merely passive receivers of messages, though this probably varies with audience, message and context. Audiences can interact with messages, not merely accept them, so the audience reaction itself may mutate the mass communication. For example, the mass grief that followed the death of Diana Princess of Wales was not initially a creation of the mass media, but once the popular response began to emerge, this was then taken up by the media and fed back to the audience.

A useful account of issues in audience research is Stevenson (1995), from which a key extract appears in O'Sullivan and Jewkes (1997).

4.3 Broadcasting

Broadcasting is large-scale communication through media such as radio and television, aiming for 'generic' audiences, rather than aiming for narrowly targeted audiences (sometimes called 'narrowcasting'). The simplest idea in broadcasting is that you send out your message to everyone who has the potential to receive it (e.g. everyone who can afford a television set), and assume that a high proportion of that audience will want it, rather than trying to identify beforehand those people who want it, and only directing it to them.

Because of the indiscriminate nature of broadcast signals, it is difficult to get meaningful feedback, or otherwise complete the communications cycle, hence the need for audience [4.2] research. Narrowcasting also can require smaller bandwidth than broadcasting ('bandwidth' is the capacity of a communications technology to carry information) and so can save money on the infrastructures needed to transmit the messages. Broadcasting research often looks at the organizational and political rationale behind particular communications initiatives (see Barnard 2000 and Geraghty and Lusted 1998).

4.4 Censorship

Censorship is a process whereby some elements of a communication are deliberately removed for a particular purpose. Usually censorship is performed by a particular authority acting on behalf of either a powerful agency, or an intended audience.

In the first case, the audience might not want the censorship, but the authority has decided to remove particular parts of the message because they are deemed to be against the interests of either the audience or the authority. In the second case, the audience have determined that they do not want to receive communications of a particular kind, and have established the authority to act on their behalf. An example of the former would be political censorship, and of the latter, some forms of film censorship or restrictions on Internet access.

Censorship can operate at a personal level, too, as an individual may consciously or unconsciously ignore certain signals in the belief that they are undesirable (e.g. some people may not read some kinds of books because they do not believe the information is 'healthy'). People may also censor their own behaviour or knowledge in order to maintain a particular personality [4.37] or sense of identity [4.22].

4.5 Class

'Class' is used to characterize social division, and, as such, is an important concept across MCCS. Class is fundamental to sociological analyses of communication, and is the heart of theoretical perspectives such as Marxism [5.27]. The idea that large groups of people operate in very similar ways, with similar interests, objectives and behaviour is also the basis of most economic theory and market research. Most approaches to effective communication, such as advertising, rhetoric [4.42] and 'political spin', are founded on the assumption that large groups of people respond in similar ways to certain kinds of signs or messages. Demographic analysis is also the heart of much social research, with the standard definition of socio-economic groups being as follows:

A: Upper middle class
B: Middle class
C1: Lower middle class
C2: Skilled working class
D: Other working class
E: Lowest level of subsistence

Bernstein [5.4] argues that class affects communication codes [4.6].

NOTE: *The word 'class' is used in other ways in MCCS literature, such as in descriptions of different 'word classes' or different 'classes of communication'. Usually it means the same as 'classifications' or 'types', so should not be confusing.*

4.6 Code

Most models of communication [4.32] suggest that there is a difference between the 'message' (the thing a speaker or sender wants to convey), the signals or signs used to convey that message, and the code which is the system within which those signs are meaningful. A simple example would be the desire to convey the message 'everything is alright', the decision to use a 'thumbs up' sign to convey this message, selected from the code of non-verbal communication [4.33].

So we can see the process of communication as taking a message and 'encoding' it through the choice of a particular set of signals from a particular code. The receiver or hearer of our signals then 'decodes' them, by recognizing the code (we hope) and trying to turn those signals back into a meaningful message, which makes sense to them.

To convey one message or meaning, we might choose from many codes, including language, non-verbal communication, semaphore, smoke signals, blues guitar solos and a large number of others. So a code may be very simple, and easy to describe, such as the finite set of signs used in Morse code, or it may be a complex, evolving set of ambiguous [4.1] signs, such as the English language [4.26].

4.7 Cognition, cognitive psychology

'Cognition' simply means 'thinking'. Cognitive psychology is that branch of psychology which deals with how the mind actually works, looking at such things as the working of memory, the locations in the brain which are active during different kinds of thought process, the speed at which certain kinds of activities happen, and so on. Cognition includes such things as memory and perception [4.36], and cognitive psychology studies these, including such aspects as how the brain works, how understanding develops, how children learn (see Piaget [5.29]), and whether some codes [4.6] are easier to understand than others. Cognitive approaches to communication are sometimes criticized because their focus on the individual mind favours an information-processing model of communication, which sees the mind as a passive receiver and processor of information, not actively engaged in an external social network.

4.8 Communications and media technologies

Communications technologies have existed at least since people first scratched a cave wall with a flint. Each technology tends to spawn its own studies, because of the functions it offers and the limitations it sets.

- *Writing.* Chapter 3 explores many aspects of writing, but not the technologies of writing. An entertaining, illuminating and far-ranging book on writing which includes technological considerations is Sharples (1999), and my own book *The Computer, the Writer and the Learner* (Williams 1991) has a lot to say on the subject, though some of it is a little out of date now.
- *Print.* Print technology is a less fashionable area for modern MCCS, except for those who are interested in the production of print. It tends to be studied as the history of print and typography, including contemporary trends in desktop publishing and online communication. Both Sharples (1999) and Williams (1991) have something to say on the latter subjects. For history of print, look at Hall (1996). Jacobson's book on information design (Jacobson 1999) gives some insights, and books such as Lichty (1989) and McLean (1980) applied information on print technologies.
- *Radio.* Also a slightly neglected area for study. An excellent guide to the study of radio, from many different perspectives, is Barnard (2000).
- *Television.* TV is, of course, a popular technology for study, partly because it is a popular technology per se, and partly because it is so pervasive in western culture. Being an enormous communications media, it also spawns a very large academic literature, as there are many aspects that can be examined. A good book which gives examples of many of these is Geraghty and Lusted (1998).
- *Film.* Even more than television, film has developed its own wide range of studies and perspectives, and film studies is a discipline in its own right (see Hollows et al. 2000).

Despite all these technologies, the phrase 'communications technologies' is usually used to refer to new technologies, digital technologies, which in some sense involve computers. The fashionable phrase is 'information and communications technologies' (ICTs), which, in some sense, store or manipulate information, produce communications, provide information through varieties of media, and have a range of cultural impacts.

We can look at technologies from three communications perspectives, each relevant to different purposes of this book:

- as a phenomenon designed for communicative purposes;
- as a tool for practising communicators;
- as a technological phenomenon which carries cultural meaning.

The first of these is a reasonably standard definition. The telephone was designed for people to communicate through. That makes it a communications technology (albeit, these days, a somewhat old-fashioned technology to study; see Fielding and Hartley 1987). The second is really the same as the first, simply looking at a technology from the point of view of someone trying to use it rather than someone trying to study its communicative implications, for example [3.4]. The third, though, could apply to almost any technology at all: a washing machine or a car can be seen as a technology which communicates, just as any other cultural artefact can carry meaning. And so it can be looked at semiotically [4.44], like any other cultural artefact.

In talking of communications technology, the third idea is generally put aside. We do not generally consider cars and washing machines to be communications technologies because they were not designed to permit a range of communications. They were not intended to be used as tools of variable communication; even though they do carry meaning, and may be thought of as technologies that communicate. If the key function of the technology is to communicate, then it is a communications technology; if its key function is to wash clothes or transport people, then it is not a communications technology, even if it is a technology which communicates.

This simple distinction is generally unproblematic, except in one rather fuzzy area. We can look at the communicative value of a car or washing machine (its semiotics, perhaps; its connotation [4.43]), and we can look at a computer in the same way, considering the computer not for its communicative power as a communications technology, but for its 'hidden' communications as a cultural artefact. However, it is possible to argue that the functional communicative value of a piece of communications technology, and its communication of 'hidden meaning', as a cultural artefact, may interrelate, and perhaps even depend on each other.

Take, for example, the common phrase 'user-friendly'. This is a phrase derived from the idea that communications technologies should be designed so that their functions are easy to use: people find them easy to learn, little or no work is required to get the desired results. In order to *be* user-friendly, a technology has to *appear* user-friendly. You can't separate the two. All the hidden meanings, the connotations of the technology, have to reinforce the idea that this is a comfortable, friendly, usable machine. Because if they don't, people will be less likely to use it and therefore it will be failing in its function.

Here we have an instance where form and function interrelate (see McLuhan [5.26]). Some designers would say that a well-designed technology should look like what it is, so that it is natural to use, whatever purpose it is designed for. If that is the case for a communications technology, then its form will reflect (or convey) its function, which is to communicate. It will communicate its communicative purpose.

So, when talking about ICTs, be very careful about the perspective from which you consider them. Are you concerned with their semiotics, their communicative functions, or their impact and implications in actual use? And do these relate to one another?

4.9 Content analysis

Many forms of media and cultural investigation involve the analysis or deconstruction [4.16] of texts or discourses [4.17]. One useful and easy technique is content analysis, a method for examining the content of texts. It is used frequently to explore texts such as newspaper stories, where the analyst will try to identify the different meanings which are being brought into play in a story. The idea is that you read a text looking for and counting instances of specific kinds of content. For example, a story about royalty will inevitably use words and concepts to do with royalty (such as 'kingship', 'royal family', 'throne', 'rule', etc.). This is an archetypal 'idealist', quantitative [6.6] approach to gathering data.

But to what extent does that same story trade on content to do with, say, 'family' or 'tradition' or 'loyalty'? You could look for the words 'family' and 'tradition' and 'loyalty' to try to answer this question. However, if the story was using expressions like 'follow the flag', 'since the battle of Waterloo', 'sitting around the breakfast table together' to convey those meanings, no simple analysis, such as a list of words, would capture these more subtle meanings. And, of course, much common discourse uses precisely these sort of complex references rather than a simple literal statement of what is meant. In content analysis the aim is to identify, list and analyse all the words and phrases (elements of content) which carry specific meanings. (See also 'connotation' in [4.43].)

You can also use computer tools for a form of content analysis, though generally they are less subtle than is needed for connotative meaning [4.43]. Most often they offer a combination of word-frequency analysis, concordancing and collocation analysis.

Word-frequency programs 'count words' like word processors do, by simply counting instances of each particular word form. By looking at the frequency with which particular words or groups of words are used, you can make some judgement about the prevalence of particular features in the text analysed. For example, I used word-frequency analysis to compare the ways press headlines, an online discussion group and a government report talked about cloning. It showed some important differences in the way that the language was used by the three 'discourse communities' represented by these three text types. It seemed, for example, that the online discussion group used many more words concerning ethical and religious issues than the press headlines.

A concordance is a list of all sentences (or phrases) in a text, or collection of texts, arranged alphabetically by key words. These can be compiled by hand, but this takes a great deal of time (reputedly an early biblical concordance took twenty-five years to compile). Computers are faster. Essentially a concordance program goes through the text listing all the word tokens in alphabetical order, and recording the immediate 'cotext' associated with each token of each word (the cotext is the words immediately before and after the word we are interested in.)

Collocation means 'co-location', that is, words which are found close to each other. Such analysis might be used, for example, to compare how many times a writer uses 'war' and 'hate' together with the number of times he links 'war' and 'love'. Sometimes such observations prove interesting in themselves – for example, we might find that the word 'important' collocates frequently with 'teaching' in a university handbook, but not with 'learning', suggesting perhaps that the writer had a hidden bias towards authority in education, teaching people being more important than their learning.

Because content analysis focuses on counting instances of features, rather than directly interpreting the text, it can be presented as an objective method. However, the selection of items to count in the first place amounts to a theoretical bias (e.g. the researcher is interested in royalty rather than power, and thereby misses the fact that there are many more instances of a power vocabulary than a royalty vocabulary). Word-frequency and collocation programs limit this problem, as the researcher is presented with all the word counts, and then can select from, analyse and interpret them based on the actual data.

4.10 Context

'Context' is one of those words you will encounter over and over again, without anyone offering anything like a useful definition. It is something of a catch-all word, usually used to mean 'all those things in the situation which are relevant to meaning in some sense, but which I haven't identified'. For example, we might talk of how the 'context' of a communication affects the way people understand it. All this really means is that similar communications might be interpreted differently in different circumstances, which is pretty obvious. (If someone says 'I like fish', you will understand different things depending on whether they are in a pet shop or a restaurant. This is one aspect of language's systematic ambiguity [4.1].)

So context can be a very imprecise idea, but it is also very useful, because it can refer to many different aspects of communicative situations. How you interpret it will depend on the context in which it is used(!). Typically, it will be used to refer either to one or more of:

- the cotext (i.e. other words used recently, and the kinds of language in use, such as question and answer, or greeting, or insult);
- the physical situation (time, place, speaker, setting, etc.);
- the knowledge and beliefs of the participants in the communication (such as

whether one person thinks the other is lacking in knowledge; or whether both participants believe they are working towards an agreement);
- the historical circumstances leading up to the communication.

Price (1997) proposes an embedded model of context to try to clarify this situation a little, by typifying different kinds of context. A communication will be inside a functional context, itself inside a situational context, itself inside a discursive context, inside a social context. This helps distinguish the different scopes of the idea of context, but does not really solve the practical difficulties of trying to relate meanings to context.

If you encounter a discussion of context, and it is not clear which of these is being meant, or the relevant aspects of these are unclear, seek clarification. Ask the tutor, or ask the participants, or do some research.

Context can be particularly important in dealing with content analysis [4.9], as it can create or remove ambiguity [4.1].

4.11 Convention

Conventions are like rules, but have less force. If a rule is in operation, then breaking it usually results in an automatic sanction (if you break the law, you are punished; if you break grammatical rules, you aren't speaking the language). However, flouting a convention may lead to disapproval or difficulty, but does not necessarily result in it, and any sanctions are generally either mild or a matter of discretion rather than necessarily imposed.

Rules are usually established by authority in some sense, and generally enforced by that authority (criminal law is an obvious example). Conventions are usually established by 'custom and practice', that is, they tend to emerge from the way people habitually act over time. 'We do it that way because that's how we've always done it.' A set of conventions constitutes a tradition, and a set of communicative conventions will make up a cultural tradition, such as a genre [4.18].

Examining the conventions which make up a particular cultural tradition or communicative practice can be illuminating not only for their own sake (as you learn about the practice itself), but also because of what it shows about the human condition generally. Many cultural theorists operate from the basis of examining a set of cultural practices and extrapolating from them to a more general theory of culture or communication. The structuralist [4.48] approaches of Lévi-Strauss [5.24] and Saussure [5.32] and the functional analysis of folktale by Propp [5.30] are good examples of this.

4.12 Conversation analysis

Conversation can take many forms and so can be analysed in different ways. The simplest form of conversation is probably face-to-face communication involving only two people. This is referred to as 'dyadic' (a dyad is a pair of people), and much of it can be analysed in simple terms as the use of 'adjacency pairs', in which a certain form from one speaker triggers a related form from the other. For example, a question may result in an answer; a leavetaking may trigger another leavetaking.

These common structures have led some researchers to write of 'conversational rules'. However, the regularities in simple dyadic conversation can develop in various different ways (a question would not necessarily result in an answer, for example: it might result in another question or a threat); and in more complex situations (e.g. where one person in the dyad has power over the other, or where there are several people involved in the conversation) the interactions can be much more difficult to tease apart. It is safer, therefore, to see conversation as operating through a set of conventions [4.11], rather than rules.

So conversation analysis seeks to establish the range of conventions that might be working in any given set of conversations, and uses these to describe and analyse what is happening in particular conversations. For example, analysis of when interruption is 'allowable' in conversation can show you when people are interrupting inappropriately, and this can tell you something about the interrupter's desire to dominate the other participant (see also Discourse and Discourse Analysis [4.17]).

4.13 Critical linguistics

Critical linguistics approaches are largely described as a reaction to what Norman Fairclough [5.9] calls the 'arid formalism' (Fairclough 1995a) of the earlier, and more traditional, descriptive linguistics [4.28]. This reaction is motivated partly by the feeling that such approaches yield relatively few insights for the amount of effort they require, and partly by a desire to explore the interplay between language and power, or language and ideology [4.23] within media (and other) texts.

The trick with critical linguistics is to know what you are looking for and recognize it when you see it. Arguably, therefore, critical linguists, with their concern for ideology and power relations, inevitably find evidence of ideological positions and domination in the texts they examine. But they see that as the point. Critical linguistics is about laying bare these underlying meanings or intents, and the possible tensions between them. Whether they believe that such meanings are the most important, or merely some amongst many, probably depends on their reasons for analysing.

For example, if we look at a political speech with a view to exposing the relations of dominance that underlie it, or if we look at a news broadcast with a view to exploring its 'underlying' tensions between the need to inform and the need to entertain, we are probably carrying out our analysis within a context of a particular position on how politicians ought to operate or what news broadcasts properly should be doing. In other words, 'critical' in the phrase 'critical linguistics' has two meanings:

- It critiques the text it is examining.
- It does so from a perspective which sees that text as representing an issue or problem; it sees the text as symptomatic of a wider social issue or political argument.

We might also suggest that the texts used by critical linguists are critical in a third sense – those texts are chosen which are seen as, in some sense, critical examples of the problem, key texts in the discussion. You choose the best examples for the job.

This means that critical linguistics lays itself open to charges of lack of rigour and objectivity. Texts are often approached with a particular agenda. They are analysed with a view to finding features which encode particular meanings that are being looked for. They are offered as evidence of trends or tendencies as if they are seminal, as if they necessarily show that many other texts must be similar. So the agenda of critical linguistics can be seen as somewhat self-fulfilling. Often a text seems to be selected because it offers such features, not because it has some external importance. In other words, critical linguistics is explicitly motivated by an agenda beyond analysing language. (For examples, see Aubrey 1982 and Chilton 1985).

But this accords with the fundamental claims of critical analysis:

- No text is neutral – it will always have an agenda, a purpose; it will always try to set up relationships between author and audience.
- Analysis is rarely a simple or a neutral exercise. Rarely do analysts pick a text to analyse simply for the sake of it. They will generally want to show something or to make a point, and for this purpose will select aspects of the text to look at and organize their observations on it with that purpose in mind.

This is why this book emphasizes the importance of 'critical reading' of texts [2.3]. To be a good student, to get yourself to the point where you are worth the 2:1 you want, you need to develop in yourself a critical attitude to texts, of all kinds, which does not take anything on face value, which looks for evidence and validity at each point.

4.14 Culture

Naïvely, we tend to think of culture as a set of products or forms (a group of paintings, a library of novels, a cathedral). However, these are really only part of what culture is, perhaps even, from a certain perspective, its by-products. Culture is essentially a set of processes, practices and values which belong to a particular social group, a society. It is how that social group goes about the business of representing [4.41] itself and the world it recognizes, how it selects particular material outcomes as of value, how it establishes and maintains those values through the particular discourses [4.17] it uses.

Some aspects of a culture will therefore have a material face: discourses are necessarily conducted through media [4.30]; representations normally have a physical form, although that may be more or less transient. A culture is often tied to a particular ideology [4.23], so that analysis of the culture or its artefacts may reveal that ideology (or, perhaps, the fact that competing ideologies or value systems are at work). Within a given culture, subcultures may also exist: practices and ideas that relate to the overarching culture, but go their own way by reacting to it, or interpreting it in specialist ways. A subculture is generally associated with a particular group [4.19], possessing its own identity [4.22].

Early cultural theory, much of which emerged from literary studies, tended to see culture as being a 'superior' artistic or literary activity (the concept which is probably still the commonest sense of 'culture' in everyday speech: 'we spent the weekend in Paris getting a bit of culture'). This view can be seen in some of the writings of Leavis [5.23], for example. However, theorists such as Hoggart [5.17], Hall [5.15] and Williams [5.39], by analysing popular and mass culture on the same terms as the 'elevated' cultures, and by shifting the notion of culture from a focus on products to processes, succeeded in arguing that 'high culture' [4.21] is of no superior status to 'low culture', merely that they have different status related to the social groups that produce and value them.

4.15 Cybernetics, cyberspace and cyberculture

Properly speaking, 'cybernetics' concerns controlling systems through information. However, its common contemporary use is more general, referring to the use of information in almost any context [4.10] involving communications technologies [4.8]. Messages carried through these technologies are conceived as existing in a complex 'cyberspace', a term coined by the science fiction writer William Gibson, in a seminal novel for the postmodern [4.40] age, *Neuromancer* (Gibson 1986). In one sense cyberspace is quite real, being the aggregate of all electronic information systems and the messages held by those systems. But in another sense it is simply imaginary, a convenient model of the 'space' in which all these messages are held, as a way of trying to conceptualize a complexity which is so large and so fluid that no-one can readily describe it, let alone analyse it.

Cyberculture, then, is the culture manifest through the information held in cyberspace, the interface of cultural and technological concerns. Of course, there is no one cyberculture. There are sounds, images, texts, social exchanges, virtual realities, games, fora, information 'spaces', databases, webcams, chat rooms. Cyberculture has many different facets, some of which tie to non-electronic culture and communication, and some of which seem to maintain a more or less independent existence.

4.16 Deconstruction

In its common uses, 'deconstruction' is simply a fashionable word for 'analysis'. However, the emphases are rather different. 'Analysis' suggests a neutral process, aiming to expose what is inherent in the communication being analysed. It appears that analysis is an objective process using neutral tools.

But 'deconstruction' is done with a purpose, and the tools used are chosen for that purpose. People who deconstruct a communication recognize that they are coming from a particular perspective and therefore that it would be a pretence to suggest their approach was 'objective'. Following Derrida [5.6], they would argue that a truly neutral analysis is impossible anyway, as all meaning is seen as a provisional negotiation. In place of objectivity, they offer as clear a statement as possible of the rationale behind their approach – the process they are using, the perspective they are adopting, and the reasoning behind it.

'Deconstruction', as expounded by Derrida, is the specific process of exposing the contradictions in structuralist [4.48] accounts of meaning. The analyst starts with a structuralist construct, an observed pair of terms in a binary opposition (a pair of mutually dependent meanings, such as war/peace, love/hate). This opposition is deconstructed by showing that the two terms are mutually dependent, and generally that the preferred term (i.e. the one which is privileged in the culture [4.14]) only has its special status because of the other. For example, 'peace', which is usually seen as the normal and preferred state existing between two nations, means no more than 'the lack of war'. Without the possibility of conflict, 'peace' has no meaning. Although people profess to wish there were no such thing as war, without it they would not be able to conceive of peace. War is therefore necessary in order to experience peace.

One problem with this approach to analysis is that it does not resolve anything. It exposes the inadequacy of a 'tight' analysis, but puts little in its place.

Often deconstruction takes the form of a looser analysis of a communication or other cultural artefact with the general aim of exposing the way it works, *from a particular point of view*. Implicitly it accepts Foucault's [5.10] argument that no discourse [4.17] is neutral, and that all an analyst can actually do is represent one discourse in terms of another, so it is important to be as clear as possible about the terms of reference, the discourse, in which the deconstruction takes place. At its loosest, the analyst is actually doing little more than 'reading critically' – extracting elements from a text on a more or less personal basis, whose insights are only as effective as the analyst may be adept and experienced. But the same issues arise when one considers semiotics [4.44], content analysis [4.9] or critical linguistics [4.13].

4.17 Discourse and discourse analysis

'Discourse' is used in several ways in communications, media and cultural studies, but normally it names a focus on the products of communication, the output, the form, the text or the practice. So analysing discourse is a fundamental activity for much academic activity, and types of discourse analysis are found in a wide range of fields.

Approaches to discourse range from the rather abstract, sometimes difficult to understand (such as those of Foucault [5.10] and Derrida [5.6]), which often tend to claim that all human acts are 'discourse' (because they all have a cultural, hence communicative, element to them), to quite simple, even mechanical, models of particular sorts of discourse, such as some forms of conversation analysis [4.12].

4.18 Genre

A genre is a type of cultural product, such as a type of film, TV programme or literature. Genres are generally typified by form and by content. The form is often related to the function, but also may be constrained by other factors. For example, situation comedies are typified by humorous content, a small cast, a family focus and are half an hour in length. Only the first of these characteristics is related to function (it would not be a comedy if there were no humour); the others result from commercial requirements, such as the cost of actors, and the time slots available.

4.19 Group communication

Communication between small groups, such as working groups, teams or families, is loosely classified as 'small group communication'. As the communications vary quite markedly depending on the type of group being examined, and small groups shade into dyadic (two-person) conversations, on the one hand, and mass (large group) communication on the other, talking about small group communication, tends to be a little imprecise. There are, however, some processes and characteristics which seem typical of small groups, whatever the kind of group (e.g. that different members of the group tend to assume different communicative and social roles [2.4.6]), so such study can be enlightening. Generally, small group communication is studied within the field of social psychology (see Argyle [5.1]).

Groups generally seek to maintain themselves through a sense of group identity [4.22], which may involve characterizing the activities of their membership in such a way that those outside the group are clearly identified. This may be done through stereotyping [4.47] those outside the group (the 'out-group') in such a way that they are significantly 'opposite' to the in-group (a form of binary opposition [4.48] which defines the identity of the group). Or the in-group may develop discourses [4.17] and conventions [4.11] recognized only by them, and so unfamiliar or problematic for the out-group. Extreme examples of this are secret societies, such as the Masons or the Ku-Klux-Klan, who identify each other by 'secret signs'.

More pervasive in society, however, are groups who maintain their elite or specialist status, and thereby their power, through specialist terminology and practices. Most academic, professional, technical and sporting groups fall into this class: the transition into the group (becoming a member, becoming accepted) is about learning the appropriate modes of communication (see High Culture and Low Culture [4.21]).

4.20 Hegemony

The idea of hegemony is that one political group or ideology seeks to dominate others that may be (potentially) in competition with it. Raymond Williams [5.39] shows that the word 'hegemony' entered English firstly with the general meaning of 'dominance', then was most commonly used to mean 'political predominance', particularly in the context of the 'great powers' dominating other nations or cultures (Williams 1983). However, its most common contemporary use emerges from the Marxist [5.27] tradition, especially associated with Gramsci [5.13], where hegemony is not merely used to characterize 'matters of direct political control but seeks to describe a more general predominance which includes, as one of its key features, a particular way of seeing the world and human nature and relationships' (Williams 1988: 145).

So the idea is that a particular group seeks to dominate others in its culture (let us say, the ruling elite in the UK), and exert control not merely by controlling the economic and political infrastructure, but also by influencing and controlling all forms of representation [4.41] which might carry relevant political messages. From this notion comes the idea that different social or political groups seek to assert their dominance by achieving hegemony (whereby all other groups accept, implicitly or explicitly, the dominant world view) so that no other way of viewing the world can be seen. Against this, less powerful groups will seek to assert their own competing views of the world through resistance and perhaps revolution, resistance being typically the dissemination of competing representations which challenge those of the dominant political group(s), and revolution being direct confrontation with the dominant groups, in an attempt to seize control of the infrastructure through which economic control is exerted and hegemonic representations disseminated.

To put this in rather looser terms, which are perhaps a little easier to understand: this account says that there is a tendency for those with a vested interest to assert their own world view at the expense of the views of others, in order to maintain their vested interest. A counter-view, from a more liberal perspective, might be one of 'pluralism' – the attempt to allow multiple world views equal expression, as in multi-culturalism.

4.21 High culture and low culture

High culture (see Culture [4.14]) is those cultural activities and entertainments generally the province of elite subcultural groups [4.19], groups with more power or wealth, who could afford to fund elaborate and resource-intensive activities, such as opera. High culture often also, being the province of an elite, maintains itself through a complex set of esoteric discourses that maintain and identify the 'in-group' and exclude the 'out-group' [4.19] who are unfamiliar with the conventions [4.11] of that discourse. For example, being able to discuss the key signatures of overtures or compare the minimalist traditions of John Adams with the romantic efflorescence of Verdi identifies someone as belonging to that elite subgroup.

Low culture is generally equated with 'popular culture' or 'mass culture', that is, there is a sense in which the larger the social group that a particular aesthetic or cultural practice belongs to, the less important it is. This, of course, is entirely born from notions of elitism: a small protective clique of 'specialists' with 'protected knowledge' can easily believe they have something superior to practices which everybody knows about and can do. But there is not necessarily an intrinsic difference of quality between practices within high and low culture. Is it more difficult to find an adjective to describe a wine, or to bend it like Beckham?

Arguably some 'high cultures' demand activities which are of high quality, in the sense that a great deal of resource or training is needed to carry out the practice: classical ballet would be an example where many people undergo years of difficult training to perform in expensive conditions. Necessarily much specialist expertise is needed and a lot of money and time to make ballet happen 'properly'. The same would not be true of karaoke. So one might argue that differences of quality, associated with a scale of resource, could distinguish some cultural practices from others. But such an argument necessarily accepts that power and wealth tend to achieve quality, and that lack of power and wealth tends to lead to inferior cultural practices. Such a distinction raises many questions about the words 'quality' and 'value', and their relationship to social class [4.5].

4.22 Identity

Identity has various conceptions. Probably the simplest identity concept is the personal identity or sense of self, which we all experience. When we use a word such as 'I' or 'me', we have a sense of a single, unified identity which that word refers to. This is the notion of personal self most typically explored by psychoanalysts, such as Freud [5.11], Jung [5.19] and Lacan [5.22]. However, their explorations, as well as social psychologists' analyses of personality [4.37], suggest that a person's identity is neither as personal nor as unified as we feel it to be. From the outside, much of identity is socially determined: we are socialized [4.45] into particular social groups, shaping our identity and our sense of self, with analysts such as Goffman [5.12] suggesting that perhaps our entire self-image is a function of social situations and our performance in them.

Identity is fragmented also 'from the inside', as psychoanalysts show. People do not have to suffer from mental illness to have conflicting feelings, to present themselves differently in different circumstances, to believe their own lies about themselves, to conceal from themselves their own mistakes and weaknesses, and so on. So our 'identity' as we perceive it may be very much a construct which hides parts of ourselves away and offers representations [4.41] of what we actually are. Freud's psychoanalytic theory, for example, suggests that personality is actually a series of interactions, even conflicts, between competing unconscious components: not one thing, but several jostling sets of desires and predispositions.

'Identity' may also be used to characterize the shape or sense of another person, either simply to name or refer to them (perhaps through a stereotype [4.47]) or perhaps through a more complex construct. Media stories, for example, need to identify the identity of agents in their narratives, as part of the representation they set up (see, e.g., Critical Linguistics [4.13]). In a similar way, groups [4.19] may construct identities (e.g. in practical terms, see [3.3.2]).

Because of the possible problems with 'identity' both as a word and as a concept, it is common to talk of the 'subject', a term which comes from Descartes in philosophy, and of 'psychoanalysis', when talking about the personal, subjective experience.

4.23 Ideology

According to Gramsci [5.13], an ideology is 'a system of ideas'. This system will belong to a particular social group or culture, and effectively dominate its way of thinking.

The word 'ideology' is often used disparagingly, to mean 'the [incorrect] ideas and ways of thinking' of a particular group, or to suggest that the group slavishly adheres to a set of rigid ideas, compared with 'our' more open and liberal ideas. In other words, 'ideology' sometimes has negative connotation [4.43]. For example, some people will talk of Marxist ideology as if it is necessarily a bad thing, because it is an ideology.

However, it is arguable that all social groups and all cultural phenomena carry an ideology of some kind, and that the issue is not whether a group have an ideology, but which ideology they follow. People tend to be disparaging of ideologies which are radically different from their own, or which have been consciously and explicitly moulded, rather than emerged over time as a set of cultural practices. We can argue that a cultural tradition, a set of conventions [4.11], represents an ideology, because it contains a set of ways of perceiving the world (including other people) and interacting with it. Ideologies tend to determine what is seen as of value or worth within a culture, and thereby to control behaviour to some extent, and socialization [4.45] is the process where that control is exerted. Arguably, one ideology within a society will seek to assert its hegemonic [4.20] dominance over others.

So, for example, the idea that we should all work to a pattern of nine till five, five days a week, for a wage, represents a particular complex ideology about work being a valuable thing to do, about the duty of people to work in order to 'earn a living', about the 'best' times to work. We have learned these ideas through the gradual socialization or acculturation that has worked on us since we were children, making it clear that anyone who does not work for a living is in some sense reprehensible. Any expression of this ideology, as it works in the interests of the ruling classes, is arguably an example of hegemonic discourse.

Stereotypes [4.47] tend to operate quite strongly when ideological differences are debated, because the ideology tends to carry the 'norm' for the culture, and a stereotype is a simplified version of what that norm might be.

4.24 Information society

The 'information society' has been talked about since the advent of computers, but particularly with the rise of the microchip and microcomputing in the 1980s.

Discussions of the information society often face two complexities. Firstly, it is hard to be clear what, exactly, is being talked about under the heading. Is it purely a technological concept of information that is under discussion, or is it information in a wider sense? If it is technological, what are the relevant technologies? For example, does everything that might be called 'information technology', or 'communication and media technology' [4.8], need to be considered, or is it only a subset? If a subset, then which, and why?

These are important questions, for, if the technology is left vague, the argument tends to float around, making use of any technologies that happen to fit that argument, rather than leading to a full discussion of actual technologies. For example, a discussion which only concerned itself with the telegraph and virtual reality environments would have very little to talk about, because there is little connection between these technologies, and they emphasize very different features of communication.

Secondly, discussions of the information society often mutate into visions of a utopia (an ideal, perfect world) or a dystopia (the opposite of utopia, a problematic, maximally disfunctional world), with little relationship to concrete accounts of the technology. This usually results from the tendency of discussions of communication and media technologies to become speculative, because of the constant technological change we are constantly experiencing. Discussing today's technology is out of date by the time it becomes public, and always influenced by the promise of future technologies. Speculation in this area is fraught. Sometimes apparently wild accounts turn out to be valuable (McLuhan [5.26] is a good example of this). Sometimes quite carefully argued accounts, based on good evidence and well-informed analysis, prove completely awry. (If you read the introduction to Williams and Hartley (1990), you'll see some examples of both types of prediction.)

It is undoubtedly the case that rapid developments in communications, media and information technologies have led to major social changes, the most common way of characterizing this being 'postmodernism' [4.40]. However, to characterize the sets of changes as leading to either a utopia or a dystopia necessarily misses the point, as it is the interaction of a whole series of cultural changes that characterizes the postmodern condition, not the linear projection of a single set of changes. In some ways, the concept of '*an* information society' is itself at fault. What we are getting is 'information societies', different realignments of particular cultural groups along or against particular technological boundaries. No-one now, for example, sees word processing as a destructive or divisive technology; the idea seems almost absurd. However, chat rooms, text messages, neural networks (computer models of mental process and problem-solving), virtual learning environments: all have their adherents and their detractors, according to how those technologies align with particular concerns (e.g. the concerns of educators, of political pressure groups, of parents).

4.25 Interpersonal communication

Communication between individuals is referred to as 'interpersonal'. It might seem slightly odd to have this term, for surely all communication is between people? The intent here is to characterize the social communication between people as individuals and in small groups [4.19], rather than in large social groups, organizational [4.34] or national contexts. Interpersonal communication focuses on such activities as conversation [4.12] and social skills. Some of the practical impacts of these is discussed in [2.4.5], [2.4.6] and [3.3.2].

4.26 Language

In general we are pretty clear what a language is: English is a language. So are French and Finnish. They are distinct verbal codes [4.6], with a long and complex history. At their simplest, they consist of a list of words (a dictionary or vocabulary) with associated meanings (the semantics [4.43] of the language) and a set of rules for putting them together (the syntax of the language), as well as rules for speaking them (phonology) and writing them (graphology).

However, language can take many forms. In academic study, we refer not only to spoken and written languages, but also to non-verbal language [4.33], visual language, and so on. In these uses, 'language' generally means a complex system of signals, which may make up one code or several codes, employing a particular medium, and used for complex purposes in different situations. Using the word 'language' in this way is really an analogy with spoken or written language, rather than an exact use. For example, it is not obvious whether, when we talk of 'a visual language', we automatically mean that it has the equivalents of words, grammar, regional variations [4.27], internal patterning [4.35], and so on. (Kress and van Leeuwen 1996 is a useful book on visual language.)

4.27 Language variation

A problem with trying to characterize language is the many variations it can exhibit. English is perhaps one of the most complex languages in this way, because it has many different variations, but most languages have different varieties. Typically a language will vary according to:

- *region*: 'regional dialect' (such as the varieties of English commonly referred to as 'Cockney' or 'Geordie');
- *class* [4.5] *or social group* [4.19]: 'social dialect' (e.g. the language you use with your friends in the pub may be rather different from that you'd use with the vice-chancellor of your university in a committee meeting);
- *situation of use*: 'register' (such as 'the language of sports reporting');
- *individual speaker*: 'idiolect' (e.g. if you habitually mispronounce or misuse particular

words, or favour certain phrases – a friend of mine ends almost every statement with 'to be honest', even when he's not being honest!).

Read Freeborn et al. (1993), Montgomery (1986) and Trudgill (1983).

4.28 Linguistics

Linguistics is the study of language in general, and also of particular languages. Early linguistics tended to be 'prescriptive', that is, it tended to tell people how they *should* use language. This role is retained to some extent by those who try to encourage or train a particular set of language uses (such as the parts of this book which try to persuade you that certain uses of language are best for particular purposes). The study of rhetoric [4.42] is a major aspect of prescriptive accounts of language, although in general the emphasis is on how language *could* be used for particular purposes, rather than what it *should* be used for.

Most modern linguistics since Saussure [5.32], however, has been descriptive. It aims to describe what language is and how it is used, and maintains a neutral stance concerning the values of language practices. Linguistics has many different branches. A few of the most notable are:

- phonology (which looks at the sound systems of language; see Speech [4.46]);
- lexis and morphology (which look at words and word components);
- semantics (which looks at meaning [4.43]);
- grammatical analysis (which looks at how words, sentences and phrases are strung together – see Chomsky [5.5] and Halliday [5.16]);
- text linguistics (which looks at the way texts are constructed, and discourse analysis [4.17]);
- pragmatics (which looks at uses of language for particular purposes, e.g. speech acts – see Searle [5.33]). Rhetoric [4.42] can also be seen as applied pragmatics;
- sociolinguistics (which looks at language in social contexts – see Bernstein [5.4], Labov [5.21]);
- psycholinguistics (which looks at language as a psychological phenonomon, arguably a branch of cognitive psychology [4.7]).

4.29 Mass communication

Mass communication is generally conceived as communication *to* the masses, rather than *by* or *from* the masses, arising largely from sociological studies of the mass media, but, of course, existing as a phenomenon since ruling elites sought to manage those ruled through communicative media (see Marx [5.27], Gramsci [5.13], hegemony [4.20]). The earliest form of mass communication is generally thought of as print, because print offered the first medium through which identical messages could be produced and disseminated in the mass.

Most often, discussion of mass communication centres on the modern media of newspaper, film, TV and, more recently, information and communications technologies [4.8]. The interactivity offered by recent digital systems changes the conception of mass communication somewhat. Simple models of mass communication by which small groups communicate messages to a largely passive mass audience become less valid. Use of digital technologies can be thought of as 'collective communication', communication which occurs in the mass, but which is maintained largely through many overlapping organizations and small groups (e.g. through small networks on the World Wide Web).

More sophisticated models of mass communication have generally recognized that the mass audience is not one homogeneous mass, even when seen as such by those sending out mass communication messages. So examinations of mass communication have often looked at the relationships between media production (the means by which mass messages are produced) and media reception (the processes by which mass audiences [4.2] receive and respond to such messages).

In the mass, audiences may be largely passive receptors of messages, in which case broadcast [4.3] messages, such as universal advertising on TV, can be an effective communicative strategy. Or audiences may actually be more fragmented, dividing into different types and groups (see Class [4.5]), and have to be addressed by different means (so called 'narrowcasting'). Or segments of the audience may have different degrees of communicative sophistication (e.g. modern audiences may generally maintain a very sceptical or critical attitude to advertisements), so effective mass communication tends to evolve in a spiralling relationship with its audiences (see Media Uses and Gratifications [4.31]).

This 'evolution' of communication processes is one factor in so-called 'postmodern' [4.40] communications, where the message maintains an ironic or self-reflective attitude to itself, internally representing part of the attitude of the audience as a way of getting that audience to identify with the message and thereby take it on board.

4.30 Media

All communication has to take place through a medium of some kind, and that medium will limit the communication in some ways, and permit various features to exist at the same time (see, e.g., McLuhan [5.26]). Often a form of communication is highly defined by the medium it employs, but there is always a dynamic between what the medium initially sets up, and what users do, or try to do, with it.

Think of texting on mobile phones, for example. A mobile phone is essentially a device for talking at a distance, without being tied to a particular transmission or connection point. But its digital transmission also meant that there was capacity (technically, 'bandwidth') for transmission of information other than voice signals, such as the ASCII codes for text (ASCII stands for American Standard Code for Information Interchange).

It costs virtually nothing to add transmission of text to voice transmission, as the amount of bandwidth needed is so small (comparatively speaking). Consequently it can be offered very cheaply to consumers. Cheap communication is a good choice for simple messages, especially where immediacy is not too important. So many people choose to text rather than talk when their messages are brief, simple or don't require immediate contact with the receiver.

But this communication is very limited. ASCII text has a limited range of signs, so any sophisticated meanings are difficult to communicate. And it takes much longer to type a message than to speak it, so even brief messages can be time-consuming. These two big limitations would surely mean that texting would remain simply a gimmick alongside the 'real' purpose of mobile phones, spoken communication.

But, as everyone knows, this turned out not to be the case, because people found ways of getting round and adapting the system to convey messages more efficiently (using less time) and more expressively (using 'smileys' or 'emoticons' = 'emotive icons'). Both these devices already existed in email practice (smileys have a long tradition in computer communication, and abbreviation, of course, is a standard response to over-complex information). They were simply taken over, adapted and then highly developed in texting, and in consequence a 'new'(ish) popular, creative form of communication was created.

But, on the face of it, it seems odd that a medium created for spoken (natural) communication has been as successful as a medium for the much less natural process of writing, especially as people by and large tend to resist the idea of written communication wherever possible.

4.3 I Media uses and gratifications

Audience effects theory assumes that mass communication [4.29] has an effect on its audiences, influencing them and making them behave in particular ways [4.2]. 'Uses and gratifications' theory suggests that audiences should be looked at not as passive consumers of mass media messages, but as active seekers of such messages (see also the discussion of the active audience [3.1.4]). Audiences seek to use the mass media for their own purposes, and seek gratifications of particular kinds from those uses. For example, they may seek entertainment through diversion, or they may seek information for decision-making. They may use the mass media for training, or for self-analysis and self-understanding.

As such, the theory emphasizes the apparent choice that individuals have in selecting the media they want for the purposes they identify. However, some media research shows that, far from exercising individual choice on each potential occasion of encountering mass media, people have well-engrained habits: they tend to read the same newspaper that they always have; they watch the same programmes on TV at the same time every week. Whilst one could rationalize some of this habitual behaviour as 'systematic choice' (i.e. once I've decided that the *Daily Record* meets all my needs, I don't have to re-make that decision later), the theory takes little account of social conformity or of the influence of ideology [4.23] within subcultures.

It seems likely, therefore, that a useful theory of how audiences interact with mass media messages must combine some element of 'effects' with a uses and gratifications element.

4.32 Models of communication

A model is an attempt to construct an abstract representation of a class of phenomena which shows the key characteristics of the phenomena in a generalized way. In other words, it is a kind of description of what language [4.26], say, or communication, is, in an abstract sense, a representation [4.41] of a theory.

Many models of communication have been proposed. Most are either adaptations of the early model proposed by Shannon and Weaver [5.34], or reactions against it. As a model aims to offer a generalization that can be applied in many, if not all, situations, it seems unlikely that one universal model of communication can be created. Consequently, the main use of such models is to set up a general description against which particular cases can be examined. From this perspective, the best way to use a communications model is to choose one that seems a reasonable match to the kind of communication being examined, and then attempt to map each part of that communicative situation to the model. Sometimes this will work perfectly, and the model is 'proven' to work for that situation. Equally often, the model will be found to be inappropriate in some ways, in which case it will be necessary either to adapt the model or to find some explanation of the situation which accounts for the difference. Models, therefore, can be useful ways of trying to describe what might be 'expected' and thereby point out the unusual or unexpected elements that need particular explanation.

Shannon and Weaver's model distinguishes a transmitter, a signal and a receiver (Figure 4.1). The transmitter selects a message to transmit from an information source. The transmitter encodes the message in a signal, by selecting from an available code [4.6], and transmits that signal through a communications channel. The receiver receives the signal, decodes the message and stores it. Whilst being transmitted, noise can enter the system, interfering with the signal, and degrading it. If so, the signal as received will be different from that sent, and the message that is decoded may differ from the one sent.

Almost all other models of communication start from this point and either enhance it, modify it or argue against it in advocating a different model. We have to remember that it is an engineer's model of telecommunications, not a model of social or psychological reality, and at that level it makes perfect sense. When we try to apply it to different human communicative situations, however, it becomes problematic, requiring modification.

For example, most human communication is two-way, so feedback of some kind from receiver to sender needs to be incorporated into the model. Noise might not just be physical noise but could, for example, result from the psychological state of

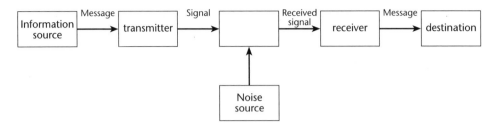

Figure 4.1 *Shannon and Weaver's model of communication (used with permission of the University of Illinois Press)*

the sender or receiver, which might 'interfere' with the process, so perhaps noise or interference should be allowed at all points in the model. Human beings can communicate about communication, so they can monitor, and seek or give feedback on all aspects of their communication, including the monitoring of noise. Therefore, perhaps the possibility of feedback loops could be allowed across all aspects of the system, including loops which combat the noise.

Clearly the Shannon and Weaver model is useful, but much of its use is in highlighting aspects of particular instances of communication which need further clarification or modelling.

4.33 Non-verbal communication (NVC)

A key idea in MCCS is that anything a human being does can be communicative. One area which is high in communicative power from the receiver's point of view, but largely unconscious or unintended by the originator, is non-verbal communication. It is pervasive in human face-to-face (f-t-f) interaction, as people are always giving off non-verbal signals that they are generally unaware of. By extension, it can be important in other forms of communication which are derived from f-t-f communication, such as acting, modelling, photography, video-conferencing, cartoons, virtual reality constructs, and so on. In Peter Jackson's film *The Lord of the Rings: The Two Towers*, for example, the effectiveness of Gollum, an animated character that people were moved by, is strong testimony to the communicative power of modelling NVC.

There are many forms of NVC, key ones being as follows:

- *Gaze.* A self-explanatory category, but one confounded a little by the range of activities that eyes can engage in: for example, pupil dilation (expansion), which generally indicates interest, arousal or fear; frequency and length of looking; use of the various muscles around the eyes to 'hood' them for sultry effect.
- *Facial expression.* The most obvious facial movement which conveys meaning is the smile, of which there are many kinds. Other obvious facial expressions are frowning and scowling. In fact, most emotional states have an equivalent facial expression, usually created by the movement not of just one part of the face, but of several.
- *Gesture.* The movement of the hands, and some other parts of the body (arms and

legs in particular), enables the formation of particular gestures. Whereas facial expressions have some degree of constancy across cultures (but not universally so), gestures tend to be more culturally specific.

- *Vocal expressions.* Often vocal expression is not listed as NVC, because it's a use of the voice (or, at least, the organs of speech). But NVC stands for non-*verbal* communication, that is, communication without words, not 'non-vocal' expression. There are many sounds that we make with our speech organs which are not words but do convey meaning: a range of clicks, sighs and snorts which can convey such things as mild disapproval (represented usually as 'tut tut'), exhaustion or contentment (both are deep sighs – what's the difference between them?) and scatological sounds.
- *Physical appearance.* This is rather a catch-all category for those elements of human presentation which can vary meaningfully, but which are generally not biologically constrained. For example, gestures and facial expressions are created, but also limited, by the muscles we have, the relationships between different bone structures, and so on. But our dress, makeup, perfume, hairstyle, and so on, whilst they may convey much about us, are generally not a function of our biological inheritance, or at least not very strongly limited by it. Most people with hair can have any hairstyle. Most people can wear any kinds of clothes.
- *Posture.* How we stand and sit. For example, 'Postural echo', where one person unconsciously mirrors the position of another, is generally interpreted as a sign of agreement.
- *Proxemics.* How close people are to each other, and under what circumstances.

There can be some practical value in knowing about NVC, but its application is not always straightforward. For example, it can be useful to know that folding your arms in an interview tends to look like a barrier, protecting yourself from the interviewer, or that leaning forward shows a sign of interest, so the former should be avoided, whilst the latter is worth cultivating, if it feels natural.

4.34 Organizational communication

Organizations communicate meanings through messages, just as individuals, small groups [4.19] and large groups do. Organizational communication is generally studied in the context of business communication (see, e.g., Hartley and Bruckmann 2002) but, of course, there are many organizations which are not businesses, such as the United Nations, charities, schools and hospitals. As you might expect, the kinds of communication found in organizations relate in part to group communication (e.g. how meetings run) and in part to sociological accounts of large-scale communication (e.g. in corporate communication, where large organizations attempt mass communication [4.29]).

However, organizations often have their own communication processes whose explanation generally relates to the way the organization itself operates, making organizational communication a distinct branch of study. Analysis of how communication works in any given institution often means an associated analysis of other working practices and organizational structures.

It is not difficult to see the kinds of issues that might typically exist in an organization's communications. For example, there is often a tension between the formal communication processes (those established by the organization itself, with specific and explicit purposes established to fulfil given functions) and its informal communications (e.g. corridor and office conversations and staff email exchanges). Some people feel that their organizations work *despite* the formal communications processes (i.e. they depend on the informal communications that take place). Other people are highly suspicious that the most important communications in their organization are informal (e.g. 'corridor decisions') and that the formal communications processes are set up merely to pay lip service to notions such as 'democracy' and 'accountability' in the organization.

4.35 Patterning

One way to characterize the whole enterprise of MCCS is to say that it is the examination of patterns in human activity, as these are essential for communication.

More specifically, analysts generally look at two dimensions of patterns in communication. These are often referred to by the hugely unhelpful words 'syntagmatic' relationship and 'paradigmatic' relationship. The first of these is pattern in sequences, that is, patterns in time, such as a musical sequence, or the structure of a narrative. Section [3.1.7], for example, in describing ways of structuring writing, uses some ideas of structural sequences to characterize certain genres [4.18]. The second concept, paradigmatic relation, is a pattern of substitution. For example, all the possible notes that could go in a particular place in a musical phrase, or all the possible words that might go in a sentence at a particular point are in 'paradigmatic relationship' with each other.

There are different kinds of sequential relationship and different kinds of paradigmatic relationship. If we take a simple sentence, for example, such as:

The red ship sailed over the horizon.

We can see that the word 'The' precedes 'red', and 'ship' precedes 'sailed'. But it is also true that the phrase 'The red ship' precedes 'sailed' – one syntagmatic structure is word order, and the other is phrase order. In fact, describing sentences like this can create simple grammars of the language [4.26], sometimes known as 'phrase structure' grammars (see Chomsky [5.5]). Because we can see two kinds of sequencing, we can also find two kinds of paradigmatic patterning, substitution of the elements at both these levels. We can, for example, substitute 'blue' or 'green' for 'red'. This is substitution at word level. But we can equally substitute at phrasal level, such as 'The blue boat' or 'The ice floe' or even 'Three pink battleships filled with marshmallows'.

By looking for all these rules of sequencing (or combination) and substitution, we can develop a grammar of a language. However, such structures can also be found in other kinds of communication codes [4.6]: the observation, for example, that in the code of dress we can substitute 'shirt and tie' for 'T-shirt', and 'pinstriped trousers' for 'faded jeans'. The combination of 'shirt and tie' with 'pinstriped trousers' makes sense: it is a recognized combination meaning something like formal business wear. The combination 'T-shirt and jeans' also makes sense, as 'informal, casual wear'. But 'T-shirt and pinstriped trousers' is not a 'meaningful' combination. We can wear both items together, of course, just as we could say 'the sailed blue ship red boat', but it's not meaningful according to the code. By analogy with language, we can say it's an 'ungrammatical' combination, and so we could talk about a 'grammar' of dress. A grammar of dress would be a set of rules for all the possible syntagmatic structures that make sense, and all the possible substitutions of items of clothing that are possible, within the code of a particular culture

This leads to the suggestion, made by structuralists [4.48] such as Lévi-Strauss [5.24], that many (perhaps even 'all') codes could be described in such a way: as structures made up of sequences and substitutions.

4.36 Perception

Perception is how we see things. However, this apparently simple statement hides a very complex aspect of human psychology, upon which important elements of communication depend.

Firstly, there is the physiology of perception, by which data from the outside world are taken in by a human being (through the sensory organs: the eyes, the ears, the nose, the mouth and the skin). These processes are largely outside the province of students of culture and communication, yet they are obviously key factors in how we can make sense of the world, and how we can share our sense-making with others. If our physical organs are not reliable, for example, or are wildly different between different people, then relating the sensation of one person to that of another might be fraught with difficulty. (Wittgenstein [5.40] takes this point to its extreme, arguing that no two people can ever have exactly the same experience and therefore never understand exactly the same thing by a particular sign.)

Physical sensations are interpreted by the brain. However, cognitive psychologists [4.7] have shown that this is by no means a simple process of 'receiving' data and assembling it. The brain does many complex things in order to make sense of the world, including making up for all sorts of omissions and compromises. As a simple example, the eye acts like a lens to receive light and pass it back through the optic nerve to the brain. But the optic nerve cannot itself receive light, so there is a 'black spot' in the eye where the optic nerve is attached. We never perceive this hole in our sight, because the brain makes up information to fill the gap, based on the information received immediately around the optic nerve.

But perception is further complicated by cultural factors. How we see and interpret things is a function not merely of how our brain works physiologically, but also of how it has been taught to work, through socialization [4.45] and acculturation. (You can find a brief account of this related to optical illusions by A.R. Luria in Corner and Hawthorn 1989.)

4.37 Personality

We all know what personality is, but find it hard to describe easily: it's a combination of personal characteristics in an individual which dispose that person to act in particular ways, where choices are available. A personality is a set of characteristics from all those possible characteristics which human beings can have, related to, but neither determined by nor determining identity [4.22]. Personality affects interpersonal communication [4.25] and group communication [4.19] but is also manifest through non-verbal communication [4.33].

4.38 Phenomenology

Phenomenology is a philosophical position which argues that we should deal with the world as it appears and not as we assume it to be. In other words, people should interact with the phenomena they encounter, rather than their interpretation, expectation or presupposition of what they would encounter. From this perspective, people, hence communication, are always embedded in particular situations, experiencing particular phenomena. Any abstraction of or generalization from that situation ignores some of the particularity of that situation, and therefore may 'miss the point', and so theories of communication which are not grounded in actual events make no sense.

4.39 Positivism

The nineteenth-century French philosopher Auguste Comte developed the notion of positivism, a philosophy which elevates the scientific method above other modes of inquiry and declares that investigations not amenable to scientific methods are not worthwhile. In the positivist view only empirical evidence (crudely speaking, 'observed facts') are legitimate data for study, and if a phenomenon cannot be observed or measured, then it is meaningless to attempt to study it.

From this viewpoint, any metaphysical (i.e. 'beyond the physical': abstract, theoretical or mental) investigation is meaningless, even nonsense. Much cultural and media theory therefore sets itself against positivism, because social movements, psychological causes and cultural meanings are clearly not measurable and, in most cases, if not actually metaphysical, are certainly difficult to observe with any accuracy. There is, however, some ideological tension within MCCS where issues such as 'modelling', 'observation' or 'measurement' occur.

For example, a descriptive linguistics [4.28] which sought to measure detectable changes in intonation patterns in speech [4.46] in order to try to model how differences in pitch related to differences in meaning would be called reductive (reducing the complexity of meaning to over-simple ideas) and positivist (by subscribing to the scientific method, necessarily limiting observations to those of little consequence). Durkheim's [5.7] original conception of sociology has been criticized in this way, for example.

Conversely, those who find themselves opposed to the more speculative, metaphysical or florid accounts of cultural theory (as the writings of Lacan [5.22] and Derrida [5.6] have sometimes been treated) suggest that the lack of empirical data in such accounts makes them little more than poetic: excursions into linguistic fantasy.

Part of the difficulty in this field lies at the heart of its origins: the notion of meaning that lies at the heart of Saussure's [5.32] and Peirce's [5.28] writing. The simplest concept of signification has both a physical, observable component, the signifier, and a mental meaning associated with that physical component, the signified. Those with a positive bent tend to focus on the signifier, and the systems which signifiers belong to. Those with a metaphysical bent tend to focus on signifieds, whose attachment to observable phenomena tends to be subordinated to conceptual (de)construction [4.16].

4.40 Postmodernism

Postmodernism is the sense that the world is fragmented and disjunctive, lacking overall coherence, and that meaningfulness largely exists through overlapping relationships between partial discourses. There is no single knowledge, only 'knowledges', and the prevalant discourse is avant-garde: experimental, fluid.

Inter-textuality is an important idea here: the notion that texts acquire meaning by relationship to other texts. In the postmodernist view, this is a central, perhaps the only, means by which communicative messages develop. There are multiple codes [4.6], multiple ways of communicating, and the relationship between them is how new meanings are constructed. This might be explicitly cross-referential, in which one text cites or refers to another one as its basis. Or it might be implicit, and subtle, where relationships are vague, partial, allusive, ironic, metaphorical, adaptive: a wide range of uses that one text can make of another, making it a good example in many ways of a postmodern entertainment.

The cartoon series *The Simpsons* is an excellent example of how texts create complex communications, by embedding one kind of communication within another, and building their effect through inter-textual relations with other culturally significant texts. For example, 'Itchy and Scratchy', the Simpsons' cartoon within a cartoon, represents a complex communication with its audience. It is firstly an allusion to *Tom and Jerry*, and similar cartoons, which pit animals against each other in mock and exaggerated violence. By making that violence as extreme as possible, 'Itchy and Scratchy' offers a comment on the nature of such entertainment: why is hitting a cat with a frying pan funny, but disembowelling it with an electric drill not a source of humour? At the same time, the cartoon is an example of the kind of humour it is critiquing, and the audience laugh at it and mock themselves.

Of course, *The Simpsons* also communicates in many traditional, simple ways. The humour of its stereotypes [4.47], pratfalls, insults, running jokes, misunderstandings, puns, character weaknesses, and so on, is characteristic of both cartoon and situation comedy cum soap opera. Just as frequently, however, the Simpsons' humour steps outside these traditions to comment on them, or to subvert them, or to pit them against each other. In addition, it uses many explicit inter-textual devices, particular references to other cultural artefacts and genres, to create much of its humour (either by poking fun at the referent, or simply by juxtaposing two radically different world views). These are postmodern devices, the self-referential interaction of communicative elements, using some part of a communication to make reference to itself, or to another part, and thereby violating the established norms for the genre.

Postmodernism is not the same as post-structuralism, although arguably they go hand in hand. Post-structuralism is characterized as the exposure of structuralist [4.48] accounts of meaning through deconstruction [4.16]. (See also Derrida [5.6] and Lyotard [5.25].)

4.41 Representation

An event or phenomenon happens or is created. We can call this 'presentation'. Thereafter, any account or reproduction of that one-off occurrence is a 're-presentation'. For example, during the Iraq war, Coalition troops were killed by fire from their own side, so-called 'friendly fire'. Once this has happened, it was over, and any attempt to talk about it, replay the video, interpret what went on or why it happened is a 'representation' of the actual event. Even if we simply summarize it as 'this tragedy' or 'the friendly fire accident', we are representing it in a particular way.

This concept is important in MCCS because representation is the way that all events are 'mediated' through a medium of some kind and necessarily affected by the processes that make that medium communicative. A representation is not the thing itself, and therefore it must be an interpretation, or reinterpretation, of that thing. Mediation of an event, representing it in some way, necessarily involves selection of some parts of that event, implicitly deciding what is 'important' or 'significant' or 'foregrounded' (brought to the attention) from all its possible features.

So representation is a way of establishing a relationship between the communicator (such as a mass media organization, or a writer) and the event, and also a relationship with those who will receive that representation. It is therefore a way of seeking to establish a relationship between that event and those people you are communicating with. For example, I have no way of knowing if 'friendly fire' incidents in the Iraq war were truly friendly fire or not. I have only media representations of these events to go on (mainly newspapers and TV). They, in turn, are dependent on their sources, which may be first-hand accounts, or may be indirect reports, or may be actual recordings of the events; but in all these cases they are mediated – a recording of an event is not the event itself. Can we be certain that the recording shows what we think or believe it shows? Would a recording from a different angle show something different? What does the recording tell us about the events immediately prior to the event recorded, or about its consequences, or about the motivations of the people involved?

Media theory argues that representation is a primary means by which power relations are established, as well as other relationships (although some would say that all relationships are power relationships). The way an event is represented establishes an interpretation of that event which is either accepted in some degree, or rejected, by those who receive it; and this 'debate' over its acceptance is the tussle over the control of this event (or rather 'control of the representation of this event'), because whoever has that control, whoever's representation is accepted, becomes the dominant person or organization in that communication, and thereby acquires power over the subordinate. (See Fairclough [5.9] and Critical Linguistics [4.13].)

4.42 Rhetoric

Rhetoric is the art of persuasion. Everyone has heard of a 'rhetorical question'. This is a question for which no answer is expected; it is being used for a particular purpose, usually as a way of making a strong statement (e.g. see [3.1.8]). This use of a question for a specific persuasive purpose is one example of rhetoric in general – the use of particular language devices and methods for specific impact and effect.

Rhetoric was a key to effective communication in Ancient Greek and Renaissance cultures, part of standard education. In the USA, rhetoric forms an element of many communications and English courses with this purpose. In the UK, rhetoric is generally taught only within the context of the study of literature (where analysis of particular effects is often part of close textual analysis), but aspects of rhetorical practice are often found in training on speaking, advertising, marketing, handling the media and technical communication. Rhetorical analysis can be useful for understanding how persuasive communication works.

4.43 Semantics

Semantics is about meanings and the study of meanings. We talk about the 'semantics' of English, that is, the meanings of English words. Semantics as a study is not just about word meaning, though, but all the range of meanings that can be found in language (such as phrasal meanings, idioms, and the ways that grammatical choices may affect meaning). Semantics also looks at the relationships between meanings such as 'synonymy' (sameness of meaning), 'antonymy' (oppositeness of meaning) and 'entailment' (one meaning incorporates another one).

The dictionary definition of the meaning of a word, that is, its commonly accepted meaning, is generally called its 'denotation'. A word denotes some thing or idea or relationship in the world of meanings. So denotation is meaning as a general class of events or things. For example, the denotation of the letters 'p-a-g-e' is not the particular page you are reading at the moment, but all the possible pages in all the contexts in which a thing we'd call a page might occur. In this sense, words don't mean things, they mean ideas.

Saussure [5.32] developed this idea, arguing that meaning relations are systematic across a language, and so it is the *difference* between signs which creates the system of meaning. This can be a difficult idea to grasp. Saussure's notion is that, because signs in a language are arbitrary (not connected in any obvious way to the thing they stand for – see Semiotics [4.44]), they acquire meaning not just by what they are used for, but also by what they are *not* used for. For example, we do not use the word 'page' to refer to a blank piece of paper that is not part of a book. We'd probably call that a 'sheet of paper' or simply 'paper'. The different signs mean different things because of the way they are used; but also they cut up the world in a particular way. 'Page' and 'paper' divide the world into bits of paper bound together in books with print on, and blank bits of paper not bound together. This is one of those binary distinctions that Saussure founded his theories upon.

When we use a word in a particular context to indicate a particular thing, such as if I say 'this page that you are reading at the moment', then that use of the word is given a concrete *reference*. I use the word form 'p-a-g-e', whose denotation is something like 'part of a book with writing on it', to refer to the specific instance of it you have in your hand or on your desk. So denotation is part of the underlying system of language, and reference is a particular use of language for particular purposes on particular occasions. This means that we can 'abuse' the language. We can take a word whose denotation is *x* and use it in a particular instance to refer to an instance of *y*. If I say to my son 'Why don't you feed the dog', even though we don't have a dog, he will probably still understand what I mean, because we have a cat.

When analysing meaning, we can generally distinguish a second kind of meaning that a sign, symbol, word or artefact can have, namely its 'connotation'. Connotation is a separate idea from denotation, being the meaning which people associate with the sign, irrespective of what its defined or systematic meaning might be. For example, both the signs 'nag' and 'equine quadruped' mean the same thing: they have the same denotation, which is *horse*. But we think of 'nag' as being a decrepit, run-down, flea-bitten old horse: that's the connotation of the word. 'Equine quadruped', however, connotes something like 'posh, snooty, jargon; an upper-class or elitist way to talk about a horse'. These kinds of connotation are the additional meanings we often draw on when we make stylistic choices [4.49]. They are also the sorts of meaning which can be most illuminating when analysing a text using approaches such as content analysis [4.9] and semiotics [4.44].

Because of the many different elements of meaning, most words, phrases and other signs can suffer from ambiguity [4.1]. Necessarily, because a sign has denotative meaning in the system, but could be used to refer to an infinite number of situations, signs are generally systematically ambiguous in terms of their potential use.

4.44 Semiotics

Semiotics is the study and analysis of signs. Signs may have different relationships with what they stand for.

- They may appear similar to the thing they stand for. Peirce [5.28] calls such signs 'iconic'. For example, the road sign representing a winding road is a pair of parallel winding lines, a stylized picture of such a road.
- They may be connected to the real thing they stand for. Peirce calls such signs 'indexes', such as smoke being an index of fire.
- They may have an arbitrary relationship, that is, no obvious connection, with the thing they stand for. Peirce calls such a sign a 'symbol'. For example, there is no reason why a particular idea should be called 'money' or 'l'argent' or 'dosh'. These are just arbitrary collections of sounds and letters used to signify the particular idea. Saussure [5.32] says that all signs in language are arbitrary.

We can, of course, find signs of different types in relationship to one another. For example, the iconic pictures on the doors to Gents' and Ladies' toilets (which bear some relationship to the thing they stand for) may be accompanied by the words 'Gents' and 'Ladies'. The words are arbitrary, but the pictures of a human form are iconic. Yet both these types of sign in this case are culturally dependent. Understanding particular linguistic signs depends on knowing the language they belong to, of course. But the visual sign is also culturally specific: there are cultures where wearing a skirt would not be sufficient to signal gender difference.

So signs also need someone to understand them. You cannot have a sign, or a sign system, without someone to interpret that sign, because it has to connect with something in someone's head (the 'receiver', in Shannon and Weaver's [5.34] model of communication [4.32]). Peirce called that mental 'idea' the 'interpretant'. Saussure said a sign is made up of a 'signifier' (the sounds, or letters, or image) and a 'signified' (the mental image or idea connected to that signifier).

Signs can be looked at as abstract systems, in the way that Saussure looked at language [4.26] and Lévi-Strauss [5.24] at culture. For Saussure, therefore, the language system is a set of connections between different sets of *signifier and signified*, and he thought that the connection would be the same for every speaker of a language. In other words, all native speakers of a language understand 'the same thing' by a particular signifier. This is essentially the idea of 'denotation', the systematic meaning of words in language (see Semantics [4.43]).

However, semioticians such as Barthes [5.3] do not seek to establish complete structural [4.48] accounts of how a sign system or code [4.6] might work. Instead, they focus on individual representations [4.41], or small collections of them. For example, you might conduct a semiotic analysis of a series of television adverts for shampoo or cars to see what kind of signs were being used, and what they were signs of.

Signs may carry all sorts of meanings. These may not always be obvious, as many messages work by conveying implicit signals that the reader or viewer is not aware of, and the signification may be quite complex, buried in subtle and detailed relationship with other signs, other sign systems, other representations or entire subcultures. So semioticians are much more concerned with analysing connotation than denotation.

For example, the meaning carried by the colour red can be quite different in different contexts [4.10]. On a traffic light it means stop. On a fire engine it means 'fire' and 'speed'. It can connote 'hell' or 'the devil', 'sin', 'sexuality', 'Manchester United', 'anger' and 'blood'. None of these are the exact meaning of 'red', they are all possible connotations (see Semantics [4.43]). So deciding which of these possible meanings might apply in any given semiotic analysis depends very much on how the signs are decoded in relation to other signs and systems.

4.45 Socialization

This is the process by which an individual is brought into, or made an acceptable member of, a particular social group [4.19]. Typically we are socialized as we grow up by our parents, relatives and peers, who gradually train us to adopt the conventions [4.11] of the social group and behave in ways traditionally found acceptable in the group. Socialization can be one way that dominant ideology [4.23] is expressed and communicated to individuals. It is also a powerful communicator of other cultural values, such as what is of 'worth' in the group, and what is the 'right way' to behave in particular communicative situations.

We are socialized to behave in particular ways and to communicate in particular ways, according to the social groups we belong to (e.g. family and class; see Bernstein [5.4]).

4.46 Speech

Speech is perhaps the most obvious form of human communication. However, like many aspects of communication, when you come to examine it, it's not entirely clear what it is. We can describe with a reasonable degree of accuracy various sounds that can be made with the so-called vocal organs (they are 'so-called' because none of them were actually evolved with speech as the primary purpose). However, not all the sounds that can be produced count as speech, and some sounds count as speech in some languages and not in others.

Furthermore, there are some sounds which can be made in one language without changing meaning, but do change meaning in other languages, and there are some sounds in a given language which 'count as' the same, even though they are different. For example, the 'l' sound we use in 'lid' is different from the 'sound' we use in 'dull' (the first is produced towards the front of the mouth and known as 'clear l'; the second is produced near the back of the mouth, and called 'dark l'). Yet they both count as 'the same sound' in English.

Similarly there are sounds we produce that convey meaning but are not part of our speech: sounds such as the ones we usually represent as 'tut tut' or 'hmph!', which would be called non-*verbal* communication [4.33].

The sounds that can be produced by the vocal organs are called 'phones' and their study 'phonetics'. Because those sounds can exist in different relationships with each other, notably in binary opposition, and because different sounds have different functions within a given language, the study of the sound systems of language (rather than just the sounds themselves) has its own name: 'phonology'. A sound considered within a given language is called a 'phoneme' (so phonology sometimes is called 'phonemics').

Speech, according to Saussure [5.32], is arguably the most important form of communication, as it is the first we learn as children, and historically predates writing in the development of civilization. Most forms of writing are derived from speech. Kress [5.20] (1989) explores the issues associated with the primacy of speech over writing.

Speech is also an important area for study because of its many variations. Not only are there many different languages spoken in the world, but each has its own internal spoken variations (see Language Variation [4.27]).

4.47 Stereotyping

Stereotyping applies a simplified group characterization to any particular person. For example, we might say 'he's typically French' or 'she's just what you'd expect of a schoolteacher'. What we are doing here is saying 'all the French' or 'all schoolteachers' have similar characteristics, and this individual is representative of those characteristics.

It is, of course, perfectly possible to make generalizations about groups which are true and reasonably objective (after all, this is what sociologists often aim to do). All the French are European, for example, and all schoolteachers are adults. But these truths are not really characteristic of stereotypes. When we talk of stereotyping we usually mean generalizations that are not reasonable, or reasoned, but over-simplifications applied to large social groups, such as a race or a nation or an occupation.

In other words, stereotypes tend to be negative. They tend to be used to typify someone in a very simple way, as a means of classifying him or her, in order that an 'instant' attitude and relationship can be established. By using a stereotype, someone avoids the need to find out what the person is really like, and can use a simplistic form of communication, saving a great deal of effort, but necessarily establishing a false picture, one which generally operates to the detriment of the person stereotyped.

So stereotypes are popular representations [4.41] of social identity [4.22] that enable simplified communication. Often the stereotype is historically derived and embedded in all sorts of communications and cultural media, such as literature, ethnic jokes, film roles, popular art, cartoons, situation comedies. Therefore study of stereotypes can tell you something about the cultural heritage and perception of the particular group and about the psychology of communication. Because stereotypes are often held by one group of another equivalent, perhaps competing, group (e.g. similar ethnic jokes operate between different neighbouring countries), they also tell you something about inter-group communication [4.19].

4.48 Structuralism

Saussure's [5.32] linguistics described two kinds of patterns [4.35] in language [4.26], patterns of sequence (syntagmatic) and patterns of substitution (paradigmatic). Lévi-Strauss [5.24] took up this idea and applied it to the anthropological study of culture.

Structuralism looks beneath texts to explore the underlying structure. It is founded on Saussure's notion of 'binary opposition'. Signs in a system have meaning by virtue of not being other signs in that system, and the key definer of a term is the opposite of that term. Each term in a binary opposition requires the other for both to be meaningful, such as 'hot/cold', 'birth/death', 'light/dark'. The important characteristics of the system within a text are the relationships between pairs of elements in the system, rather than the nature of those elements themselves.

So, Lévi-Strauss's analysis of myth finds it based on different representations [4.41] of the opposition 'culture/nature'. Or a structural analyst of the Sherlock Holmes stories may note that the relationship between the 'elements' Holmes and Watson is that of superior intelligence to inferior intelligence, and this opposition gives a structure throughout the story: the relationship between the intelligence of the Holmes and Watson investigative team is superior to the police investigators' intelligence; men's intelligence is superior to women's intelligence; the intelligence of 'good' is greater than that of 'evil'.

We could say that this analysis shows the 'underlying meaning' of the Holmes stories; that these pairs carry, through the narrative, the main story movements; that the tension between these oppositions holds much of the suspense and mystery in the stories, that the moral tone is equated to superior thinking, and so on. We would have an explanation of how the 'underlying meaning' of these stories works in terms of the oppositions they set up.

In a similar (but much more extensive) way, structural analysis can be applied to any coherent set of texts (or discourse [4.17]), such as myth or folktale or kinship patterns or advertisements, and used to expose underlying structures, patterns of opposition. Its accounts can be insightful, if the oppositions identified are key ones, prominent in the discourse.

The post-structuralist view goes beyond this level of analysis to deconstruct

[4.16] it, by showing how the apparent opposition is dependent on something else, suggesting that structuralist analysis will always over-simplify as any apparent opposition can be read differently (see also Derrida [5.6]).

4.49 Style

Arguably all communication is a matter of choice [3.1.9]. Style is determined by making a series of compatible or interrelated choices 'of the same kind'. For example, consistently choosing informal words, an informal syntactic structure and the medium of 'chat' would all assert a particular style of communication.

Styles of language are studied in a branch of linguistics [4.28] called 'stylistics'. Sometimes this has a literary flavour, and sometimes a wider remit for studying language choice.

4.50 Technological determinism

The strong version of theories of technological determinism is that technological change causes social change. A weaker version is that technological change influences social change. This is one of those areas where 'common sense' may be at variance with theoretical perspectives. Whilst it might seem obvious that the invention of the microcomputer changed society (and many books have argued and explored this), such a view sees society as essentially 'one thing' awaiting the technology, then consuming it, and reacting to it. Does it really work like this?

It might be more reasonable to see technological change as itself socially determined. People identify needs, and try to address them. People make discoveries, and try to fit those discoveries to perceived problems. Organizations wish to make money from innovation, so seek ways to innovate in an economic context, taking into account the nature of particular groups of consumers and their desires. Designers, writers and broadcasters, including writers of science fiction, speculate about the nature of possible technologies, their pros and cons, the social and personal needs they might address, the values and drawbacks of particular concepts. Social, commercial and economic history tends to focus on an innovation and influence it: for example, microcomputers have been designed with all sorts of different keyboards, usually innovations aimed at speeding up typing; but the keyboard that is used throughout the English-speaking world is the QWERTY typewriter design, intended to slow typists down (because on the original mechanical typewriters fast typists jammed the keys).

All of these influences suggest that technology is as much shaped by society as a shaper of it. But to suggest that this was the entire case would also be an over-simplification as there is clearly an interaction between social forces and technological processes, almost a dialogue, whereby needs and uses subtly alter. Sometimes this is a very explicit process. For example, the whole focus of what is called 'user-centred design' in technology is to involve potential users in technological development at every stage of development and this often leads to technologies which could not have been envisaged by the technologists.

Sometimes the process is much more subtle. For example, if you consider the relationship between computer gamers and computer games, the whole history of games development has been through a complex series of discourses which include:

- economic exchange between the gamer as consumer, and the developer;
- complaints and requests answered or avoided, through chat rooms, marketing questionnaires, user testing;
- fashions in game genres and other related media;
- innovation of consumers themselves (e.g. in hacking into code, pirating software, adapting originals, customizing games).

All of these processes interact all the time in shaping the development of new games technologies for games players. As with the debate about media audiences (see Audiences [4.2] and Media Uses and Gratifications [4.31]), the links between technological and social change are not one-way.

5

Forty key thinkers

Introduction to the chapter

Like the previous chapter, this one looks at the kind of information you might have to deal with as a good student of MCCS. It gives a brief account of forty key writers and analysts. Some have had a historical impact, being the sources of key ideas in the analysis of MCCS, whilst others are more recent theorists who, though they may not have had such a fundamental impact, may well be more important to you as a student trying to get to grips with the range of the subject. As far as possible I have tried to select a few contributors from each of the many different disciplines that contribute to our area. This means, of course, in a limited space, that some have had to be missed out.

If you would like a rather more substantial list, Edgar and Sedgwick (2002) provides a comprehensive and readable account of over eighty cultural theorists. This book has a strong focus on the philosophical underpinnings of cultural theory. However, it contains a few inaccuracies, and it has no remit to cover theorists with a largely communications or media rather than cultural bent, so read it selectively. Lewis (2002), meanwhile, does a very good job of integrating discussion of many key thinkers in the context of larger discussions of movements, themes and theories.

There are cross-references linking the thinkers in Chapter 5 to ideas in Chapter 4. There are also suggested readings for most of these thinkers, although for some I have suggested introductory readings or extracts, rather than the original texts. Many of the writers listed below are advanced reading, and in some cases their writing only occasionally connects with the concerns of a media, communications or cultural studies student.

5.1 Argyle

Michael Argyle is the social psychologist who has probably had most influence in the study of human communication, largely through work begun in the 1970s. Much of his work has focused on communication in groups and interpersonal communication, although, being a social psychologist, he is also concerned with other group processes, not merely with communication. His work is of less relevance to media and cultural research, although some of his social analysis can be applied to the study of organizational culture and intercultural communications.

His books are particularly readable, and have been very popular, probably as much for their subject as their style. His accounts of non-verbal communication, for example, have done much to interest people in wider aspects of social communication, and by advocating a detailed approach to social skills analysis, his research has impacted on the everyday world of practical communication. He argues that to understand (and thereby improve) group and interpersonal activity, people's skills can be analysed, categorized and evaluated, just as for any other area of learning or training, and he provides many approaches to doing this sort of analysis, usually by offering models of what might be going on when people interact.

An extract on non-verbal communication by Michael Argyle appears in Corner and Hawthorne (1989), but Argyle's key text – Argyle (1994) – is well worth reading, as is Argyle (1988).

5.2 Bakhtin

Mikhail Bakhtin was a writer, critic and analyst exiled from the Soviet Union and writing in the first half of the twentieth century, although his writings were not well known in the west until they were translated in the 1970s. A key idea of Bakhtin's is that language is always a material dialogue. This is different from the ideas of structuralists [4.48] such as Saussure [5.32] and those who followed him, and many linguists, such as Chomsky [5.5], who see language as essentially a structured system which can be abstracted from actual practice. Language, for Bakhtin, is always a material practice, an actual activity, not an abstract set of structures, in which a dialogue is carried out between a speaker or writer and a hearer or receiver (see Models of Communication [4.32]) but which, crucially, is carried on in the context of previous communications. So he suggests that you can only understand what is going on in language by looking at the actual relationship being established between the participants, and other discourses [4.17] they have knowledge of. Communication is necessarily social and inter-textual.

This view is, of course, radically different from the model implied by the conventional engineering speaker–hearer model of communication. In this model messages are transmitted from a sender through signals (signs) to a receiver, and the receiver decodes or (in slightly more sophisticated models) reacts to, the message sent. The 'space' between sender and receiver is unimportant, unless it interferes with or modifies the signals being sent. Bakhtin sees the emphasis here as completely the wrong way round. The relationship between speaker and hearer, or writer and reader, is the crucial element in the communication, that which constrains, determines and is facilitated through actual practice.

In Bakhtin's view, the model of communication which sees 'messages' 'sent' to 'receivers' through 'structures' is a monologic view of communication, rather than 'dialogic'. Language is seen as coming from an individual source, not as a dialogue or negotiation between two or more communicators. Rather than thinking of one language system used for one social purpose by a communicator (the monologic view of language as a single system), Bakhtin prefers to see a culture as containing multiple, overlapping languages, referred to as 'heteroglossia'. He suggests that a culture is maintained by lots of different languages, modes of communication, which all members of the culture maintain and can switch between at different times, according to situation and need.

This view is similar to that of sociolinguistics, that branch of linguistics [4.28] which looks at language embedded in social situations: we have a number of codes [4.6] we can use, and we move between them according to the current social context, including the relationship we wish to establish with others in the communicative situation. Bakhtin's ideas are also helpful for practical communicators, by making them see communication as an interaction with other people, thereby not merely 'taking the audience into account' but fundamentally designing your communication to engage other people [3.1].

Bakhtin's view also offers insights into postmodernist [4.40] ideas of the world: that there is no single, unified way of communicating, but only *ways* of communicating, between which we can move with greater and lesser degrees of sophistication; and that there are tensions between the ways we might communicate, pulls in different directions, according to the different dictates of situation, participants, other discourses [4.17] and the language [4.26] itself.

A useful account of Bakhtin is in Bertens and Natoli (2002). Readings from Bakhtin can be found in Morris (1994) and Jaworski and Coupland (1999: 121–32).

5.3 Barthes

Roland Barthes is one of the earliest and most influential of semioticians. By showing, through several seminal applications of semiotics [4.44] to different cultural activities, that sign systems are embedded in almost all human activities, Barthes not only sensitized theoreticians to the need to account for the symbolic throughout cultural activity, but also gave practical methods for the application of semiotic analysis. So he illustrated the presence of communication structures where others (e.g. in the light of Derrida [5.6] or Lévi-Strauss [5.24]) merely asserted that such structures could be universally found. Detailed analysis of different kinds of cultural texts in Barthes's practice suggests that, whilst subtexts, connotations [4.43], conflicting ideologies [4.23] and complex communication patterns [4.35] could be found in almost any cultural artefact, it is unlikely that such patterns could easily be brought together in any single model of culture or communication.

Barthes's practice, like that of many semioticians, is not a methodology as such, and certainly not easy to replicate. It depends very much on the sensitivities, experience and knowledge of the analyst, suggesting that semiotics in many ways corresponds to literary criticism, which in some respects it developed from: an intelligent application of experienced insight, rather than systematic application of a discipline or rigid set of principles. Cultural analyses of this kind depend on knowledge of the cultural context and a willingness to examine what might lie beneath surface signs, repeatedly asking the question 'what is this a sign of?' and not always accepting the most immediate or direct answer to that question.

Essentially semiotic analyses like those of Barthes are concerned with examining the connotations that signs gather, rather than their denotations (see Semantics [4.43]). Connotations often work at an unconscious level, and are less systematic than the denotational backbone of a communications system, which is why there can be no formal analytical method.

Four of Barthes's most influential works are: *Elements of Semiology* (Barthes 1967), *Mythologies* (Barthes 1972), *S/Z* (Barthes 1975) and *Image, Music, Text* (Barthes 1984). A useful account of Barthes is in Bertens and Natoli (2002). The best way to understand Barthes, and the approach to semiotics which he established, is to read a series of his analyses. His account of denotation and connotation can be found in Cobley (1996: 129–33), of language and speech in Elliott (1999: 48–60) and of modern myth in Durham and Kellner (2001: 122–8). Additional material can be found in Sontag (1982).

5.4 Bernstein

Bernstein was an early sociologist interested in education and language, using a generally sociolinguistic approach. His early work focused in particular on the way different classes communicate, a focus which created controversy, as he was seen as suggesting that working-class language lacked the characteristics of middle-class language. This is generally known as 'deficit theory', the idea that one code [4.6] is deficient in relation to another.

Bernstein constantly maintained that his theories did not amount to a deficit theory. His primary theoretical contribution was the notion of 'restricted' and 'elaborated' codes (outlined in Bernstein 1971). His empirical fieldwork found that working-class speakers used restricted codes, that is, codes that are very specific, and highly dependent on the particular context. Conversely, the middle classes used an elaborated code, which was more generalized, universal in application and not dependent on context.

For example, controlling children through a restricted code might include language like 'Don't hit your brother with that pillow. Your mum won't give you that 50 pence.' Here the attempt to regulate behaviour is carried out by focusing on very particular aspects of the situation. An elaborated version of the same situation might be: 'Don't attack people. It's not nice behaviour.' In the first case, the demand is on the specific act, and a specific penalty that might apply. In the second, the act is generalized into a kind of act, and the sanction is general moral disapproval, rather than a specific punishment.

It is easy to see how this can be read as 'deficit': it seems to suggest that those who use restricted codes are not capable of seeing the wider horizons. Bernstein argued that neither code was better than the other, merely that they were more appropriate to the contexts of the particular classes, the working classes having to deal with the minute details of production and the middle classes with the more general concerns of management and organizing. Bernstein suggested that schools (and the education system in general) were more geared up for the reproduction of elaborated codes, so that working-class individuals operated from a disadvantage within it, thereby accounting for class differences in educational performance.

The key text is Bernstein (1971), from which a useful extract appears in Corner and Hawthorn (1989).

5.5 Chomsky

Noam Chomsky is probably the most influential twentieth-century linguist after Saussure [5.32]. In the 1950s Chomsky elaborated the notion that the grammar of a natural language [4.26], such as English, could be represented by a relatively simple set of formal rules. These rules he called a 'generative grammar', because the rules, if properly described, were supposed to generate (i.e. produce) sentences of the language, and only sentences of the language. Chomsky's idea was that if you got the rules right, you would produce from those rules the sentences of the language, and no other sentences, and that therefore you had a complete description of the language in those rules.

On top of the basic generative rules he also postulated a set of 'transformational' rules that took the basic structures represented by the core rules (called 'phrase structure' rules, which describe the 'deep structure' of a language) and transformed those structures into more complex ones. For example, one transformation rule would take the simple active sentence and produce a passive version of it by transforming it. (For more on active and passive see [3.1.9] and Halliday [5.16].)

Chomsky claimed that his rules specified the 'competence' of the language: that is, the set of all things that would be known to create 'legal' sentences in the language. He distinguished this from 'performance', which was the way people actually used these rules in practice, with all the attendant errors and mistakes that people are used to. (This is similar to Saussure's notions of *langue* and *parole*.) So the structure of a grammatical, meaningful sentence would be the output of competence, but actually uttering such a sentence in a real context for a particular purpose would be an example of performance.

Chomsky was not interested in examining performance, as he saw language as the rules which defined competence. By making the distinction between competence and performance, he was able to claim:

- that he was talking about an idealized model [4.32], a description of the language in principle, and not about what any person or group of people actually knew, so there was no sense in looking inside people's heads to verify his model;
- that all the oddities of real speech were mistakes and peculiarities of actual performance, unrelated to the actual system in the underlying language structures.

Chomsky's account was found to be a powerful one. Much of its value came from the fact that the transformational generative (TG) approach offered a lot of explanatory power using relatively few rules, whereas much more complex accounts of the language which had preceded Chomsky tended only to provide descriptions rather than explanations. Linguists liked the idea that they could explain lists of features of a language by representing them as just a few simple rules. (For example, a grammar of ten rules can generate an infinite number of sentences, some of them infinitely long.)

However, Chomsky's approach is not without problems. Firstly, despite his claim that he was not describing actual cognitive [4.7] states (i.e. what really went on in people's heads), some people nevertheless tried to determine experimentally whether the sorts of transformations that Chomsky outlined were actually how people's minds worked. (And, indeed, it is arguable that Chomsky himself shifted the ground sometimes, and seemed to be talking about what went on in people's minds even when he claimed not to be.) Interestingly, some research does seem to show that it takes people longer to process passive sentences than active sentences, suggesting that there is an extra activity associated with the mental acts of creating or understanding a passive: as if an underlying simple structure was 'transformed'. However, there has not been any sustained evidence that the rules outlined by Chomsky really are the rules of a language as used.

Secondly, no-one has satisfactorily developed a complete TG grammar (or indeed a complete grammar of any kind) which, on the one hand, satisfactorily and completely deals with all the regular features of a particular natural language, yet, on the other, does not generate non-sentences as well. This is not necessarily a problem for the serious linguist, as most linguists tend to regard all living languages as developing, changing and somewhat unstable phenomena: you can't fully define what 'the English language' is, so how could you write a complete grammar of that language? Such linguists are happy to play with incomplete grammars, because the oddities, the omissions, the non-sentences, help us understand some of the peculiarities and boundaries of the language being studied. However, it does call into question the idea that the TG approach is the best way of doing things.

Thirdly, Chomsky relegated everything not accounted for by his grammar (except for vocabulary and the associated semantics) to the realm of performance, thereby discounting all elements of context and social situation. The sociolinguists and functional linguists who have worked after Chomsky clearly show that this misses the point in many cases (e.g. Labov [5.21] and Halliday [5.16]), and cultural theorists such as Bakhtin [5.2] would claim that Chomsky's approach is completely inappropriate for analysing real communication.

Finally Chomskian accounts, whilst they might explain many of the regularities of language, generally are only able to do so for the most regular and least interesting elements of language, being completely unable to deal with other interesting regularities. For example, his account struggles with features such as phrasal verbs or idiomatic phrases (strings of words with their own distinct meaning, such as 'never the twain' or 'put 'em up'), which are clearly used intact because of their meaning, not their structure, and are preserved for social and contextual reasons.

Chomsky's importance is partly for the clarity with which he was able to specify quite elegantly many regularities of language, partly because he showed that simple accounts could have a great deal of power, and partly because (like Saussure [5.32]) he seemed to offer a scientific approach to the study of language. But probably his main impact has been in ensuring a huge reaction against such comparatively simple modelling in the growth of functional and social accounts of language which reacted to his work.

In the latter part of his career Chomsky has switched his concerns much more to a critique of US foreign policy than linguistic research. He is one of the most respected of left-wing critics of the international implications of US policies.

Smith and Wilson (1979) provide a good review of the linguistic impact of Chomsky's linguistic work. Read Chomsky (1957) and Chomsky (1965).

5.6 Derrida

Jacques Derrida is a French philosopher most widely known for his concept of 'deconstruction' [4.16]. He can arouse strong feelings, as those who espouse his ideas are fierce proponents whilst those who disagree with him (such as Searle [5.33]) appear to feel that his ideas have very little rigour or merit. This hostility to his ideas arises partly because he persistently seeks to challenge the roots of much modern philosophical thinking, and partly because many of those who have taken up his ideas (such as literary analysts and media students) would not readily be recognized as philosophers. His approach uses more literary expression than is traditional in philosophy (whose tendency to emphasize precision and exactness has led to conventions of very tight and exact language), and this makes his writing difficult to interpret yet also more attractive to a wider range of readers.

In consequence, Derrida, more than most philosophers, sees his ideas altered and diffused as they are disseminated by people who have either misunderstood or taken a different meaning from his writings. (Of course, from a postmodernist [4.40] perspective, which sees academic ideas as context-dependent discourses which will inevitably change as they drift through different contexts, this is more or less inevitable. But Derrida leaves himself open to reinterpretation more than most philosophers do.) Arguably, Derrida is easy to read but, because of that, hard to understand.

Derrida has a rationale for this approach, however. His position is 'post-structuralist', which is to say it is a reaction against (or a development from) structuralism [4.48]. Derrida sees structuralism as endemic to the western philosophical and academic traditions, with their rigidity and their attempts to determine single, simple and fixed interpretations. For Derrida, meaning is only temporary. It is a provisional construct which exists at a particular time as a negotiation between reader or hearer and text.

Structuralism [4.48] is founded on the notion of binary opposition, but deconstruction [4.16] exposes the underlying instability of such oppositions: they depend on something else. Structuralist accounts are shown to work only in a context which allows them to make sense. If you read a binary opposition in a different way, you find that the 'system' that a structural analysis identifies can be seen to be just as much as a construct of structural analysis as of the texts themselves.

A characteristic example of Derrida's view of semiotics is the extract in Cobley (1996: 209–24), 'Semiology and Grammatology: Interview with Julia Kristeva'. For an account of Derrida and postmodernism, see Bertens and Natoli (2002), and for his significance for cultural theory, see Lewis (2002: 164–70).

5.7 Durkheim

Émile Durkheim is regarded as one of the founding fathers of sociology. His analyses, mainly published in the early part of the twentieth century, established fundamental principles of sociology, such as the notion that societies are held together by more than the actions of individuals, and he explored differences between different kinds of society, such as pre-industrial and post-industrial societies. Durkheim also established many of the key principles of sociological investigation, favouring what might be loosely called a 'scientific' approach to sociological study (an approach that is generally characterized, usually negatively, as 'positivism' [4.39]), and making extensive use, for example, of social statistics. His central beliefs, that societies operated according to logical rules and in meaningful patterns, and in ways that could not simply be accounted for as an aggregation of the separate actions of individuals, remain the guiding principles of modern sociology.

Extracts from Durkheim's works can be found in McIntosh (1997: 179–248) and Worsley (1991: 29–33), and a useful introduction to Durkheim as cultural theorist is Lewis (2003: 45–50).

5.8 Eco

Umberto Eco is a semiotician well known for his novel *The Name of the Rose* (Eco 1998), which attracted a mass audience when it was turned into a successful film with Sean Connery as the lead. The novel uses the genre of detective story, and the patterns of exploration and discovery it permits, to examine the nature of meaning. By placing the murder mystery in a medieval setting, the meanings Eco explores come from the realms of the symbolic and the spiritual, and he examines the ways these are 'revealed' through reading. This reflects Eco's more academic concerns with the nature of texts and textuality, as well as with medieval history.

For Eco, texts are typically 'open', capable of multiple interpretations, those interpretations depending on the experiences that readers bring to bear, including experiences of other texts. In this his position is similar to that of Derrida [5.6].

So, for example, the way a reader approaches *The Name of the Rose* will depend partly on that reader's knowledge of the conventions of detective fiction, of medieval history, and of Aristotle's theories of text. Aristotle's *Poetics* is an important element of the plot: Aristotle wrote his *Poetics* in two parts, one on Tragedy, which survives, and one on Comedy, which has not survived. The plot of *The Name of the Rose* partly concerns the possible discovery of the missing part.

So in a quite literal sense it is a story about the search for interpretation (Aristotle's interpretations of comedy) and how those interpretations might impact on the world (some characters fear the outcome and try to prevent it); the plot is also about how the 'detective' interprets the information available to him, and 'reads' it in making sense of the 'mystery'. It is also about the nature of 'mystery', which, in one interpretation, is a holy secret only to be revealed by religious enlightenment yet, in another interpretation, is the mundane application of reason to facts, the treatment of evidence in the real world. Eco therefore makes an equation between the detective and the scholar, and the tension that exists around 'fear of discovery'.

By such means, exploring the ambiguities [4.1] in the textual conventions [4.11] readers are familiar with, Eco very cleverly creates an unconventional murder mystery (because part of the detective's task is, effectively, the decoding of meanings in texts), which is also a philosophical exploration of the nature of meaning and understanding, and the processes of interpretation which people live through to create such understanding. The book can be read in part as an exploration of the conflict between reason and spirituality, but it is actually more complex than that, as the actions of the detective effectively assert that the application of reason *is* a spiritual act. Eco suggests that revelation in a holy sense and in the mundane sense can be the same thing, if the God-given insights of human intelligence are applied honestly.

In this Eco also betrays some of his own scholastic concerns as an academic: the apparent belief that the proper activity of human beings is to hone and apply their analytical intelligence is central, of course, to the academic enterprise (see [2.3]) in the search for truth. So *The Name of the Rose* is actually a good text for a student of media, communication and culture to read, for not only does it explore many of the relevant issues, it is also a parable for a student, a model of how good academics should apply themselves.

Eco's academic approach to semiotics can be found in Eco (1977). An example of this approach is the extract 'How Culture Conditions the Colours We See', which is in Cobley (1996: 148–71). Discussion of Eco and postmodernism [4.40] is in Bertens and Natoli (2002).

5.9 Fairclough

Alongside Gunther Kress [5.20], Norman Fairclough has probably been the major proponent of critical linguistics [4.13], the attempt to use descriptive linguistics [4.28] as a critical tool in the analysis of discourse [4.17], generally to reveal underlying ideological or political subtexts in discourses.

In his very readable book '*Media Discourse*', Fairclough (1995a) looks at some of the ways language is used in media texts. He presents this as an account of three kinds of construction, following Halliday's [5.16] systemic or functional account of language. These three constructions, arguably carried by all media texts (in Fairclough's view), are:

- representations (how the world is represented) [4.41];
- identities (how people in media stories are referred to);
- relationships (the links between different people or groups involved in the story, including, for example, the reporter and the audience).

These constructions are central to the critical linguistic account of how language operates in media discourse, but are inevitably the source of much debate themselves, and applied to many other language contexts [4.10], not merely media texts. It can be argued, for example, that in any text which, in some sense, tells a story there will be representations of the real world, identities set up for participants in the story, and relationships established between those participants. But this view can degenerate into a very simplistic analysis, as the sort of formal analyses which critical linguistics might object to, such as sometimes found in narratology (the study of narrative structures), would also suggest that, to be meaningful, any story must have actors who interact in a limited world (see, e.g., Propp [5.30]).

Fairclough (1995a) gives a good introduction to key concepts in critical linguistics, though the collection of his papers in Fairclough (1995b) is a more comprehensive and developmental overview. Fairclough (1999) discusses inter-textuality.

5.10 Foucault

Michel Foucault's account of discourse [4.17] amounts to saying that all human communicative and cultural activity is construed as 'discourses'. His is probably the most expansive approach to discourse, arguing that no human can escape participation in discourses, that discourses are socially determined, that all meaning is determined by the place of a particular communicative act within its discourse (or, alternatively, between discourses of different kinds), and that discourses are largely driven by historical processes.

Foucault is hard to classify. Like many other thinkers who have had an impact on cultural theory, his work was not really bounded by traditional disciplinary categories: in a very real sense, he was interdisciplinary in his analyses. (For a brief discussion of interdisciplinarity, see section [1.3].) In a single word, he was a 'philosopher'. His central interests were analyses of knowledge, not merely knowledge in particular areas, but the nature of knowledge itself. 'Epistemology' is the study of knowledge, but Foucault's work does not sit squarely in the epistemological tradition. He was a historian as much as a philosopher. For him, knowledge was inseparable from the particular historical processes, and consequent social structures, created by, and resulting in, power relations.

For Foucault, the popular adage 'knowledge is power' was literally true. This adage is generally used to mean 'if you have knowledge that some one else doesn't have, then you have power over them'. Foucault's view, however, was that all knowledge constitutes power relations of particular kinds. For him, there could be no 'absolute truth' or 'objective' knowledge, because all knowing is done by people in particular social and historical contexts, and those contexts constitute power relations, in which knowledge is one, key, component.

For example, consider the situation of a student in a university lecture room. That student is more powerful than the hopeful applicants for next year's places on the course: she knows more about the course, more about the application process, more about the subject area than they do. Her particular history means that, in any competition with those hopeful candidates, for example a bursary, she stands a better chance. The historical process that has led this student to this place gives her power through the knowledge she has acquired by virtue of that process.

At the same time, the same student also sits in relationship to her peers in the classroom: she is perhaps seen as an expert on using the Internet, so others come to her for advice and help, which enables her to dominate them in particular social interactions. ('I'll sort out your browser problem for you, but you'll have to be in at seven for me to do it. Have the kettle on.') And she sits in relationship to the tutor in the classroom: she is quiet, well-behaved, controlled in that situation by the 'authority' in front of her; anxious to acquire the specialist knowledge that this lecturer possesses, and which he is doling out to her in order to apply his rules of assessment and performance to her in seminar questions, essays and exams.

If the lecturer suddenly asks her a question on the information he has just given out, what will be the correct answer? Will it be her own personal opinion? Perhaps she dare not give that, because of the power relationship. Even if she believes it to be 'correct', it may differ from the 'facts' that she has just been presented with? No, more likely she will repeat the information given out, because that is 'correct' in this power relationship. But suppose the night before the lecture she has been reading the latest journal article, which presents new evidence that disputes the facts just given out by the lecturer. Assuming the tutor has not read the article (it was only published yesterday), the power relation has subtly shifted. She has power over him, even though he doesn't know it: she has the power to dispute his carefully constructed observation, show up his lack of scholarliness on this subject, embarrass him in front of the class and assert her own superiority of knowledge. She decides not to do this, reasoning that keeping the knowledge hidden ultimately gives her more power in this relationship, for when it comes to the test, the essay, she will be able to mobilize her special knowledge and impress the tutor.

Foucault is not particularly interested in micro-analyses at this level, but he does argue that the 'subject' (the self – see Identity [4.22]) is constituted by these power relations, that is, by the knowledge people possess by virtue of their social roles. What you know 'defines' you in an important sense for Foucault, as it both is determined by and it determines the power relations that constitute the infrastructure of social relationships.

Foucault's focus is on the particular historical studies of particular power relations (constituted through knowledge), therefore his analyses are always about specific historical or social phenomena. Such an approach follows naturally from his analysis of the nature of knowledge. His own knowledge, his own approach, has to be defined by particular power relations, the particular history which has led him to be where he is, so he cannot step outside that and look for some 'independent' or 'objective' historical, social, cultural or epistemological truth. In his view, there can be no such thing even for him, because the knowledge he is creating or mobilizing is dependent on the power relations that define his own self. Accepting this, he can only explore constrained historical or social situations and tease out the knowledge and power relations that constituted them, as they were (or, more accurately, as they appear to have been, given his particular standpoint at the time of analysis).

The consequences of this view appear to be that there is no truth, and no objective knowledge, which will stand the test of time, but there is knowledge which is true now, because it can be used in terms of existing power relations. When you are sufficiently distant (in time or circumstances) from a particular phenomenon, you can examine its knowledge constructs, its power relations, because they do not involve you in any direct sense. What you are doing, through analysis, is translating the knowledge that lay within that system (and which does not apply in the translator's system) into knowledge within the translator's system, which thereby transfers power to the translator.

Foucault's theories are complex, and his approach changed during his professional life, so trying to understand all he says is difficult. It is probably also unnecessary for an undergraduate, as long as you remember the key points:

- Knowledge is not absolute, but embedded in particular social (hence power) relations.
- Knowledge and power are inextricably interrelated.
- Both are historically constituted.
- The subject, the self, is defined by its knowledge constructs.

Readable introductions to Foucault are Bertens and Natoli (2002), Danaher et al. (2000), Lewis (2002: 170–6), Merquior (1991) and Storey (1997: 96–100). An indicative extract is in Jaworski and Coupland (1999: 514–22) and three other extracts from his writings can be found in Calhoun et al. (2002: 185–218). His key text is probably Foucault (2002), although this is a very difficult starting point for someone new to his ideas.

5.11 Freud

This is probably one of the best-known names in this list, because of people's fascination with Sigmund Freud's insights into the sexual motivation of much human activity. Freud was, of course, the first psychoanalyst and established the field as a legitimate profession. His central interest in dreams was largely motivated by the belief that they give the analyst insights into how the psyche operates without the interference of conscious thought. He aimed to lay bare the workings of the unconscious, and one reason for the pervasiveness of his thinking is the systematic way he did this. His account of human personality [4.37] is articulated as a set of internal conflicts between different elements of personality, generally established early in personal development as a function of the relationships between a child, its parents and, to a lesser extent, its siblings.

From the viewpoint of a student of culture, Freud's writings offer a grounding for the understanding of the notion of the 'self' and its 'identity' [4.22]. If we see meaning as being interpreted by an 'I' that perceives and constructs the world around it, then the nature of that 'I' is crucial to the understanding of what meaning is and how it works. Psychoanalytic theory essentially takes apart the notion of the 'I', suggesting that, in fact, the self is itself a construct, partly (perhaps wholly) defined in terms of the world it finds itself in (i.e. in early childhood, the world of the parents). Jacques Lacan [5.22], in particular, developed the implications of this viewpoint, strengthening its relevance to MCCS rather more than Freud did.

Freud wrote a great deal. His best-known work is *The Interpretation of Dreams* (Freud 1975). You can find a brief extract in Corner and Hawthorn (1989), and a rather quirky, but approachable, introduction in Appignanesi and Zarate (1992).

5.12 Goffman

Erving Goffman was a sociologist concerned with interpersonal communication [4.25], which he described as 'encounters' between 'actors'. He was interested in how communication is used to manage social encounters, such as how first impressions are created, how communication is used both to control the way we are perceived and the different techniques people use to present themselves in particular ways and communicate particular things about themselves. Goffman's approach was grounded in 'symbolic interactionism', that is, the idea that all human interaction is fundamentally symbolic, with what is going on 'front-stage' in an encounter being dependent on a hidden 'back-stage' which it is symbolically related to.

He was interested in various aspects of interpersonal communication, including non-verbal communication [4.33], as well as social behaviour, and saw the self as fundamentally constructed through social interaction. His view of speech [4.46] was that it could not be analysed independently of the interaction it formed part of. He also looked at how social behaviour adapts to different contexts, such as how people learn to behave 'appropriately' in prison, through socialization [4.45], suggesting that a great deal of social interaction is not just about conforming to the situation but being perceived as *competent* in that situation. We want to be perceived not simply as fitting in, but as being capable and adept in that social situation, as it enhances our status and self-image.

Corner and Hawthorn (1989) includes a short extract by Goffman on how we present ourselves to others, taken from Goffman's seminal work, *The Presentation of Self in Everyday Life* (Goffman 1971). For a student, the collection of readings in Lemert and Branaman (1997) can be a useful starting point. You can also find short extracts on the social situation of talk in Giglio (1972: 61–6), another in Jaworski and Coupland (1999: 306–20), and a collection of relevant writings, including an analysis of lectures, in Goffman (1981).

5.13 Gramsci

Antonio Gramsci was an Italian Marxist, most of whose writings were composed in prison, where, having been imprisoned by Mussolini's Fascist state in 1928, he spent the last nine years of life. On his thirty-three prison notebooks, some of which have not yet been translated into English, together with his letters from prison, Gramsci's strong reputation rests.

The notebooks cover many different areas of Italian history, culture and society, and (as readers might expect, given the circumstances of their creation) do not form a logical coherent project. However, Gramsci's writings established him as one of the most influential Marxist intellectuals. Central to his thinking is the idea of hegemony [4.20]. He argued that the great mass of people within a culture accept, and consent to, the will of a ruling elite through hegemonic processes, that is, processes which employ the power of the dominating group to influence and persuade the subordinating group to accept the ruling group's ideology [4.23]. Hegemonic assent is seen as working not primarily through the actions of the state, but through 'civil society', those people who dominate the economic and intellectual processes of a society, and who therefore profit by alliance with and acceptance of the ideology which enables that profit. It is in their interests, therefore, to maintain, develop, support and disseminate ideas and social and economic processes which keep the state ideology dominant.

For example, owners of large newspapers make money by selling their papers. In a society such as the UK, which thinks of itself as free and democratic, one way to sell newspapers is to offer views which appear to challenge government positions. However, it would not be profitable to challenge the notion of democracy (as conceived in that society), or ideas such as the need for stable government, the need for an unrestricted media, or the benefits of a capitalist economy, as such challenges would undermine both the power base of the government of the day and the ability of a newspaper to make money by challenging such a government. Whilst appearing to conflict with the government's views, the 'free, capitalist press' in the UK fundamentally reflects and reinforces the ideological foundation of that government.

An introduction to Gramsci can be found in Bertens and Natoli (2002) and another, placing him in a wider Marxist context, in Lewis (2002: 97–100). A selection of his writings can be found in Gramsci (1971). Extracts by Gramsci on ideology [4.23] can be found in Durham and Kellner (2001: 43–7).

5.14 Habermas

The German Jürgen Habermas is seen by many as one of the most important contemporary intellectuals. He achieves this position partly because his ideas oppose the more fashionable postmodernist [4.40] views that prevail in cultural theory. Whilst postmodernism sees knowledge, communication and culture as disjunctive, fractured and relativistic (i.e. composed of many different world views, each dependent on a particular social and cultural history, which cannot be escaped from and cannot be reconciled), Habermas defends the unfashionable concepts of reason, humanism and universality.

Habermas argues that people can rise above, or argue through, the prejudices and biases inherent in their particular cultural contexts [4.10]. Central to his ideas is the notion of 'communicative action', manifest in the 'public sphere' of public debate. The public sphere is that forum of communication which exists between state and individual or private social group. Habermas sees the public sphere, manifested as the mass media and its public debate, as the place in which, through open, committed and frequent communication, people can work towards an enlightened and rational view of issues. This open communication, he believes, will lead to reconciliation of divergent views, and hence solutions to social and political problems. This public debate is 'communicative action', social dialogue through which reason achieves social improvement. Reason, in Habermas's view, is as a universal quality (i.e. a capacity which all people have in the same way, and is not culturally determined).

Habermas's thinking therefore integrates philosophical and sociological approaches in a desire to achieve political impact.

An extract from Habermas's writings, in which he discusses the public sphere and how public opinion acts as a mediator between society and state, is in Durham and Kellner (2001: 102–7), taken from Habermas (1989). Another can be found (with two other extracts) in Calhoun et al. (2002: 358–76). A brief, contextualized introduction to Habermas is Lewis (2002: 101–3).

5.15 Hall

Stuart Hall is a cultural theorist with a strong interest in the mass media, and one of the defining voices in British cultural studies. He was the second director of one of the most important groups in the UK studying culture from 1969, the Centre for Contemporary Cultural Studies at Birmingham University. As such he has overseen many research projects in subcultures and media research. In many ways the Centre was the foundation of a UK cultural studies, as a reaction to the prevalent study of high culture [4.21] in academic institutions, an orientation which had been established by Richard Hoggart [5.17] as first director. Hall's approach was largely a Marxist [5.27] analysis of mass communications [4.29], alongside politicized analyses of ethnicity and identity [4.22]. For example, he was one of the leading left-wing analysts of Thatcherite policies in 1980s Britain. His Centre was also one of the first to pursue feminist approaches to cultural research in the UK.

Papers by Hall and other members of the Centre are in Hall et al. (1980). An extract on 'Encoding/Decoding', and how that relates to a Marxist analysis of television, is in Durham and Kellner (2001: 166–76). Lewis (2002: 133–8) and Storey (1997: 63–71) give brief introductions to Hall's approach, and Hall's own view of cultural studies can be found in Storey (1997: 31–48), but perhaps the best text is Morley and Chen (1996), which collects writings both by Hall and about him, including interviews.

5.16 Halliday

Michael Halliday is an influential Australian linguist whose work is often seen in contrast to more formal Chomskian approaches to language study [5.5]. Hallidayan approaches nevertheless have a strong grammatical and representational element of their own; the key difference is in what they aim to describe.

Hallidayan linguistics is often called 'systemic linguistics' or 'functional grammar'. These names suggest its emphases. The Hallidayan approach aims to capture the functions of language in use, the systems of meaning, social code [4.6], context [4.10], register and style [4.49] by which socially embedded language actually communicates (see Language Variation [4.27]). The emphasis in Chomskian grammar is to construct abstract models which represent the rules of the underlying language (the competence of native speakers). The emphasis in Hallidayan grammar is to construct models of how bits of language actually function in context, with as much concern for performance as competence. Put simply, Chomsky is concerned with the stabilities in language, the constants, whereas Halliday is as much concerned with language variation and fluctuation in particular contexts.

At the heart of Hallidayan grammar are descriptions of the choices that are available to language users. Such grammars tend to be written as networks of possible choices, described in terms of the constraints upon choice, and the linguistic consequences of making particular choices: for example, the choice between active voice and passive voice, discussed in [3.1.9]. Such choices are not independent of other choices you might make: for example, if you were aiming to write 'reader-friendly Plain English', then this contextual requirement would tend to constrain you to choose the active voice. But if you wanted to write 'formal academic prose in the tradition of psychology', then you're more likely to be constrained towards the passive voice.

So language choices tend to go along together to some extent, and relate to context. A 'style' of language is essentially language associated with a particular context, a type of language where the same types of choices are made again and again. This is one reason why the key to effective communication is to know why you are writing, and who for, and to make choices appropriately. Hallidayan grammars offer some tools for formalizing the description of your choices.

Hallidayan approaches to language can have competing emphases, for example, arising from a belief that the complex net of choices dependent on social context are so complicated and so particular to circumstances that they cannot be usefully formalized in any way, and the best way to analyse them is to describe their very particular sets of rules and activities. This brings the study of language much closer to certain cultural studies perspectives: for example, there is a lot of similarity with Barthes's [5.3] approach to semiotics [4.44] (that each cultural artefact has its own particular communicative code) or Foucault's [5.10] belief that all discourses [4.17] are specifically determined by historical and cultural context. It would seem that, in principle, it is not too difficult to move from a Hallidayan perspective – which sees the communicative value of language as essentially constructed by its social context – to a cultural perspective, which sees culture [4.14] as entirely determining, and determined by, specific context.

Extracts from Halliday's *Language as a Social Semiotic* (Halliday 1978) can be found in Cobley (1996). Pages 88–93 give an introduction to the notion of language as a social semiotic (a social sign system) and pages 359–84 give an excellent overview of sociolinguistic questions and the structure and function of language elements in the context of language variation [4.27].

5.17 Hoggart

Richard Hoggart was the first director of the Centre for Contemporary Cultural Studies at Birmingham University, succeeded by Stuart Hall [5.15]. Through his 1957 book *The Uses of Literacy* (1981), Hoggart did much to establish the field of cultural studies in the UK. His working-class origins, coupled with his training in literary criticism (very much in the mould of F.R. Leavis [5.23]), led him to apply his critical skills to popular culture. *The Uses of Literacy* is the result of this exercise, and offers analyses of popular culture for ordinary readers, showing them the values of their culture and at the same time the value of critical analysis. The richness of his analysis also showed that there was a worthwhile academic enterprise to be engaged in: the treatment of popular culture in the same way that elevated or elite culture had typically been treated. By applying the same tools to both kinds of cultural products, Hoggart also effectively made both political and intellectual statements: if similar tools can be used in both cases, to produce similar sorts of understanding, by what criteria is one form of culture preferred over another? Why are some forms of communication privileged? Much of cultural studies implicitly or explicitly addresses these questions, and generally concludes that the differences are a function of power relations, and not any inherent quality of the cultural enterprises themselves.

Read Hoggart (1981) and the account of Hoggart in Lewis (2002: 126–9) and Storey (1997: 46–54)

5.18 Jakobson

Roman Jakobson was a linguist who took a formalist approach to poetics. In other words, he examined literature (and some other kinds of text) focusing on the system and structure of literary forms, seen from a linguistic perspective. A similar approach was taken by Vladimir Propp [5.30], the Russian formalist, to the study of folk- and fairy tales.

An important observation of Jakobson's, around which he based much discussion of literary text, was the difference between 'metaphor' and 'metonymy'. He noted that metaphor in language works by similarity or analogy between a subject and the word or phrase used to substitute for it. For example, 'a snowy skin' substitutes 'snowy' for 'white'; or 'she built a house of lies' substitutes 'built a house of' for 'told many'. Metaphor, therefore, is an act of substitution, using the paradigmatic [4.35] dimension of language.

'Metonymy', on the other hand, works by contiguous, or sequential, links. The subject is indicated not by a substitution, but by mentioning something related to that subject in reality. For example, in the sentence 'Downing Street today has announced a new policy', 'Downing Street', the place where the Prime Minister works, is used instead of 'the Prime Minister'. Or in 'torches searched the evening night for the criminal', it is not the 'torches' that are doing the searching, but the people holding those torches. So metonymy is a relationship of connection, rather than substitution, that is, a syntagmatic [4.35] relationship.

An example of Jakobson's approach to language can be found in the extract 'Shifters and Verbal Categories', which examines language which refers to language, in Cobley (1996: 292–6), and another in Jaworski and Coupland (1999: 54–62), with selected writings in Jakobson (1971) and commentary on Jakobson in Hawkes (1983).

5.19 Jung

Carl Gustav Jung was a student of Freud, later to develop ideas in opposition to Freud's. A key idea of Jung's is the 'collective unconscious', the notion that people have, in some sense, shared memories, social memories, at an unconscious level, which enables similarity of understanding in radically different social or cultural situations. Exactly how such a collective memory would work has never been clearly explained, and the idea readily shades into mysticism: Jung's ideas are often espoused by 'New Age' mystics. At the same time, the idea is a potentially powerful one: it is not difficult to believe, for example, that everyone dreams of similar monsters because of the fears of our primitive ancestors.

Jung also suggested that people carry out their social obligations and maintain their social roles by presenting what he called a 'persona' to the outside world, a public face which disguises the underlying personality. Thus Jung is suggesting that the self is something other than what we see, and that social interaction and interpersonal communication [4.25] are not carried out by our true identities [4.22] but by a construct. This theory is in direct opposition to those, such as Goffman's [5.12], which see identity as primarily a function of social interaction.

Many excerpts of Jung's writings are gathered in Jung (1998), with Robinson (1992) and Storr (1973) providing good introductions to his ideas.

5.20 Kress

Gunther Kress has been a key figure in critical linguistics [4.13]. He has also a particularly strong interest in visual communication, arguing, for example, that there has been a shift towards visualization in cultural communications over the last fifty years, and exploring the relationships between analysis of verbal and visual communication. We can see this most obviously in the prevalence of icons on computer screens (the pervasive use of GUIs, 'graphic user interfaces'), but Kress suggests that it is a more universal communicative trend found in a range of different genres [4.18], from children's books to scientific and technical documentation.

See, for example, Kress and van Leeuwen (1996), an extract from which can be found in Jaworski and Coupland (1999: 377–404), and another in Cobley (1996: 172–80), discussing some of the ways that children decode images. In the same volume the extract 'Social Processes and Linguistic Change' discusses how writers develop their writing in response to social constraints, leading to conformation to genre conventions [4.18, 4.11] (in Cobley 1996: 299–313), whilst Kress (1985) and Corner and Hawthorn (1980: 85–93) introduce his linguistic ideas.

5.21 Labov

William Labov was one of the first linguists to develop sociolinguistic approaches to language, arguing that studying language outside its social context missed critical elements, and tended towards theories of language that over-simplified or misrepresented the true ways that language worked. He showed, for example, that apparent irregularities in non-standard varieties of English were actually perfectly regular, and that grammars of dialects could be established. It is partly due to work by such linguists as Labov that the notion of privileged or 'good' forms of a language have largely been dropped. Instead linguists regard all varieties of language as of equivalent value or importance, showing that some varieties (such as Standard English, Received Pronunciation, academic English) have been accorded privileged positions because of the power accorded to them by particular social groups.

Read Labov's writings in Giglio (1972: 179–218), Giglio (1972: 283–307) and Jaworski and Coupland (1999: 221–35).

5.22 Lacan

Jacques Lacan was a psychoanalyst who argued that our sense of identity is constructed symbolically through language. As a strong proponent of Freud's [5.11] notions of the self and identity, he extended Freudian ideas to suggest how the earliest formative stages of the child determined its symbolic thought. Lacan linked Freudian ideas to concepts of the symbolic in the accounts of the structuralists Lévi-Strauss [5.24] and Saussure [5.32]. His ideas are hard to grasp, but in the simplest form he suggests that the division between the child and the parent, as perceived in early childhood, constitute both the desire and the difference upon which symbolic life is founded. Initially the child perceives no separation from the parent. Upon realization of separation, then desire for re-union is created (in Freudian terms, the Oedipal or Electra relationship of the son wanting the mother, the daughter the father), which is the foundation of the sexual self, and the perception of difference establishes the elementary symbolic system: the core symbol for the child becomes that newly perceived other, the image of desire. Because the division creates the particular desire, it also creates the symbol of desire in general, and the particularities of the relationships (how love is manifest, how it is restrained, how it is interfered with by siblings, etc.) constitute the initial elements of a symbolic system through which the child begins to make sense of that world.

Lacan's ideas therefore influence discussion of 'identity' [4.22], 'subjectivity', 'the real', and 'the imaginary'. For a student who wants to explore notions of the self and identity, and who finds psycholanalytic approaches insightful, Lacan may provide useful concepts. However, his thinking is difficult to negotiate: his ideas are perhaps most suitable for third-year and dissertation work, rather than everyday studies.

A good example of Lacan's writing is his somewhat poetic account of the relationship between the unconscious and Saussure's account of signification, in Cobley (1996: 186–94, an extract from Lacan 1977). Here he suggests that the one-to-one correspondence between signifier and signified is not as fixed as Saussure proposes. Introductions to Lacan are Bertens and Natoli (2002), Leader and Groves (1995) and Lewis (2002: 176–9).

5.23 Leavis

F.R. Leavis was a Cambridge literary theorist who had strong ideas about the separation of popular and elitist cultures. His account of the literary 'Great Tradition', for example, sought to argue that certain key novels were the unmatched epitome of literature, against which other writings would inevitably be found wanting. Consequently, he was establishing a kind of hierarchy of worth in cultural artefacts, and much of his work was an exploration of the criteria which one could use to establish the canon of the 'greatest' texts, and whether particular texts passed the test and could be included in that canon (see High Culture and Low Culture [4.21]).

For Leavis, the central notion was that of 'tradition'. The most rewarding cultural artefacts, in his view, were those which recognized and carried forward the tradition in which they were founded. Texts which did not recognize and accord with the established tradition were necessarily lacking in moral and spiritual validity, because they were divorced from the cultural tradition which was their heritage. Leavis's view seems to have been that, in well-established 'high' cultures, such as that manifest by the English novel, a process of moral refinement was at work, gradually evolving an increasingly elevated view of the world and human relationships. Thus the texts within the 'Great Tradition' tended to be those that examined complex moral or emotional problems with deep insight and moral purpose. Almost by definition novelty and popular traditions would lack such refined and clearly articulated purposes. For this reason popular culture, which grew up quickly in response to new forms or new media, generally was inferior because out of touch with the moral heart of English tradition, often being a superficial response to fashionable media. There is a strong nostalgic sense in Leavis's thinking, and a feeling not merely that high moral purpose is associated with an elite literary tradition that goes back to Chaucer, but also that the elite culture goes hand in hand with an elite class.

Leavis's great strength was in his articulation of the value of textual analysis in understanding. Although he would not have expressed it this way, he was a strong advocate of decoding or deconstructing [4.16] text in order to understand it. His version of 'deconstruction' was 'literary criticism'. His central exercise was close analysis of text, designed to reveal the underlying moral or spiritual worth of the humanist discourse (or its lack, in the case of those texts which failed to pass the test). Because of his elitist message, Leavis tends to be neglected, but his exegesis and rigour make him well worth reading, even if the results sometimes make you want to throw the book across the room.

Read Leavis (1993), Leavis and Thompson (1977). For discussions of Leavis's views see Lewis (2002: 117–21) and Storey (1997: 28–35).

5.24 Lévi-Strauss

Claude Lévi-Strauss was an anthropologist who studied culture and myth from a structural [4.48] viewpoint. By noting different variants in cultural forms, such as art, narrative and kinship structures, and the variations in myths across related groups, he identified cultural systems and structures encoded in those forms and myths. These structures concerned the basic social rules of the cultures maintaining those myths, relating, for example, to such social taboos as incest, murder and kinship.

His primary technique he called '*bricolage*': the gathering of cultural fragments, almost as an ad hoc process of finding 'interesting' features of a culture: the stories that were told at key moments; the cultural practices associated with birth, death and marriage; and features such as dress and food. Why he decided to record some features rather than others is largely unexplained in his writings, but this approach of collecting or noticing 'interesting' aspects of a culture has always been a major technique of anthropological study, and indeed other social studies where the researcher is, in some sense, within the culture, such as 'participant observation' [6.6.6].

Once the features have been noted, the structural anthropologist's task is to arrange those features so that they betray their differences and similarities. Lévi-Strauss took the notions of vertical, or paradigmatic, and horizontal, or syntagmatic, relationship from structural linguistics.

Leach (1985) is a good introduction to Lévi-Strauss, as are Hawkes (1983: 32–58) and Boyne (2000). Probably the most approachable of Lévi-Strauss's books is Lévi-Strauss (1968).

5.25 Lyotard

One of the most influential writers on postmodernism [4.40], Jean-François Lyotard suggests that postmodernism results from a move from society built upon the economics of physical commodities to one where knowledge and information are prevalent commodities. So the postmodern 'move' is signalled by the advent of communications technologies [4.8]. As essential communications tools, computers establish a pervasive concept of what is 'information', what is 'communication', what counts as 'knowledge', and so on. The models of communication that emerge from these prevalent technologies (e.g. that all meaning can be represented digitally, that 'information processing' is what goes on in people's heads and therefore the fundamental way of characterizing communication) amount to a hegemony [4.20] established and maintained through the technology.

Lyotard goes beyond this, though, to develop a critique of the nature of scientific knowledge, arguing that the form of knowledge which emerges from science/technology is necessarily fragmented (the scientific method, for example, can only establish partial truths, not 'truth'; and scientific accounts can only make sense within particular discourse [4.17] communities). This fragmentation is seen as societies abandon what Lyotard calls 'grand narratives' (central stories or ideas which govern the whole of a society, such as Marxism or Christianity) and instead promulgate a host of 'little narratives' which exist in partial conflict and partial overlap with each other. 'Truth' is abandoned, and in its place there is only a collection of partial truths, from which societies and individuals make selections according to need and circumstance.

Lyotard's key work is *The Postmodern Condition: a Report on Knowledge* (Lyotard 1979), but this is a difficult text, and not introductory by any means. An introduction to his work can be found in Bertens and Natoli (2002) and another in Lewis (2002: 225–30), whilst useful extracts on the postmodern condition can be found in Docherty (1993: 39–46) and Elliott (1999: 317–26).

5.26 McLuhan

'The medium is the message' is the popularized phrase that summarizes Marshall McLuhan's thinking. His idea is that what we do with a medium, how we use it, *is* the message that it conveys. The medium constrains, and also liberates, certain kinds of meaning. What a new technology adds to existing communications necessarily is the meaning we want to convey through it.

For example, each new idiom of popular music (Thrash Metal, Rave, Trance, Hip Hop, etc.) does not merely allow certain kinds of message (what we might call particular 'content'), it is its own message. Or, each new communications technology does not simply facilitate existing messages, what it adds to existing content is the new message: its 'meaning' is what society wants to convey – faster, interactive, dynamic, networked.

McLuhan develops this notion at length, offering ideas similar to Bakhtin [5.2].

For example: 'Manuscript culture is conversational if only because the writer and his audience are physically related by the form of publication as performance' (McLuhan 1962: 84). Here the suggestion is that writing (i.e. handwritten text, as opposed to printed text) is like a conversation, because as the writer formulates her or his unique expression, she or he is engaging in a performative dialogue with a reader. Writing is not merely an act of recording, it is, in Bakhtin's terms 'dialogic' and in Searle's [5.33] terms 'performative'.

McLuhan's writings in the 1960s in many ways proved prophetic, although they probably helped to bring about the future they envisaged. In *The Gutenberg Galaxy* (McLuhan 1962), for example, McLuhan suggested that electronic communications would arrive that would shape the world in ways that typography and print had previously. We now see that many of his detailed projections were accurate. For example, his phrase 'the global village' (McLuhan 1964), intended to characterize the fact that increased availability of faster communications would necessarily reduce the perceived distances between cultures, is now commonplace, characterized as globalization: the need to see many communication and social issues in a global context, because speed of communication means they will be felt globally.

McLuhan's style makes him quite readable, though sometimes problematic, even irritating. In *The Gutenberg Galaxy*, for example, he writes in short sections of a couple of pages, each headed by a dramatic declaration, such as 'Schizophrenia may be a necessary consequence of literacy', which is his way of summarizing the idea that writing separates thought and action (although he actually goes further than this, suggesting that a phonic alphabet, a spoken code which can be remembered and replicated, provides this division). Another example is 'With Gutenberg Europe enters the technological phase of progress, when change itself becomes the archetypal norm of social life.' This is an exact predictor of the 'information society', with its emphasis on perpetual innovation, lifetime learning, and the sense that communication and culture are fragmented and fluid, constantly changing.

Read McLuhan (1962) and McLuhan (1964), or start with the extract from the latter on 'the Medium is the Message' in Durham and Kellner (2001: 129–38).

5.27 Marx

Perhaps the most influential social scientist the world has yet seen, Karl Marx's economic and social analysis has not merely created a strong intellectual tradition, but has also been the root of many social and political revolutions, in a quite literal sense.

Central to Marxist thinking is the idea that economic and social history follow a more or less inevitable sequence determined and realized by the economic relations of social classes. Capitalism is the economic development based on the investment of capital, where wealth is held by a relatively small class of elite and powerful people. It depends for success on continued economic growth (i.e.

continual production of items of economic value). This in turn requires the exploitation of a working class as it is their labour which generates the value in products.

This power relationship is managed by control of the means of production (i.e. the tools and structures through which the labouring classes produce value – such as factories and equipment owned by the investors). It is also controlled by various social processes which manage and maintain the hegemony [4.20] of the ruling system. For example, the dominant world view is maintained by placing ownership of mass communication in the hands of the same capitalists who control the means of production, such as newspapers and satellite TV companies being owned by the same shareholders who run oil companies and manufacturing plants. In other words, particular communication practices lie at the heart of the means whereby capital controls its labour. In Marx's words, 'the class which is the ruling *material* force of society is at the same time its ruling *intellectual* force' (Durham and Kellner, 2001: 39).

However, capitalism is inherently unstable and will, in the Marxist view, lead to revolution, whereby the labouring classes will seize control of the means of production and labour for the collective good, not merely to accrue profit for the small ruling class. Revolution follows from understanding. As the working classes recognize the nature of their position, and question the hegemonic view imposed by those with the power, alternative messages are constructed which question that hegemony – and the very fact of questioning it means that it no longer exists. Communication, therefore, is critical to the challenge of existing order.

There are many difficulties in the Marxist position, but it has had sufficient power to attract a large number of intellectuals, such as Lyotard [5.25], Habermas [5.14], Hall [5.15] and Gramsci [5.13]. In particular, the notion that history and the social interaction of classes are the fundamental determiners of communication seems a very powerful idea. Many different approaches to communication show that at least part of the meaning being carried by communicative practices is some form of power relation. So the agenda of some analysts, such as critical linguists [4.13], is precisely to expose such relations.

An extract by Marx and Engels on the relationship between the ruling class and dominant ideas is in Durham and Kellner (2001: 39–42). Other readings can be found in McIntosh (1997: 13–109) and Worsley (1991: 431–6). An introduction to Marxist ideas of culture can be found in Storey (1997: 101–34), and a good account of Marx and those who have developed his theories is Lewis (2002: 75–106).

5.28 Peirce

Charles Sanders Peirce was an American scientist, mathematician and philosopher who provided probably the earliest account of signs (he died in 1914), which still constitutes the basis of our understanding of semiotics [4.44]. He is also credited with founding the philosophical school of 'pragmaticism'. A pragmatic view, for Peirce, is one that deals logically with facts, and aims for as precise and complete an account as possible, but recognizes that in many cases perfect or absolute definitions and explanations are impossible. However, rather than resorting to metaphysical theorizing at the point where facts and observation give out (an approach which Peirce dismissed in scathing terms), the pragmatic view is that, if the facts take you no further, then you can go no further. Metaphysical speculation, in this view is merely empty words.

His sense was that the human universe was everywhere made up of signs, and that many of the disciplines and sciences that people use to examine the real world were actually concerned with the interpretation of signs. Put crudely, facts are signs of reality.

Peirce distinguished different classes of sign: an icon is a sign which in some sense represents what it stands for; an index has a causal connection of some kind with what it stands for; and a symbol has no relationship to what it stands for, the relationship is merely conventional. Signs, as described by Peirce, are thought of as having three components (not the two-part 'signifier' and 'signifed' of Peirce's contemporary, Saussure [5.32]). David Macey summarizes the view as 'the sign . . . is something which stands *to* somebody *for* something' (Macey 2000: 294). In other words, in Peirce's thinking a sign is not merely a relationship between a signifier and signified, but there is also a 'someone', who is effectively the intermediary between the two. Peirce's vocabulary for these ideas has not been widely adopted, but the idea that an interpreter must necessarily exist to mediate the relationship between a sign and what it stands for is, of course, a critical one.

Peirce published no book in his lifetime, though he did write many essays, largely in science journals. The first volume of his selected writings (including some which were unpublished before his death) is Peirce (1992). An extract can be found in Cobley (1996: 48–60) and there is a contextualized introduction to Peirce's ideas in Lewis (2002: 150–1).

5.29 Piaget

Jean Piaget's work on the cognitive [4.7] development of children (they way they learn, in particular) is important for communications work which aims to assist learning. For example, work on the design of learning materials, on speech therapy [4.46], on accessibility in websites, can all benefit from addressing the kinds of issues explored by Piaget and other developmental psychologists. However, the most obvious relevance is in examining children's communication. This can be a fascinating area, as we have all seen how children acquire different language functions [4.26] at different stages of development, and how they spend a great deal of their time in language play.

Before Piaget, study of child language development largely focused on differences between adult and child language. Piaget, however, 'concentrated on the distinctive characteristics of child thought, on what the child *has* rather than what the child lacks' (Vygotsky 1962: 9). This approach proved enlightening, as it allowed Piaget to describe what children actually did (and what could be deduced about the way they thought from what they did), rather than treating them as miniature adults who could not quite achieve what adults could achieve.

Hawkes (1983) has notes on Piaget, and Gruber and Voneche in Piaget (1977) offer comments and many extracts, or read Piaget (1932).

5.30 Propp

Vladimir Propp worked in the tradition known as 'Russian formalism', which is to say he was concerned with examining the functions and structures of texts. His impact on cultural thinking largely resulted from one text, *The Morphology of the Folktale* (Propp 1971). In this book Propp examined a collection of Russian folktales, looking for their 'underlying structures', in a manner similar to structuralism [4.48], but focusing on the functional elements of folktales, rather than binary oppositions.

By analysis of actual folktales, Propp suggested that the key elements of the tales were the functions fulfilled by characters in carrying plot forward. He observed the following:

- The functions of characters are constant. They remain stable across tales, even though they may be fulfilled by different characters in different tales.
- There are a finite number of functions, thirty-one according to Propp's analysis.
- The sequence of functions is identical across tales, so they all have the same structure.

He also noted that the thirty-one functions were distributed across seven 'spheres of action', by which he meant that groups of functions tended to cluster together, to form particular character types, such as 'villain', 'helper' and 'hero'. So these roles in the tale are typified by the kinds of functions they carry out.

Proppian analyses of the functions of characters within narratives have been conducted for other kinds of narrative. Sometimes these seek to identify whether Propp's exact typology applied to other kinds of discourse, and, interestingly, it does seem to map onto some classes of discourse, for example, particular film genres such as the Western, and classes of newspaper story, such as heroic rescues. This leads some analysts of narrative to suggest that there are certain narrative patterns which underlie classes of story-telling, such as the 'hero story'.

Read Propp (1971) or the account in Hawkes (1983: 67–73).

5.31 Russell

Betrand Russell was a philosopher of language who tried to establish a highly logical approach to meaning, attempting to characterize and analyse meanings through formal and abstract logical analysis. His work, with that of A.J. Ayer, is characterized as 'logical positivism', following the scientific tradition of positivism [4.39] established by the French philosopher Auguste Comte. He is mainly of interest to students of communication and culture because of the reaction against his position by philosophers such as Wittgenstein [5.40], who first took up Russell's ideas and then strongly rejected them, and Searle [5.33]. Russell's approach examined meaning without any consideration of context or the experience of individuals, looking for general semantic principles. As such he shared an approach to communication similar to that of Chomsky's [5.4] early work (though Chomsky was concerned with syntax rather than semantics [4.43]), in trying to model fundamental communication principles.

If you are interested in logical approaches to describing meaning, you might like to look at Ennis (1996), a logical approach to critical analysis [2.3], which follows very much Russell's way of thinking. An introduction to Russell and selections from his writings can be found in Carr (1975).

5.32 Saussure

Ferdinand de Saussure is generally regarded as the father of structural linguistics. Saussure (1974) in many ways defined modern linguistics [4.28]. His three key principles still guide linguists:

- Linguistics should be synchronic (looking at language in its current state), not diachronic (looking at historical development).
- Linguists should study *langue* (the underlying language system), not *parole* (the particular individual aspects of speech).
- Speech is more important than writing (cultures have speech before writing; people learn speech before they learn to write).

Saussure also suggested that the principal way that signs acquired meaning was in distinction from other signs. Speech sounds functioning in the system of a given language are separated by minimal 'distinctive features' which divide one sound from another. For example, the /p/ sound in /pop/ is distinct from the /b/ sound in /bob/ by virtue of a single sound ('voicing', a vibration in the throat). The same distinctive feature separates other sounds in English, /f/ and /v/, /k/ and /g/.

These priorities suggested that human communication could perhaps admit of systematic scientific study in the ways that, say, animal biology might. In fact, whilst others have also made similar claims (e.g. Lévi-Strauss claimed that he offered a scientific method for the study of culture and myth), such claims have largely proved difficult to maintain. The scientific study of media, communication and culture, where it has been undertaken, has almost always been found to offer either an unhelpfully narrow approach to the topic, or else a useful method leading to knowledge which then required further interpretation.

Extracts from Saussure's writings are Cobley (1996: 37–47), which outlines key linguistic principles, and Cobley (1996: 99–114), which discusses linguistic value. Or read the original text, Saussure (1974).

5.33 Searle

John Searle was a philosopher whose major contribution to communications research was to develop the notion of the 'speech act' (first proposed by another philosopher, J.L. Austin). Although developed as a position from the philosophy of language, Searle's account sits squarely with sociolinguistic [4.28] approaches to language [4.26]. His view was that any speech [4.46] was not merely a stretch of language that had meaning, but also an act, an activity which had meaning just like any other action, and this action would alter the meaning of the linguistic act. For example, if the meaning was 'the door is open', several different speech acts could use that meaning in different ways. We might be commanding someone to shut the door, for example, or suggesting that someone leave, or informing them that there is a draught: speech acts of 'command', 'suggest' or 'inform', respectively. Different contextual conditions would need to be true for different kinds of speech act to apply. For example, the act of 'promising' can only be properly carried out if the speaker intends to carry out a particular act in the future.

So speech acts describe a relationship between intention (such as 'I want to command person x to do y') and the real world, and use language but do not require a particular form of language.

The twenty-page article extracted in Giglio (1972: 136–56) from Searle (1969) is all you need to understand the essence of Searle's theory of speech acts, illustrated with the example of rules for the act of promising. (It is also in Cobley 1996: 263–81.) You may also like to read Austin (1996), which lays out much of the philosophical groundwork on which Searle's account is built.

5.34 Shannon

Claude Shannon and Warren Weaver established a simple descriptive model of the communication of telecommunications information. Theirs was not intended as a universal model of all communication, but it has been adopted by most writers on communication models as offering a vocabulary that describes the key elements of communicative acts. As a model it has many weaknesses, which have been discussed by other commentators, but as a starting model for discussing communication [4.32], it is very useful.

Read the account in Fiske (1990: 6–13) or McQuail and Windahl (1993: 16–9), or the original account in Shannon and Weaver (1949).

5.35 Skinner

B.F. Skinner was a psychologist who strongly espoused the notion of 'behaviourism'. In his view, the proper subject for psychological research was observable behaviour, and such experimental observations could be carried out through controlled experiments using negative and positive stimuli (e.g. electric shocks and food, respectively). Because internal psychological processes could not be observed or measured, they were not legitimate areas for study, but responses to stimuli were observable, measurable and therefore 'proper' areas for scientific research. As such, Skinner was an archetypal positivist [4.39], and his approach is not well regarded by most academics in the media, communications and cultural community. His view of language was that it was a particular form of behaviour, learned by 'operant conditioning', that is to say, by repeated and regular reinforcement.

Read Skinner (1974).

5.36 Van Dijk

Teun Van Dijk's approach to discourse analysis [4.17] is very much that of a linguist, looking for the structures and sequences within discourses, aiming to create something like a grammar of discourse. In his early work he developed the notion of 'text grammar', although later work loosened the strict models he initially developed. He recognizes the strong interplay between social meaning and text structures, and aims to use clear linguistic methods to reveal them. In this sense he is close to critical linguists [4.13] such as Fairclough [5.9] and Kress [5.20], although his motivation springs more from the desire to categorize and explore interesting text phenomena than the desire to expose power relationships in discourse through linguistic analysis.

Van Dijk (1991) and the extract in Jaworski and Coupland (1999: 541–58) are good examples of his work, applying linguistic approaches to racism in discourse.

5.37 Vygotsky

Vygotsky explored the nature of language, starting from a psychological base, and working with empirical data, but actually moving very much into the area of the philosophy of language. He argues that language is entirely socially determined and, as such, functions primarily for emotional and social purposes, and only secondarily in a logical and referential way.

The primary function of speech is communication, social interaction. (Vygotsky 1962: 6)

He suggests that linguistic thought develops from the internalization of linguistic behaviour, so the process of abstraction gradually develops as we learn language: initially we use it merely for maintaining social and personal relationships, and only gradually do we learn to manipulate it as an internal set of codes for thought, through which we can explore abstractions and hypothetical constructs.

Read Vygotsky (1962), the seminal work.

5.38 Weber

Max Weber is often seen alongside Durkheim [5.7]. Like Durkheim, Weber thought that social processes could be described and explained in terms of logical theory and general rule, but he believed the explanations had to be grounded in a science of the social, and not import methods from the physical sciences. The raw material of such explanations were the meanings which people subjectively attributed to social acts. For example, Weber distinguished four broad classes of social acts, derived from the way people saw them: purposeful acts (aiming to achieve a concrete goal, such as build a bridge), value-oriented acts (representing a particular social value, such as promotion to achieve social rank), emotional (such as the hatred of a lynch mob) and traditional (such as celebrations at festivals).

Weber felt that such categories of social action were needed, for he believed that Marx's [5.27] ideas of economic determinism were too rigid to explain many kinds of radical social change. Particular cultural factors were needed, in Weber's view, to be associated with economic factors in order to explain particular social changes, so a model of social phenomena which saw them as strictly determined had insufficient flexibility.

Extracts from Weber's writings can be found in McIntosh (1997: 113–75), including lists of further readings, and a useful introduction is Lewis (2002: 50–3).

5.39 Williams

Raymond Williams was a cultural theorist whose work was grounded originally in literary studies. Williams was one of the pioneers of cultural studies and the examination of popular culture in the UK. His argument that many forms of discourse had value, or values, emerged from readings of high culture [4.21] as well as low, and he had a strong affinity with Hall [5.15]. His seminal book *Communications* (Williams 1962) did much to establish the field of communications study as a worthwhile enterprise in the late sixties, with both a social and an educative agenda.

You can find a discussion of Williams in Lewis (2002: 129–31) and Storey (1997: 54–9), an extract from Williams on mass communication in O'Sullivan and Jewkes (1997: 18–27), and on cultural studies in Storey (1996: 168–77), or read Williams (1961), Williams (1962) and Williams (1983).

5.40 Wittgenstein

Wittgenstein was a Cambridge philosopher writing early in the twentieth century, but most of his influential writings were not published until after his death, with much of his impact on intellectual development coming in the 1950s and 1960s.

Wittgenstein developed two radically different notions of the nature of language, its relationship with the world; and its (inter)dependence on culture. His earlier thought is represented by the *Tractatus Logico-Philosophus* (Wittgenstein 1969), in which he argues that language is entirely dependent on connections with the real world, through reference to real things in it. This is a position arising from the thinking of the 'logical positivists', philosophers of language such as Betrand Russell [5.31] and A.J. Ayer, who, following the positivist [4.39] tradition, aimed to construct a logical representation of meaning.

Wittgenstein later rejected his early views, however, and in *Philosophical Investigations* (Wittgenstein 1972) moved towards a position which is much closer to postmodern [4.40] views of language and meaning, seeing language as entirely learned in specific cultural contexts (at its simplest by imitation and repetition). Consequently, meaning is inherent in those cultural contexts. His argument is essentially that no word has meaning except by virtue of the way it is used, so everyone's understanding of the meanings of particular words is a function of the contexts in which they have used them and heard them used. 'Naming' a 'concept' and 'naming' a 'thing' are, for the later Wittgenstein, the same thing: using a word in a particular way to summarize a collection of particular experiences.

Wittgenstein calls the ways we use language in different, culturally determined, contexts, 'language games'. He suggests that we learn language by playing such games (with our parents, our siblings, our peers and our teachers), and this is not hard to see: for example, the babbling games parents play with babies in which the sounds of language are explored; playground language games; jokes; conversations; essays – almost all uses of language in real situations are bound by particular conventions [4.11].

However, at its extreme, Wittgenstein's view seems to suggest that 'true communication' (whatever that might mean) is impossible. Because he sees meaning as grounded in the particular experience of each individual, he argues that no-one can ultimately know what anything means to someone else, because we all experience the world differently. If we hear the word 'red', we all have been attuned to see a particular property of the world as signalled by that word. And, whilst a logical view might be that 'red' signifies a particular set of wavebands in the visible range of the electro-magnetic spectrum, that hardly captures anything at all of the particular experiences I have had when I 'make sense of' that word: I remember a particular pair of red trousers hung in a chapel; I think of the scarlet I painted childhood models in; I remember a sunset shared with a particular person; I remember the red hair of a sweetheart and the red cheeks of my children in the cold; I hear the sound of Jimi Hendrix's 'Red House' – all these are particular experiences, particular shades of meaning which come together in my 'understanding of the world'. And the physiological and psychological impact they have had on me cannot be related in any direct sense to you, with all your particular experiences and understanding of that word.

A word such as 'red', therefore, is a vague counter, signalling some sort of commonality in experience, some shared meaning which we can recognize as belonging to particular contexts, which we have learned to use in those contexts because that is what our cultural experience has taught us to do; but, fundamentally, what we each know by that word is different. And when I use the word to you, I don't communicate my experience of it, I play a game: I lay a cultural counter down, meaning something to me which fits the context of use, and you pick it up, as appropriate to the context of use, but as fundamentally meaning something different to you, in terms of your experience.

It would follow, from this view of meaning, that you can't really study what words mean for individual people in their own minds. The consequence of Wittgenstein's position is that all that can be talked about is the social (or cultural) construction of meaning. And, in fact (though Wittgenstein does not say this), what you are actually doing in talking or writing about the social construction of meaning is reconstructing that meaning so that it fits a different set of cultural contexts. In other words, the study of language (and, by extension, all human communication) is not about 'discovery' or 'revelation', as if there was something to be found or some hidden meaning to be revealed. It is perhaps better conceived as 'translation' – the mapping of a set of cultural conventions in the culture under observation (supporters of Manchester United at a match, for example) into a different set of cultural conventions (academic conventions for the analysis of communication, say).

This is perhaps akin to what Foucault [5.10] intends when he sees everything as discourse [4.17], and academic commentary merely as the movement of a set of meanings from one discourse into another: discourse about discourse. 'Knowing' in such a view is about translating the studied phenomenon into a context you recognize and are familiar with, and which is accepted by others in the culture you belong to. For the academic, 'knowing' is about placing a studied phenomenon into an elaborate and carefully constructed discourse of academic discipline in the subject area. But for the football supporter, 'knowing' is about being able to select the right chant for the task and tailor it to the name of the player who's just scored: fitting the particular context [4.10] into the communicative tradition of those you belong to.

For an introduction to Wittgenstein in a cultural context, read Lewis (2002: 147–50). Wittgenstein (1972), though complex, is an enthralling account of the philosophy of language.

6

What gets good marks in media, communication and cultural studies?

Introduction to the chapter

Given that the good MCCS student has acquired effective communication skills and assembled appropriate information, these need to be directed to the specific tasks of getting good marks. So this chapter advises on assessment techniques. Whilst Chapter 3 outlined the communicator's skills, this chapter focuses on the specific problems of using those skills most effectively in an *assessed* context.

The chapter is structured in the following way:

- an overview of differences in grading [6.1];
- general hints on ways of improving performance [6.2];
- advice on essay writing [6.3];
- advice on examinations [6.4];
- advice on dissertations [6.5];
- approaches to research [6.6];
- avoiding plagiarism [6.7].

6.1 What do marks mean?

Table 6.1 sketches key differences in performance between different classifications of assignment, and what they mean. Section 6.2 outlines how you can set about improving against these criteria.

Table 6.1 *How assessment is classified*

Class	What does the student do?
1st	Interpret the assignment question thoroughly.
	Offer an excellent argument built on critical analysis of relevant concepts.
	Give detailed observations, strongly supported by examples, quotation or original research.
	Show substantial underlying reading, with many citations, all correctly referenced.
	Produce high-quality presentation with a logical, cohesive structure and clear navigation.
	Include a strongly justified approach consistently interpreting the question, a focused introduction and a conclusion entirely derived from the argument.
	Possibly offer a creative approach to some or all of the tasks.
2:1	Provide a good interpretation of the assignment question.
	Provide an argument that makes good use of critical analysis of relevant concepts, with alternatives considered.
	Write a good justification of opinions and conclusions and a clear logical thread linking sections.
	Discuss key concepts and issues showing understanding of several sources.
	Produce good quality presentation and structure, with a good introduction, and a conclusion derived from detailed discussion of the question.
2:2	Discuss the assignment question, but possibly miss some aspects of it.
	Provide some relevant analysis of concepts used to support the argumentation, but offer relatively little critical analysis.
	Argue in a way that is coherent and rational, offering some justification of opinions.
	Generally provide a logical and coherent structure with clear links, introduction and conclusions but also show some weaknesses or lack of clarity.
	Make some use of examples and relevant literature, perhaps with occasional mistakes in referencing.
	Spend more time writing descriptive than analytical material.
	Include occasional personal comments without justification.
	Present in an acceptable way, probably with a few errors.
3rd	Write in a way which is mainly descriptive rather than critical, and only weakly analyses the assignment question.
	Make poor use of reference to concepts.
	Present in a way that is largely logical and coherent, but sometimes lacks clarity in argument and structure, and may be unattractive.
	Offer observations or material that are not relevant to the task.
	Offer a structure which is mainly coherent but makes poor use of the introduction or conclusion.
	Make infrequent use of examples and references.
	Present in a style with many weaknesses, e.g. poorly edited.
Fail	Fail to include sufficient number or adequate quality in:
	• reference to theory and concepts;
	• justification of opinions and conclusion;
	• logical thread between sections;
	• discussion of assignment question and of approach to it;
	• relevance of information included in the discussion;
	• coherent structure, introduction and conclusion;
	• examples and references;
	• error-free attractive presentation.

6.2 Ways to improve and impress

If you look at Table 6.1, you will see that key skills that move you up a classification require you to:

- monitor mistakes and learn from them [2.1];
- improve the relevance of your information [2.2];
- develop better critical abilities [2.3];
- develop better understanding of the links between concepts [2.1.2], [2.3.3];
- improve skills in argument [3.1.8], [3.2.3];
- improve analysis of the task;
- improve presentation [3.1.9]
- improve editing;
- increase creative thinking.

Section numbers against some of the items in this list suggest parts of the book which will help you with these skills. This section addresses the last four items in this list.

6.2.1 Know your assessment

The better your understanding of what you've been asked to do, the better you are likely to do it.

MCCS students might carry out many different types of assessment. Here's a list of the most common, annotated with relevant sections of this book:

- short and long essays [3.2.2], [6.3], [6.7];
- analyses of textual and cultural forms and practices [4.12], [4.13], [4.16], [4.17], [4.42], [4.44];
- reviews and reports [3.2.3];
- seen and unseen examinations [6.4];
- individual and group presentations (whether oral or technology-based) [3.3], [3.4];
- critical self-evaluation, peer-evaluation and role-analyses/evaluations [3.2.6];
- logbooks, diaries and autobiographical writing [3.2.6];
- individual or group portfolios of work (whether critical, creative, self-reflective or the outcome of professional practice) [3.2.6];
- group and individually produced artefacts, including productions in sound, audio-visual or other media [2.4.4];
- individual and group project reports [3.2.3];
- research exercises [2.2], [6.6];
- tasks aimed at the assessment of specific skills (e.g. IT skills, production skills, research skills, application skills) [2.4.4], [2.4.7];
- external placement or work-based learning reports [3.2.3].

On your course it is likely that you'll have to do several different kinds of task, as most universities these days subscribe to the idea that a variety of different types of assessment is a good thing. Such variety is probably good for you because it allows you to develop a wide range of skills, relevant to different sorts of contexts, and you can make up for weaker abilities in one area with strengths in another. Of course, the balance between these different types of assignment in your course is likely to be uneven: you'll probably have more exams and essays than other kinds of work, for example. You may also find that some units allow you choices of assignment types and others offer you little or no choice, which means that the units you choose may determine the kind of assessment you have.

In order to get the best marks you can, it's helpful to have a good sense of your own abilities when selecting optional units or choosing between assignment types. Don't just choose the easiest because it is the easiest: choose the one you are likely to get the best marks from. Sometimes a course appears easy because the work is undemanding, but that very fact means it is difficult to get excellent marks. For example, a unit which demands largely descriptive work is easy to satisfy but hard to shine at.

Group work can depress or improve your individual mark, depending on the kind of group you're in [2.4.6], [3.3.2], and on the weighting that is given to different aspects of the work. Practical work can lead to high marks, as can extended essays and dissertations; but delivering these higher marks often makes higher demands on your time, so will you be able to find enough time to do well on these units, given all the other things you have to do?

To help with these decisions, put yourself through a little self-analysis. There's no need to make it public in any sense, but work out for yourself which kinds of assessment you actually do better at. Are you one of those people who does better at exams? Some people actually enjoy exams because of the thrill of adrenalin-driven high performance – and they often do well – but they rarely admit to it, because it's not the sort of thing you typically let your friends know.

Or perhaps you are particularly good at the design and presentation of documents, and some sort of presentational assignment is more up your street (e.g. building a website or creating an advertisement). Or are you a very studious, research-oriented person, who likes long bouts of reading and note-taking, who enjoys constructing unusual arguments, and debating the ideas of the great thinkers in your field? Or perhaps you simply talk better than you write, and would benefit from assessment in oral presentation.

Whatever your attitude to these different forms of assessment, be honest with yourself. There's no point in pretending that you are more skilled than you are in any particular area: this sort of self-delusion is only likely to lead to later disappointment. If you are not entirely certain how good you are at particular sorts of activities, ask for advice from your tutors, or ask your friends for their views on your abilities. Or you can look for self-diagnostic exercises. Some universities offer study skills support which enables you to judge your abilities in particular areas, in order to identify the best forms of support that might be helpful.

After your self-analysis, you should be in a reasonable position to decide on your preferred assessment strategy. It may be that you want all assessments to be of the same kind, because you have decided that you are much better at that kind of assessed task than any other. This could work, of course, providing the commitment to lots of the same thing does not lead you to boredom or overload.

The opposite strategy, likely to keep you more motivated and interested in your learning, is a selection of different assessment types. This is much better from a learning or developmental viewpoint, as it requires you to develop a wider range of skills; but it does mean you are less able to play to your particular strengths (unless you have lots of different strengths!).

However, you should also consider how the overall pattern of assessment will work out: Will you have enough time to do all the dissertations and project work you are opting for? Will any deadlines coincide, making it hard to deliver different assignments at the same time? Will it be easy to obtain resources, connect with other relevant people, do any preliminary work, fit the assignment into your typical week? Do the assignments fit into your personal timetable?

Any well-designed assessment will relate directly to a set of learning outcomes (what the unit or course is supposed to give you) and associated assessment criteria (the things you are supposed to show and do through assessment which prove you've achieved the learning outcomes). The language that courses and tutors use to express these may differ from course to course, but the basic idea remains the same, because it is a fundamental one in university thinking.

So, make sure you know what the learning outcomes of each unit are. And make sure you are clear on the relevant assessment criteria for each assignment. A good tutor will generally make both of these clear to you at the beginning of a unit. Ideally it is helpful to have them *before* you do the unit, so you can analyse possible choices with care. If at all possible, get a written list or description. Some tutors will be very detailed, and quite precise, telling you all the criteria in unambiguous ways, and even suggesting how many marks might be awarded against each criterion. Some will content themselves with vaguer statements of 'the kinds of things we are looking for'. If they aren't laid out in a document, ask the tutor to detail them for you.

If you have a vague tutor, it's a good idea to try to get as much clarity as you can, so always politely pursue any areas of vagueness. If the tutor cannot be more precise, then ask for examples of what would be classed as good work against those criteria, so at least you have a model to work to.

When you have a list of assessment criteria, obviously you should work to them. But don't be too mechanical about it. Tutors often reserve the rights to adjust marks and award extra marks, treating the criteria as guidelines, not as hard-and-fast rules, and they will also expect you to satisfy requirements that might not be on the list. For example, just because a list of assessment criteria does not say 'the piece must be professionally presented and referenced in a recognized academic format' does not mean that scrappy work with no references will not lose marks.

6.2.2 Present your work effectively

The physical appearance and the organization of a document affect how it is perceived. The more attractive it is, the better disposed markers are likely to be towards it. So look at the structure, format, style of presentation, use of graphics, visual and physical design of the document, and see what can be done to increase its quality. This involves assessing that whole document against the criteria of purpose and audience need. In particular:

- Do organization and structure relate to content?
- Does the visual look and physical makeup of the document make structure clear by using space around headings and paragraphs, different font for cross-references, indentation to show the hierarchical relationship of points, boxed text for examples, and so on?
- Are navigation aids clear: for example, clear page numbers, headers or footers that orient the reader (telling them which section they're in), good cross-references to connected sections?
- Are quotations clearly identified (italics for short ones, and separate lines for long ones)?
- Are headings in a different font from body text to make them more obvious, and easy to spot when browsing?
- Have appropriate visuals been used, such as tables for summarizing data, graphs for showing trends or bulleted lists for a series of similar observations?
- Does the main body make explicit use of any included appendices?

Advice on such aspects of document design can be found in Schriver (1997) and Jacobson (1999).

6.2.3 Edit your work well

Academics are often surprised by the weakness of students' editing skills. This means it's one area where you can definitely garner extra marks, if you put your mind to it. It is easy enough to understand why student editing skills are poor: most students are not taught how to edit, they are just expected to 'do it', and most students feel they do not have time to edit [2.4.2].

The second of these is easy to avoid. Do not write your essays in such a way that they are always delivered at the last minute, depriving you of the 'extra' time you need to edit. As a minimum, work out a schedule that leaves you enough time at the end for reviewing what you have done, and stick to that schedule.

Furthermore, do not fall into the 'it's finished' trap. A piece of writing is rarely, ever, finally perfect. There's always more that can be done, more refinement that can be made. But for those of us who are not perfectionists, there has to be a cut-off point when you say 'that's as good as it's going to get'. Simply make sure that that cut-off point comes after thorough editing, not before.

Editing is a communications skill, just like any other. Good writers can be bad editors and vice versa. It should be your aim to be good at both, as each skill makes the other easier. The good editor makes sure she or he locates all errors and weaknesses in a document by the following:

- *Editing at all levels of the document, not merely words.* As well as spelling, grammar and punctuation, the good editor looks at sense, word choice, sentence length, appropriateness of style, paragraphing, layout, organization, cross-referencing, signposting, references and bibliographies.
- *Editing in all parts of the document.* As well as the main body text, the good editor looks at headings, headers and footers, contents lists, figures and images, appendices, charts, footnotes, bibliographies: in short, every occurrence of information of some kind within the document.

One way to improve the editing of your work is to give it to someone else to do. People are always more objective, and more ruthless, on the work of others than on their own work. Ask a friend to do the editing for you, or at least to read it for the most obvious kinds of problems. This approach can be particularly useful when the subject matter is very difficult, and therefore likely to be a source of error for the 'average' reader.

In return for the favour, you should also edit your friend's work. Not only does this share the burden, but it improves your own editing skills, as you will consider your friend's attempt from a relatively dispassionate point of view: you don't have the same love–hate relationship with his or her work that you have with your own.

If no-one is willing to do your editing, then the best way to approach it yourself is not to do it for a week or two. Put the writing aside and let it mature in a drawer for a fortnight. Then retrieve it, and you will find that your 'ownership' of the writing has faded. You can consider it more objectively, because you have developed some distance from it. This means you should be in a better position to give it a thorough going-over than you would have been on the afternoon that you thought you wrote the final word.

It's usually easier, and more effective, to edit by making several passes through the document, each one focusing on different aspects, rather than trying to do everything at once in one pass. Three passes should give you a good review:

- *Review for content and associated expression*: sense, coherence, relevance, and so on. Are there enough examples? Does the argument feel like a logical progression? Does the text make proper use of the graphics?
- *Edit for spelling, grammar and punctuation*, remembering to look at every element of the document, not just the body text.
- *Edit for structure and organization.* Look at the headings: Do they make sense? Does the contents page use the correct headings? Are the cross-references to the right page? Are all bibliographical citations complete and correct? Is the bibliography organized in the right way?

6.2.4 Find creative approaches

Creativity is an enormously complex, sometimes almost mystical, area to explore. There are no firm rules for it. Talking of creativity, tutors might typically say things like 'I don't know how to get it but I know it when I see it'. Even when you know some of the principles involved, making them work is not easy.

Essentially creativity boils down to two difficult things:

- *Finding connections that no-one has noticed before* [2.1.2]. Academic creativity is often about linking two previously separate concepts, or applying a concept to a problem area that has not previously been thought of.
- *Doing something new.* This may mean breaking conventions or rules, or seeing an opportunity where none had previously noticed it, or simply realizing that there was an approach or a topic which no-one had really looked at before.

If you want to try to bring a little more creativity into your academic work, here are a few examples of things you could try:

- *Find links between ideas across different units.* Don't always confine your discussion just to the material presented in the unit if there is relevant information in another unit you are studying.
- *Challenge one of the most fundamental theories or practices in the unit.* Don't make this the entire force of your work (in case there is a fundamental problem with it), but devote a little energy to making a good case for the challenge. One way to do this is to present the challenge as a 'possible idea' (i.e. not one that you necessarily agree with), that you explore as a way of 'testing' the concept you are challenging. The outcome of your challenge can then be along the lines of 'this objection to the concept actually seems to have some force, but would need rather deeper analysis than I've given here to be established properly'.
- *Combine something unusual with the standard concept or theory or approach you are adopting.* This might be another theory, or an issue or problem area, or it might be a research method [6.6] that has not been applied to that concept before.
- *Choose an application area, or example topic, which is not run of the mill.* For example, if the topic is media portrayal of violence, students are likely to choose topics such as football hooliganism, war reporting, detective thrillers, cartoon violence, domestic violence (all interesting areas; all well studied). A somewhat off-the-wall approach might be to look at portrayals of violence in, say, programming for the under fives (Is there any? How is it manifest?); or perhaps boxing programmes, where clearly the whole point is to report violence, so the issues are rather different from the media effects debate [4.2], [4.31].

6.3 Doing better in essay writing

When essay writing, bear in mind all the issues and techniques discussed in [3.1] and [3.2.2], but remember that your assessment will also be testing one or more of your:

- knowledge of communication and media practice;
- knowledge of media, communication and cultural theory;
- knowledge of sources;
- academic argument and writing skills.

The quality of your work, from a marker's viewpoint, will be a question of how well you satisfy all the relevant criteria, but also how you integrate them in your writing.

A useful approach in discursive essay writing is to have at the back of your mind the phrase 'It depends what you mean'. Almost everything in MCCS is interpretative, which means there's always more than one way of looking at something, and 'deep' understanding of that something involves recognition of those different ways of approaching it. Of course, if you question everything in your essay, you will probably produce something that is incoherent. But, if you want to demonstrate understanding beyond that of merely reproducing the textbook, show that you:

- recognize the complexity of key ideas and key issues;
- recognize that simple answers depend on compressing or ignoring more complex underlying issues and ideas;
- know that there are different competing theories or interpretations.

Consider this example:

Discuss the claim that new technologies offer a fundamentally different form of communication.

This question falls into two parts: the instruction to the student 'Discuss the claim that . . .', and a statement of a claim that 'new technologies offer a fundamentally different form of communication'. We'll examine the first part in section [6.5]. The second part acts like a hypothesis or a thesis statement (a statement which encapsulates a hypothesis, the summary of an argument). We saw in [3.1.8] how you can use the questions raised by a thesis statement as a way of structuring writing, and in [2.3.2] how critical analysis gives you fundamental questions to ask of what you read. Putting these two things together, you are in a position to write an excellent essay. Your discussion can ask questions of this thesis statement, and your essay can offer both the answers to those questions, and the further questions they demand, using the four planks of discussion, 'theory, argument, evidence, conclusions', to guide you.

A simple way to address the essay question would be to say which technologies you understand by 'new technologies', answering the first question that the thesis statement arouses: 'what are the new technologies?' You would clarify what forms of communication they seem to offer, and discuss any sense in which those forms of communication are different from previous forms of communication. In doing this, you'll probably say something about the similarities and differences between these new forms of communication and some earlier forms. Providing you use appropriate examples, and enough of them, this would probably be sufficient to derive a quite reasonable answer.

However, if you look back at Table 6.1 [6.1], you'll see that such an answer is most likely to get you a 2:2.

So a deeper understanding, taking Minto's insistence on repeated questioning to heart ([3.1.8] Minto 1991), and looking critically at the question, might start by examining *every* premise within the task. For example, instead of merely listing the new technologies you are going to talk about, you could consider the problem of identifying what, exactly, is meant by the phrase 'new technologies' [4.8]? Are there, for example, different ways of defining 'new technology'? Are there different ways of looking at technology which would see some technologies as new, and others not? Perhaps it can be argued that there are no new communications technologies, because they all have origins in some other technologies. Perhaps it can be argued that 'new technology' is a misnomer, as most of the technologies under discussion have been around in some form for over twenty years. So the notion of 'new' could be seen as problematic. You might also question the word 'technology': for example, what technology legitimately can be seen as specifically communications technology rather than, say, calculating technology or graphics technology?

When you start to think about such things, you find it's actually quite a difficult area. People talk and write as if it is self-evident what the new communications technologies are, but in fact it is by no means obvious what should be included or excluded.

In a slightly different way, you might also question the word 'fundamentally'. Okay, you can identify ways of talking about 'difference' in forms of communication (this is one of the values the examiner will find in this question, of course: 'How does the student go about the task of clarifying what is meant by 'different forms of communication?'). This is clearly a very problematic word, when you ask the question 'what do you mean by it?' In what sense is a difference in communication 'fundamental'?

It must surely mean a difference which makes communication something other than it previously was, by adding or altering it in some way, so that something truly new has been created. And, obviously, the intelligent way to handle this is to say that, whilst some characteristics of communication can change, others cannot be changed, so in that sense some fundamental elements of communication cannot be altered. So, whilst we might claim that new technologies offer mass communication [4.29] on a 'fundamentally' different scale from anything previously known, we would also have to say that many of the defining characteristics of mass communication remain the same whether delivered by satellite, cable, the Internet or digital TV.

6.3.1 Argue effectively

Most assignments will require you to make a case, either in an academic argument, or as an analysis of a discourse [4.17] or practice. The better your case, the better your marks.

Remember all the advice on critical analysis in [2.3] and apply it to your own writing. Remember the advice in [3.1.3] about the active audience, and forestall objections. But also bear in mind the following additional approaches in building and enhancing your own arguments:

- Consider different viewpoints.
- Use appropriate and up-to-date sources.
- Always back up points with evidence.
- Try to find cross-validating (mutually supporting) evidence.
- Take a critical attitude to all claims made by others.
- Take on board objections to your case and alternative viewpoints, and either incorporate them, accept them (so modifying your case) or refute them.
- Make sure structure, organization, presentation and language all fit together, representing a coherent approach.
- Make sure that references and examples are well integrated throughout your argument.

In addition, here are seven guidelines for keeping your argument solid (adapted from Berger 2000):

- Don't select evidence in a narrow way, but seek it from many different sources and viewpoints [2.2.3].
- Don't treat authorities as necessarily 'the truth'; always maintain a critical eye.
- Don't use emotional appeals or emotional language (such as irrational beliefs or appeal to prejudice). Instead, rely on logic for your case.
- Avoid over-generalizing. Don't say 'all' when you only have evidence for 'some'. Beware of absolute judgements and be prepared to use phrases like 'as a rule', 'probably', 'generally' and 'in most instances'.
- Avoid imperfect or misleading analogies and metaphors. Use them to illustrate a point, but do not rely on them as logical structures.
- Don't overplay your hand and push your argument to extremes. Take it only as far as the evidence allows, and do not be tempted to speculate beyond what you can prove from your evidence.
- Don't misrepresent the ideas of others. Make sure that quotations are accurate, your summaries of others' observations and conclusions are complete and correct, and that the opinions you cite from others are representative of their views.

6.4 Doing better in examinations

6.4.1 Knowing the topic

There are many ways of doing well in examinations, but they all depend on having knowledge in the first place. If you haven't done the work, if you don't know much about the subject area, you might just be able to wing it and pass by the skin of your teeth. But if you want good marks, you need to have plenty of relevant information under your belt. No amount of examination technique can compensate for ignorance of the topic.

Which is not to say that you need to know everything possible in order to do well in exams. Although the primary aim of unseen exams is to test student knowledge (which is one of the reasons most students hate them, of course), no examination will be able to test the whole range of possible knowledge. Examiners see unseen exams as a way of testing everything a student *might* know by assessing a sample of what they actually do know. But students tend not to be prepared to answer on any possibly topic, so generally revise simply one more than the number of expected questions.

The examiners feel they have a fair test of the student's overall knowledge and ability. The students feel they can second-guess the examiner and, by only working on three or four questions, satisfy the examiner that they would, could or should have enough knowledge on the unanswered questions. In practice, of course, examiners know that students attempt to question-spot, and revise only for limited areas of the whole course. But examiners who use unseen examinations generally still feel it is the best process they have for testing both depth and, potentially, breadth of knowledge.

Obviously the way to do well on an unseen examination is to know everything that might be known on every topic that might be asked. But, if you have that knowledge, you probably don't need this book (and you should probably be lecturing on the course rather than studying it!). So you need to know how to make the best of the more limited information available to you.

6.4.2 Revising effectively

Too many students use revision as their first encounter with some of the material they are to be assessed in. Better students, however, understand that revision is 're-seeing', looking again at material they have already looked at. A prerequisite of good revision is good-quality notes, so your note-taking skills will be tested when you come to revise from them [2.4.3].

One good revision technique is what might be called 'continual refinement'. The idea is that you start with all your notes on a topic, and read through them carefully, marking as you do the main ideas, quotes, information, subtopics, headings, issues, and so on (e.g. by using a highlighter pen). Having done this, your second stage of revision is to read through all the highlighted areas, and only those, identifying within them keywords and short phrases which encapsulate those rather longer issues. If, in the course of this second stage, you discover you don't understand any of the highlighted notes, you need to go back and re-read that particular subtopic.

Your next stage of revision is to work only from the abstracted keywords. For a given topic you might have a list of about fifteen to thirty keywords and phrases, each of which is a focal message which triggers your knowledge of the material it summarizes or represents. If it doesn't do this, either it is badly chosen, or you need to go back to the original material it was derived from and work through it once again. Eventually, when you have your refined list of (say) twenty keywords, all of which signal extensive underlying knowledge, you commit this list to memory, and it is this list which you use in the exam for planning around the actual question you have to answer.

What you should find is that, eventually, this list of keywords acts as a set of 'triggers' which more or less automatically fire off the underlying information each time you read them. You should become so familiar with these keywords that the knowledge they summarize becomes an almost automatic response.

However, learning a simple, unstructured list of about twenty topics is not the easiest of tasks. People generally find it much easier to remember structured lists, in which the twenty items are themselves subdivided into four or five groups of four or five subtopics each. These little subgroups do not need to be very sophisticated analyses of the main topic. There is more versatility possible in structures which are not too tight or too complex. So your subgroups might simply be categories like 'positive ideas', 'negative ideas', 'practical implications', 'key problems', 'main theories', and so on.

Even better would be a series of lists which are related to each other in ways that allow you to write about them in offering an argument. For example, your first group might be 'theoretical perspectives, positive views', your second 'theoretical perspectives, negative views', your third 'practical applications', your fourth 'issues raised for new research'. These four groups would give you substructures that could be reassembled in different ways according to the question you have to address. If it is something like 'Compare and contrast opposing views of x', then a sequence roughly like that given above would work, but if the question was of the form 'What theories of x best illuminate its practice?', a more appropriate structure might be one which first outlined the practical applications, then accounted for the issues raised, and then used these issues to examine different theoretical perspectives.

6.4.3 Planning in the exam

Planning is useful in an exam context, if it does not take up too much time. Using a brainstorming technique like the mind map or brain pattern can be a good practice, as it generates many ideas very rapidly. The idea is very simple:

- Write the key topic or concept in the centre of a page.
- As quickly as you can, and without pausing to think or evaluate, write a subtopic or idea that comes to mind, related to the main topic. Draw a line linking the two.
- Again quickly, and without reflection, write down another idea or keyword, suggested either by the main topic or one of the ideas you've written down. Draw a line linking this topic with the idea that suggested it.
- Continue in this fashion. Each topic is likely to spark another connection or subtopic, whose link you draw. In the end you'll end up with a diagram something like Figure 6.1.

This is a 'map' of what you know about the topic. It's variously called a mind map or brain pattern (because it describes your knowledge) or a spider diagram, because

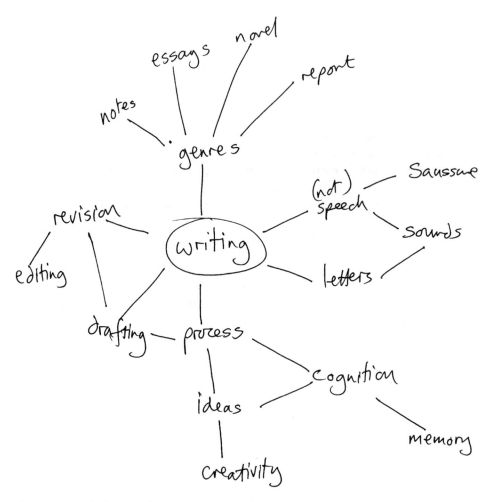

Figure 6.1 *Mind map*

of its appearance. It is an extremely effective way of rapid planning, and has the immediate benefit of offering you a possible structure as well, as each branch of the map shows you subtopics related in your mind to larger topics.

However, if the mind map does not give you a structure you are happy with, treat it as a brainstorm of ideas, and take a couple of minutes more to outline a brief structure which makes better sense of the ideas you have generated. The same technique can work in any rapid planning situation, such as when you have to give a presentation at a moment's notice.

Having created a plan, it can be useful to leave it in the exam script in a form that the examiner can consult if he or she wants to. There is no reason to delete it (unless, for some reason, the examination's rubric requires you to) and the extra information provided might be of real benefit to you if the examiner has difficulty (e.g. in deciphering your handwriting, or understanding a gap in your argument).

6.4.4 Writing a good answer

Answer the question. I am certain you've heard that advice before. But it is the key advice in doing a good (as opposed to an 'okay') exam question. The average student tends to assume that answering questions in an exam is about trotting out all they know about the topic, as specified in the lecture, and probably the essay they did for their assignment, and they typically reproduce that essay in the exam, *no matter what version of the topic the actual exam question actually addresses.*

Some, badly designed, exams do allow you to do this. But they should not. If you have already been assessed on a particular aspect of a topic, then you should not be assessed on precisely the same topic again, even if in a slightly different way.

As part of your revision, get hold of previous exam papers in your units and analyse them. You might apply content analysis [4.9] to explore the topics, and discourse analysis [4.17] to examine the typical form of the questions. If there are no previous papers, or if the tutor is new, then aim to get 'typical' or sample questions from the tutor. Some lecturers give out dummy papers as part of their exams briefing, or run practice sessions to give students a good idea of what to expect. If not, seek a tutorial with the aim of getting the lecturer to dictate to you a few examples of the kind of question you might expect.

The key to answering a question fully and appropriately in an exam setting is to analyse the exact requirement of the question, and address that explicitly and consistently. Table 6.2 gives some examples of key instructions within exam questions, with advice on how to approach such questions.

Table 6.2 *Typical wording of exam instructions*

Question task	Things to do
Analyse	Apply your critical skills to the issue or problem, taking it apart in a logical way. Explain why you have chosen your particular approach to analysis: for example, what the benefits are, or what that sort of analysis is designed to do.
Argue	This does not mean 'object to' but 'make a case'. Such a case may include possible objections, but generally only to refute them.
Clarify	This will present you with a complex area for you to give a simple account of. It is a chance to show your knowledge and your analytical skills.
Compare	Comparing involves finding the similarities and differences between two items. In the case of MCCS, the two items are probably theories or ideas, and the task is probably a test of whether you are familiar with (and can reproduce) the details of each. So the task has three parts: <ul><li>Show the examiner that you know all the key elements of idea (a) (or whatever the first item in the comparison is).</li><li>Show the examiner that you know all the key elements of idea (b) (or whatever the second item in the comparison is).</li><li>Show the examiner that you understand the similarities and differences between these two ideas, by noting all of them.</li></ul>

Table 6.2 *cont.*

Question task	Things to do
Compare [*cont.*]	But the better student, the 2:1 student, will go beyond this basic task. S/he will not only note the nature of each of the two ideas, but explain variants or modifications of each: for example, different historical variations or different researchers' interpretations. This shows that you understand that the idea is not merely a simple thing that can readily be reported in a mechanical way, but that it is a complex network of sub-ideas. You could also note the overlaps between the two different ideas, their similarities and differences, and explain why they are there. And you may enter into a brief discussion of the implications of those similarities and differences. For example, if we say that Argyle's [5.1] social psychological view of communication is like a sociological model of communication, in that they both treat the social functions of communication as primary, this is a similarity. But they are different in that the focus of Argyle's work is small group psychology: essentially the operation of individuals within groups; but sociological theory is about people in the mass and typically does not regard the behaviour of individuals as particularly interesting. This is a reasonable comparison between the two ideas of communication. But a better answer would not merely describe similarities and differences, but seek to explore and explain them, showing understanding beyond merely 'knowing what the theory is'. For example: The superficial similarity – the concern of both approaches with the social characteristics of communication – therefore disguises a critical difference in the values of the two. In the one case, we might look for explanations of communication which attribute motivation to the distinct beliefs of particular individuals, so each social interaction can be seen as a distinct activity. But in the case of a sociological explanation, individuals are not seen as having any particular motivation, independent of their social functions, so all communications of a particular kind tend to be seen as similar communications. In the first case, accounting for the behaviour of a family watching *Friends* together might be explicable in terms of the particular interests, experience and desires of each member of the family, and how these are 'managed' within the group. In the second case, these would be seen as functions of the way families interact with mass media messages, the focus not being on personal motivations but on how the mass media messages are articulated and represented through their interactions.
Compare and Contrast	Obviously, in essence, this is the same as 'Compare' except that it explicitly asks you to look at *differences* between the two items being compared as well as similarities. In such a case, make sure that you devote an equal amount of time to both aspects of the question. Examiners will normally expect you to devote about half the question to each part of the task, so do not focus entirely on similarities and just scribble a few words on differences in the closing paragraph: structure your answer in such a way that both get equal attention.
Critically discuss	This is the same as 'Discuss' (see below) except that you are expected to apply your critical skills to the discussion as well. So the opinions and views you bring into play need to have a rationale, and they need to illuminate the items you are discussing in revealing ways.
Define	Definition might be simply remembering the literal definition of a straightforward term. However, it is more likely to be definition of a complex term, for which no simple formula exists, such as 'culture' [4.14] or 'communications technologies' [4.8]. The examiner is expecting you to explore different ways of looking at these terms, not simply to come up with a glib simplification which doesn't do the job.

Table 6.2 *cont.*

Question task	Things to do
Define [cont.]	One useful technique is to start with a simple definition, which you know is inadequate. Explain why it is a reasonable starting point, then show why it is inadequate and develop a more detailed version, either by enhancing the definition you started with, or abandoning it, and offering a second one which deals with the objections you have just raised. You can repeat the process until you end up at a definition you can call 'complete'.
Describe	Make sure that your description is adequate and relevant to the task: for example, do not include irrelevant detail, and ensure that you include detail that might be useful for the rest of the question. You may also feel that the task of description is not as straightforward as might be assumed: for example, perhaps there are two views or interpretations of the phenomenon being described. In which case, either give both, or else give one and explain why you are not giving the other (this shows the examiner that you know about the other one, and that you have the critical judgement to decide which is most appropriate).
Discuss	Discussion requires you not merely to describe a particular state of affairs, but to provide a range of different views on it, which you try to reconcile, integrate or evaluate in some way. Amongst those views should be some of your own, but when you offer your own views, make it clear where they come from. Don't just say 'I think . . .', but 'I think . . . because . . .'. The 'because' element in your opinion should at least contain an argument of some kind, and preferably include evidence to back it up.
Explain	An explanation normally relates an observed fact or phenomenon to some underlying cause, or gives a rationale for a particular view or process: for example, 'Explain why ambiguity exists in natural languages', where you would be expected to explain not only why it has come about, but also what its purpose is.
Give examples, give evidence	Make sure your examples are relevant, and cover all the necessary ground. For example, if asked to give examples of non-verbal communication, you need to consider if what is required is an example of all the different kinds of NVC [4.33] (e.g. to illustrate the whole range) or simply two or three, to show that you understand what is being asked. Examples are a kind of concrete evidence, but evidence is also data, quotation, observations, and so on.
Illustrate	This is another way of asking for examples or evidence. However, it may require detailed, deep illustrations. For example, it may be an opportunity to report case study research [6.6.7].
Justify	This question asks you to adopt a particular position or viewpoint, and support it. You will need to offer evidence and argument to support the position you adopt.
Outline, summarize	This asks for a bare overview, not for detail. However, it should still cover all relevant factors. Usually this is an opportunity to display knowledge, by showing succinctly that you know all the elements of a particular area. (See Summary [3.2.4].)
To what extent	This phrase asks you to evaluate a thesis or idea. It expects a complex evaluation underpinned with reasons, justifications and arguments. It would be perfectly reasonable to answer such a question with an 'it depends how you evaluate it' answer, as there will be no correct answer to such a question. It will be a matter of debate.
With reference to	This limits the question to a particular viewpoint which you should pay specific attention to. Although you should mention the other approaches which might have been considered relevant, to show that you know they could have been used, your task is to relate the question to the explicit context given.

In addition to all the above, in all cases a good answer will seek to explore relationships between concepts [2.1.2]. If you see a valid link, mention it.

6.4.5 Use your time effectively

Exams have different lengths and different requirements, but typically have three or four questions with forty minutes to an hour for each. Although this can be a frighteningly long period to contemplate, if you know your stuff, it turns out to be very little time indeed to say what you find you want to say in the exam. You have to use time effectively to turn your knowledge into marks.

Key advice is to make sure that you answer all the questions you are supposed to. It's very simple advice, but it is surprising how many students spend two and half hours on their first two questions, and then suddenly discover they only have half an hour left for the final question. In general, three reasonable questions of roughly equal length will get you better marks than two good questions and a weak third question. This is because of the mathematics of marking.

The best way to understand this is through an example. Take the typical three-hour, three-question paper. If you spend an hour on the first question, you'll write, say, five pages of about three paragraphs a page, i.e. 15 paragraphs. Suppose you get a good mark for this (65%, say), then each paragraph seems to be worth, on average, about 4.3 marks. You might expect on this calculation that if you write three more paragraphs (one more page), taking another 12 minutes, you'll increase your mark by another 12.9 marks, giving you a total of 78. What you're assuming here is that the graph of marks against time is linear: for every 12 minutes you spend, you get 12.9 marks.

But this is very unlikely. Much more likely is that your extra 12 minutes on the first question will send your mark up by two or three per cent, to, say, 69%. This is because the marker has decided well before page 5 what kind of quality you are delivering, how much you know, how well structured your answer is, and so on: 'it's in the mid- to high 60s, I think'. You would have to make a significant difference in the additional three paragraphs to change this perception markedly.

But suppose you use the same 12 minutes to start a new question. Here you still write three paragraphs, but beginning on a new topic. Assuming it is of the same sort of quality as the previous question, your first page of the new question is likely to get you something in the region of 15 to 20 marks. If the total mark for a five-page answer comes out as 65%, then the graph of pages (or time) against marks is likely to be something like Table 6.3.

Table 6.3 *Sample marks in an exam*

Page	Mark	Total so far
1	19	19
2	16	35
3	13	48
4	10	58
5	7	65

You can see that, as time goes on, it gets harder and harder to get marks. Of course, no examiner works quite so mechanically, and the fact that you make two good points early on does not mean the examiner will then ignore the fifteen mistakes you subsequently make. But the tendency is for examiners to see an essay as belonging in a rough classification, and simply to adjust that impression as more points (or errors) are found.

Even if this analysis is only partly true, it should be pretty obvious what you should do in an examination if you want to maximize marks. Where you have a choice between adding a page to an existing answer, or starting a new page for a new question, always do the latter. You should do this even if you are on your third or fourth question which you feel you do not know anything about. It is much easier to get ten marks for a single page on your fourth question then to add ten marks to an answer which the examiner has already formed an opinion about.

So, always attempt all the questions you are supposed to. If you find that after beginning your final question you quickly run out of things to say, and you really cannot write more than a couple of pages, then by all means go back to the other questions and add new material if you have more to say. At this point your decision is different from the 'do I add a page to an existing question, or start a new question?' decision; it is of the form: 'do I add a page of rubbish to an existing answer, or a page of rather better material to a different existing answer?' The answer to this seems pretty self-evident.

What you should aim to achieve is a roughly equivalent amount of time (and therefore words) for each answer. If you can achieve this, you'll probably get roughly equal marks for each, assuming that you have been able to achieve most of the other requirements for good exam answering, as discussed above.

6.4.6 Practical questions in examination

Multiple choice tests   Multiple choice tests are used as a time-saving way to test factual knowledge, but generally of a rather superficial kind. The results are not good discriminators between students, and the pass mark is usually set quite high to discourage random answering.

If you do not know the answer to a multiple choice question, it is *always* worth a guess. In badly designed tests, it is sometimes even possible to pass through random answers (e.g. with a pass mark of 30 for a test of 100 questions, if there are three possible answers per question, random answering should get a mark of 33%). Furthermore, sometimes you find that you know the answer when you thought you were guessing: your subconscious dredges the information up, even though you were not consciously aware of it. If you have read enough and thought enough about your subject, you may have embedded the knowledge in your memory.

Otherwise, there is little that can be done to pass such tests, apart from knowing the answers. As they favour large-scale superficial knowledge, and as the questions can be difficult to design (designing believable wrong answers is quite difficult), the best way to acquire the relevant knowledge is to attend all the lectures and to read all the essential reading. Most tutors' questions will come from these two sources.

Textual analysis   The examiner may ask you to analyse a text of some kind, verbal or visual. Obviously, the aim will be to test your analytical skills and techniques, which should be relatively easy to revise. For example, you may have been taught to use content analysis [4.9], semiotic analysis [4.44], deconstruction [4.16], structural analysis [4.48], some form of linguistic analysis [4.28] or perhaps critical analysis [2.3].

However, there may be several ways of analysing the text, and the question might not make it clear what form of analysis is required. If so, you have two choices:

- Choose one possible analytical approach, and apply that thoroughly.
- Apply several approaches.

In the first case, it will be sensible to justify your choice, as part of the test may be to see what approach you use, and why. In the second, you will need to make sure that you fit the outcomes of your analyses together in some way, either by showing how they reinforce each other, or by suggesting why they appear to lead in different directions.

In either case, an analytical exercise will also be testing your understanding of theory, in two senses. Firstly, the examiners will be interested in how you select or justify the analytical method you have chosen. Secondly, they will want to see what you do with the results: what kind of information do you get from your analysis, and how do you use it?

Therefore, you should always ensure that you relate your analytical answers to some form of theoretical perspective, whether it is a critique of the method, or an interpretation of the results.

6.5 Writing a good dissertation

In essence, a dissertation is a long essay. So all of the guidelines that apply to essay writing apply also to dissertation writing [3.2.2], [6.3].

However, it is not *just* a long essay. You can't create a good dissertation just by doing the same thing as in essay writing, and merely delivering more of it. Essays are typically about 2000 words in length, dissertations are anything from 8000 to 20,000, but a dissertation is not simply four essays placed end to end. Dissertations have their own structure and rationale, and elements that you might not pay too much attention to in a typical essay become much more important in a dissertation.

Dissertations are also tests of your research and presentation skills. You're expected to do more, and better research for your dissertation, to sustain it more successfully, and to present the information as closely as you can to accepted academic conventions.

Different courses will have different rules for what should go into a dissertation and how it should be presented. So the first thing to know, if you want to write a good dissertation, is what the rules are in your institution. There will be a maximum number of words, which you obviously should not exceed, but it's worth knowing what counts towards that word total, and whether there is any leeway. Sometimes, for example, the rules allow you to exceed the total by up to 20% before you are penalized. Sometimes figures, footnotes or appendices are discounted from the word total.

Knowing these rules gives you a sense of how flexible you can be in what you write: if you know that every word counts and the penalties for excess are harsh, you'll need to write with rather more discipline than otherwise.

6.5.1 Choosing a topic

Almost certainly you'll have a free choice of the topic you will explore for your dissertation, though you'll probably have to negotiate it with a tutor, and it may have to go through a process of formal approval. Choosing a good topic is probably the most important stage of dissertation work. You've got to find a topic which is:

- *Interesting*. If you're not motivated to do it, you'll get fed up half-way through and do inferior work. If you're not interested in it, why would your readers be?
- *Do-able*. Don't go over the top. You've got to have a project that can be carried out with the resources you've got, in the time you've got.
- *Appropriate*. Your topic has got to be of the kind that's required. If the assessment asks for a project based on library research on 'popular culture', there's little point constructing a project that requires a survey on personality.

Defining a topic for your dissertation is very often the task of zooming in on a tighter and tighter specification. Start by choosing an area of interest. Then find a problem or issue in the area. Decide why it looks like a problem, then work out how it might be looked at, thinking about possible theoretical perspectives and practical methods. Then state the topic very precisely, in a single sentence, referring to the relevant theoretical perspective. You may also find that it divides into three or four sub-questions, which will be the main research questions you hope to address (see [3.1.8]).

6.5.2 Choosing a supervisor

If you have a choice of supervisor, select one who:

- knows about the subject you are interested in;
- will work well with you, helping, advising, motivating and perhaps challenging;
- knows about the research methods you want to use;
- has enough time to supervise you in the way you want.

6.5.3 Whom is the dissertation for?

The audience for your dissertation will be your academic supervisor, and probably other academics acting in the roles of additional examiners. However, to make sure that you write in an appropriate way, you should assume that your research project will be published and read by your peers, that is, other students or researchers. Your audience analysis [3.1.1] will probably suggest that these people will be:

- knowledgeable in a general sense about the field;
- ignorant about the particular project you're discussing and its context;
- ignorant of the research underpinning your research project;
- looking for a critical approach, i.e. evidence and objectivity, in the statements that you make;
- looking for general learning points arising from your research project.

6.5.4 What should be in your proposal?

Most supervisors, and some course teams, want to approve a dissertation proposal before they will let you get on with it. Make sure your proposal includes:

- a draft title, to give your dissertation focus (you can always change it later, if necessary);
- the aims of your dissertation (What is this research for? What problem or issue are you trying to address?);
- the approach to research, and the methods you might use;
- the possible theoretical base, perhaps supported with a list of relevant readings.

6.5.5 What structure should a dissertation have?

Dissertations often follow a conventional structure, of the following form:

- abstract or summary (see [3.2.4]);
- introduction (see [3.2.2]);
- literature review (see below);
- research methodology (an account of what you did, why, and possible issues – see [6.6]);
- data analysis (the results of your work, and how you have categorized and interpreted it, including problems);
- conclusions (what the data tell you about the questions you wanted to address, plus possible gaps, issues and implications);
- bibliography (a list of *all* the texts you have used in the work – see [3.2.5]);
- appendices (additional material, if needed, and optional material which may be relevant to some but not all possible readers, e.g. a glossary).

Only the literature review needs explanation. It is more or less what the name suggests: a review of available literature relevant to your project. In effect, the review is a prose record of the activities you might have carried out following the advice in section [2.2]. It can have one or more of several purposes (as well as proving to the examiners that you've read some literature and know how to summarize it). Typical purposes are to:

- find clear definitions of the problem you want to investigate, and what is already known about it;
- find inspiration;
- help you define the topic more precisely, and justify it in relation to what is known;
- identify gaps, problems, weaknesses in the current state of knowledge of the field(s);
- identify methods that might be useful, and prove that they're appropriate (e.g. to show that interviews have been successfully used in audience research);
- construct an argument for a particular approach to the intended problem;
- explore the conceptual background (e.g. to provide an intellectual history of the field);
- explore the relationships between different literatures that might appear relevant, so you can select the most suitable or synthesize them in some way;
- underpin particular ideas you are going to make use of in the main body of the work (and so show that you understand them) – this might be particularly important with terms like 'discourse' [4.17] and 'postmodernism' [4.40], which are used in many different ways;
- document your exploration of the topic, especially your early stages as you define the approach, as a systematic account of what you understand by the topic and the steps that led you to develop it.

A good literature review is an account of the literature that makes sense of it in its own terms, showing an overview and a synthesis, an understanding of that literature – in other words, giving your work its 'intellectual underpinning'. It should not be just a series of summaries or read like a diary of what you read and when you read it.

The word 'review' is important. It's another of these complex writing tasks where you have to say everything you need to say in the simplest way and briefest space, reconcile competing objectives, prove that you know everything that might be relevant without *literally* documenting everything, and establish how all the varied literature that has consumed your time during the project 'fits' the overall purpose, when (usually) half of it is unhelpful.

A common structure for a literature review is as follows:

- It follows an introductory chapter or section which lays out the parameters of the project (e.g. the problem to be addressed), so it starts by outlining what literature might be relevant to that problem.
- It outlines the purposes that the review of literature is supposed to serve, related to the stated problem and study.
- It says something about how the literature was explored or found, where this was anything other than a series of bibliographical and web searches.
- It says something about how the literature review chapter is organized.

- The bulk of the section is usually a series of accounts of the literature. Weaker reviews tend to operate text by text, becoming a list. Stronger reviews find a higher degree of organization, reporting elements of texts in the way that they fit together and reinforce, contradict or develop from each other.
- Sometimes there are sections which deal with a set of texts only to reject them. You might do this to deal with literature that proves unhelpful, but where you've spent a lot of effort that you want recognized.
- Finally, there is a summary of the reviewed texts which picks out the key points for the project, leading in to the next chapter, where those key points become the rationale for the approach.

6.5.6 Working with a large document

Because a dissertation is big, possibly the longest document you will ever have to write, it requires some techniques you won't have applied extensively in essay writing. So as you are working, make sure that:

- all ideas you put forward relate to the central thesis (e.g. they support it, contradict it, exemplify it, etc.);
- you avoid 'interesting' but peripheral information;
- you create thematic linkage across and within chapters (e.g. end each chapter with a brief summary of what it said, and give a pointer to how this connects with what will come in the next chapter);
- you link new ideas clearly to ideas already presented, using cross-references and signposts where appropriate;
- you let readers know where they are in the argument;
- you use visual mechanisms to present and summarize data (e.g. flowcharts and tables), and perhaps to guide readers (e.g. different typography for headings) [6.2.2].

Dissertations are best written in stages. Create a draft of each chapter shortly after you've completed the relevant stage of the work. When all stages have been completed, redraft all the chapters so that they fit better together, making sense in respect of each other. Then write the Conclusion. Then write the Introduction, making sure it highlights the issues that you know are going to be addressed by the main components of the work, and focused on in the Conclusion. Finally, write the Abstract or Summary.

6.6 Research work

Usually, for a dissertation or substantial research project, you will be working either from secondary data (information other people have gathered or created) generally held in a library [2.2] or you will be gathering primary information, new data for yourself using one or more research methods. Choosing the appropriate set of methods for your needs and how to apply them is called 'research design'. Research design is a too big a topic to describe in a small book, so I can only set you on your way here.

The many methods boil down to two sets of choices:

- Am I interested in quantitative (numerical, measurable) data, such as readership figures or average headline lengths; or qualitative (non-measurable) data, such as opinions and beliefs?
- Am I interested in media, forms, discourses or practices (which exist 'outside' people, as it were) or in people?

This gives you four sets of possible answers, which help you identify the kind of technique you might need, as shown in Table 6.4:

Table 6.4 *Types of research method*

	Quantitative	*Qualitative*
Discourse, text	Content analysis [4.9] Descriptive linguistics [4.28]	Rhetorical analysis [4.42] Semiotics [4.44] Deconstruction [4.16]
People, process	Questionnaire Survey Structured interviews Experiment	Focus groups Unstructured interview Observation Case study

As you can see from the table, text-based methods are introduced elsewhere in the book. So, for the other methods, here are a few notes of guidance which will help you decide if they are helpful in your case. Having decided that a particular method might be useful, you should read one or more research books on the topic. Good guides are: Berger (1991) and (2000), Blaxter et al. (1996), Denscombe (1998), Hampson (1994), Hart (1998), MacNealy (1999), Robson (1993), Rudestam and Newton (1992) and Swetnam (2000).

6.6.1 Questionnaire

A questionnaire is a research instrument, a document containing a fixed set of questions, administered in identical ways to several people (called 'respondents'). Questionnaires are usually used in postal surveys, but may be delivered online, and might be used as the basis of structured interviews [6.6.3].

Questionnaires can be cheap to administer, but may take some time to design well if they are to be effective. Because people do not like questionnaires, they need to be as simple as possible, require the minimum amount of reading and the minimum number of actions on the part of the respondent. This suggests a form requiring mainly ticks in boxes for completion, and a high degree of structure in the document. But tick-boxes can severely limit the kinds of questions you might ask, and the forms of possible answers. And a highly structured design can be quite difficult to achieve if there are many questions, especially if some are optional.

A questionnaire is only as good as the questions it asks. An attractive and simple questionnaire that nevertheless asks the wrong questions will be worse than useless (because it will generate flawed data). So do the following when designing questionnaires:

- Only ask open questions (which can have very many possible answers) after a closed question (with highly restricted answers). The closed question establishes the relevant context and the open question acts as a follow-up.
- Avoid ambiguous questions. Do not ask questions which can be read in different ways. For example: 'Is there, in your opinion, any way that the group structure could be improved?' This could be a closed (yes/no) question, a question asking for a possible way of improving the group structure, an open question (lots of possible opinions could be given) or a hypothetical question, if 'could' is interpreted as meaning 'under some hypothetical circumstances'.
- Avoid leading questions, which predispose the respondent to a particular kind of answer, such as 'Do you approve of the war on Iraq or do you support terrorism?' This is constructed as a closed question: there are only two possible choices, of which one is clearly negative. Many respondents may wish a third option, but find they have to respond by approving of the war on Iraq.
- In the instructions use clear language, giving precise options. Test the instructions.
- Use a layout which makes it clear what the respondent is to write where, in relation to which question.
- Always keep your respondents in mind. Be courteous in tone. Explain what the questionnaire is for, and how its data will be used. Give respondents simple instructions on how to return the questionnaire, and limit the costs to them as much as possible.

You should always pilot a questionnaire, preferably by giving it to a few people of the kind you intend as respondents. Almost always the pilot shows ambiguities you have missed or flaws in instructions.

Detailed advice on question design can be found in Foddy (1993).

6.6.2 Survey

A survey is a set of questions asked of a substantial number of people. Counting the answers tells you how many people think what. Surveys tend to be broad but shallow (the questions you can ask tend not to be very searching).

The most useful surveys are representative of a population, so that their results can be generalized beyond the people being surveyed. 'Population' is a statistical term, meaning 'all the people who, in principle, you might have surveyed', that is, all the people you might be interested in, such as 'all TV viewers' or 'all parents'. Usually you can't survey everyone, so you have to survey a 'sample' of the population, which you try to make representative using a sampling strategy. Sampling can be a complex statistical business, but most samples either aim to ensure that they represent all the different types within the population (this is called 'purposive sampling') or that they have a statistically meaningful sample, randomly chosen.

A purposive sample is representative because its members are each chosen for that reason, but getting the numbers right can be difficult. For example, national social surveys generally require at least 100 responses in each category of person within the sample to be statistically valid, so that is the minimum needed for any nationally representative category. But if your population has, say, 20% teenagers and 80% adults, then you would need 400 adults in the survey to keep the proportions correct (and therefore representative), making a total survey of 500 people. Of course, if you were not interested in the differences between teenager and adult, then you do not need to sample with the subgroup in mind.

A random sample avoids many of these issues. The idea is that you don't really know the breakdown of your population beforehand, but if you sample them in a truly random manner, it won't matter because the proportion of each category you get in your random sample will be representative. Unfortunately, getting a truly random sample can be hard. And sampling theory insists that a random sample may not be *truly* representative, because different random samples will throw up different actual collections of people, with slightly different characteristics.

For student dissertations, it is worth knowing about these problems, and accounting for them in your work, but you are unlikely to solve them unless you deal with a very small population. The best advice for a survey is to 'survey everyone'. That way you know it is representative.

However, surveying the whole population (e.g. all the students in your year), though practicable, can still lead to distorted data, because of the response rate. Questionnaire surveys generally do not have response rates higher than about 40%. If that 40% happen to have one opinion, but the 60% who didn't respond have a different opinion, what you report from your survey will be biased.

So anything you can do to increase response rates is a good idea. Most effective is to follow up the questionnaires (e.g. with face-to-face meetings or phone calls) politely asking if the questionnaire was received and when it is likely to be returned.

6.6.3 Interviews, structured and unstructured

Face-to-face communication works best in many situations, but can be time-consuming (e.g. compared with surveys) and has its own pitfalls. A structured interview is one which is tightly planned beforehand, in which all questions are laid out (as in a questionnaire) and the choice of answers is limited. An unstructured interview has a looser agenda, with open questions, and may change direction as it develops.

The advantages and drawbacks of the two types of interview tend to be opposed, as shown in Table 6.5.

Table 6.5 *Features of interviews*

Feature	Structured interview	Unstructured interview
Amount of information gathered	Largely known beforehand	Unpredictable
Control	Interviewer in control	Interviewee has more power to direct things
Managing the interview	Easy to do	Hard to do
Relevance	Easy to keep on track	Easy to go in different directions
Interviewee's role	Clear and obvious	May be unclear, negotiated
Design of interview	Requires effort to get it right	Easier to set up
Interviewee's knowledge	May miss what interviewee has to say	More opportunity for interviewee to offer information
Data analysis	Easy to code and count	Harder to analyse, may be lots of variable information
Formality	Tends to be formal, may make people uncomfortable and unresponsive	More 'natural', easier to get honest and open responses
Quality of information	May be superficial, but focused on purpose	Likely to get deeper insights, but much may be irrelevant
Type of data	Better for facts	Better for opinions
Timing	Efficient use of time	May be time-consuming
Skills needed	Easier to learn, because rigid	Harder to learn, depends on personality (e.g. good listening skills)

Where simple facts are to be obtained, and simple descriptive answers are required, structured interviews generally work best. Where opinions or beliefs are sought, unstructured interviews are generally better. There is no such thing as an ideal interview. As with all communication, it is conditioned by the purpose and the situation. When interviewing, remember to be courteous and avoid the same sorts of problem questions you'd avoid in questionnaires [6.6.1]. However, open questions can be used more readily, especially in unstructured interviews, because the interviewer is there to clarify any confusion or follow up any ambiguity in response. Bear in mind what you know about interpersonal communication [4.25] and conversation [4.12].

6.6.4 Focus groups

Focus groups are, in essence, group interviews. You gather a group of representative people together, and ask them questions. So many of the issues listed in Table 6.5 apply. Advantages of a focus group over individual interviews are as follows:

- It can be efficient in time and other resources.
- Participants can bounce ideas off each other, sparking additional responses.

- Different interests can be represented.
- Consensus, or divergent views, can be more easily identified.
- For idea generation, opinion gathering and 'representative voices', it can be close to people's real behaviour.

Disadvantages are as follows:

- All the processes of group communication [4.19] may interfere with information gathering.
- Different people may get different opportunities to contribute.
- The researcher needs good interpersonal skills.
- Recording information whilst managing the session can be difficult.
- Sometimes it is hard to get measurable outcomes.

If you plan to run a focus group, useful practices are as follows:

- Have a mix of people involved.
- Plan a few fixed questions, a few open questions (for general discussion) and to have at least one practical activity that involves all participants.
- Make sure everyone gets a chance to speak about all issues.
- Have one researcher managing the group and one researcher recording information.

6.6.5 Experiment

Experiments generally are not favoured by researchers in cultural and media studies because of their positivist [4.39] connotations, but are a little more common in communication studies, where cognitive [4.7] and social psychologists have a stronger interest.

The idea of an experiment is that a hypothesis (an explanation of a phenomenon within a particular theory) is tested by stabilizing all aspects (called the 'variables') of the real situation except two. Of these two, one is systematically varied (called the 'independent variable'), and the consequent effects on the other (called 'the dependent variable') are measured.

For example, suppose we wanted to see if people learned more from reading the styles of language in *The Sun* or *The Times*. We could set up an experiment in which two exactly equivalent people read exactly the same information. One person would read that information in the style of *The Sun* and the other in the style of *The Times*. We then give both people the same test of their knowledge of that information, and measure the differences in knowledge (the dependent variable). If there is a difference, we conclude that it has to be due to the difference in style of writing (the independent variable), because everything else was the same.

This little example shows you exactly the strengths and weaknesses of the experimental approach. It is a very small piece of research. If there are only two people, it will be hard to know if the results might apply elsewhere. It is a very unreal situation, not close to reality at all, so perhaps the results will bear no relation to the real world in practice. It requires a high degree of control and rigour to make sure that nothing varies in the situation apart from the variables we are interested in. It tries to normalize, or account for, things which may not be very similar. For example, can we find two people who are 'equivalent'? What does this mean?

Finally, it may be flawed in its design, despite its apparent rigour. For example, although the experimenters say that they have merely changed the style of the writing, and the information remains the same, linguists, psychologists and cultural theorists would say this is nonsense: a change of style is necessarily a change of meaning.

There are ways of guarding against all the above problems, but they make good experimental design difficult to achieve. For a student, the easiest thing is to think in terms of 'pseudo-experiments': that is to say, an activity that is as close to an experiment as possible within the learning situation, but which will probably be flawed. The idea is to explore the hypothesis, rather than definitively prove anything, and to show the issues involved, as well as the student's understanding of the experimental approach to research.

6.6.6 Observation

Some people would say that observation is not research. It's what we do all the time in real life, so it can hardly be called an academic activity. However, observation in the research sense means more than just keeping your eyes open.

Research observation usually takes one of two forms. Either the observer is a participant in the activity being observed, or else that person is separate, observing 'objectively' from the outside what is going on. Both have merits. Participant observation has the strong virtues that the observer, being closely involved in the actual activity being researched, has direct experience of it, understanding first-hand what it means, and recognizing all the particular details of the concrete situation. But the obvious drawbacks to this are that the observer may be crucially affecting the object of the research (it would perhaps have gone differently if the researcher had not been involved), and the personal experience may lead to all sorts of subjective and selective interpretations in observation and reporting.

So participant observation tends to be carried out in situations where the 'interference' of the researcher in the activity studied is unimportant and where issues about subjectivity and objectivity in reporting are ignored. For example, we can argue that researchers *always* affect the activity being studied, in all sorts of ways, that selectivity always operates in reporting, and that objectivity is simply a tactic of positivist [4.39] reporting, to be rejected. With such a view of the world, participant observation is a legitimate research activity.

More remote observation is likely to be more independent and objective, but runs the risk of missing critical elements of the activity being researched. Such observation may be direct (watching a workgroup solve a problem, say) or perhaps through recording media such as video, audio or webcam.

In participant observation, the significant aspects of the activity being researched tend to emerge from the researcher's experience of what is going on. External observation finds this more difficult, and very often starts with a clear view on what is going to be looked for, so may establish a 'precoding' scheme of classification, against which records are kept. This can be at a micro-level (e.g. recording every time one person interrupts another) or on a larger scale (e.g. recording the ways an organization seeks to convey motivational messages to its workforce). It may also employ tightly devised coding schemes, such as classifying all utterances in the situation as either 'interrupted' or 'not interrupted', or rather looser records (e.g. recording each time an 'interesting message about motivation' was found).

In some ways it can be easier to 'post-code' observations, that is, to categorize them once the entire activity is completed, which requires a comprehensive record of everything of interest (such as complete video of all the conversations being studied). It can be easier because you can review the material over and over again, until you are satisfied that your categories make sense, before you begin any actual coding, and it also means that you do not have to guess beforehand what might be interesting.

However, for a student engaged in observation, it is a good idea to be pretty clear from the outset what you think you are observing, and the classes of data that you are interested in, because post-coding can be complex and very time-consuming.

6.6.7 Case study

Properly speaking, case study work is not a distinct method, but rather an approach rousing a method. A case study is a particular, detailed study of one example – a real situation. But it is a study that can be carried out using any or all of the above methods. Case studies are a good way of conducting small-scale research, because almost everyone can find a particular real-world instance of the issue they are interested in. Case studies can also be rewarding for the researcher: simply being real-world, they may bring actual benefits to the group or organization being studied.

However, case studies can be problematic because of their very particular nature. Important issues are as follows:

- The outcomes of a case study can rarely be generalized, because it is simply one illustration of a particular set of circumstances.
- Managing the project can be highly dependent on the researcher's relationship with the situation, depending on personal factors (e.g. if you dislike the people you are studying) and resourcing issues (e.g. if the organization decides it doesn't have time for you).
- Confidentiality and ethical conflicts may arise (e.g. if your research shows a particular manager bullies his workforce through rude communications, what do you do about it?).

You can reduce the issue of generalizing by conducting several similar case studies. Whilst these will not give you statistical validity, having three case studies which show very similar things goes a long way to proving your point. And, if they show three different things, you are in the wonderful situation of being able to debate the pros and cons of competing interpretations of what is going on.

If you can establish a good working relationship with a group or organization to study, and can be reasonably certain they will be committed to your project throughout (this often comes if your research may be of practical value to them), then a case study can be a very good approach to student research. And if you can get three organizations to do this, even better.

6.6.8 Using research results

Students report three common difficulties with original research. However, they are all *positive* outcomes for student research. Remember that a student research project is about demonstrating your research skills, not about shattering new discoveries that will rock the research community.

'I've not shown anything new.'   Students are not *expected* to be original. Of course, if you do make a new discovery or develop a new approach, then you are going to interest your tutors much more, and you are setting yourself up for a first-class mark [6.1]. But that first would indicate the unexpectedness of that activity.

'I have no interesting results. They are all negative.'   Negative results are still results. If you show how you got them, explain why they are as they are, establish their relationship to the theory you've chosen, and suggest what might be needed to obtain different results, you'll have shown excellent understanding of the research project. If you set out to show that children are oppressed by teachers in the playground, and you cannot show it, isn't that good news?

Well, it may be, if the reason is that teachers do not oppress children. Or it may not be, if the reason is that there were some flaws in your theory, method or interpretation of data. Discuss both these possibilities, rationally, objectively. Show that you know what would be needed to put it right. That can easily be a 2:1 project.

'There are no obvious conclusions. My data show all sorts of different things.'   Confusing or patternless outcomes are not unusual in research, because they are usual in the real world. Reality is more complex than researchers would like it to be. This is why research generally aims for a tight question, a narrow subject area, a simple hypothesis: something that is small and easy to examine.

Multiple outcomes may come because of poor method, of course, in which case you do have a problem. But if the approach is sound, then it's the world that's at fault. Multiple results, conflicting data, problematic results, are therefore a godsend to the student *who wants to show his or her understanding of research*. You have any number of possibilities to theorize about and apply, any number of research considerations to discuss and reject, any number of hypotheses for additional testing and study, any number of theoretical perspectives that might be brought to bear. If your method is sound, and the data are weird, then the chances are your supervisor cannot explain it either, so the more you can do to suggest ways into it, the more likely your supervisor will be to recognize in you a creative intelligence struggling with a difficult problem.

6.7 What not to do in assessment

As a final word on assessment, here are a couple of warnings about practices you should avoid: plagiarism and collusion.

'Plagiarism' is passing off someone else's work as your own. Usually a plagiarist copies another person's work almost word for word, and makes no mention of the source, so that it appears to be the plagiarist's own writing. It is rare for someone to plagiarize a whole piece, such as a complete essay. More often long chunks are used, perhaps taken from two or three unacknowledged sources, and stitched together with a few original words by the student.

Do not plagiarize. It is unethical, immoral, unscholarly, cowardly and stupid. It's stupid because most lecturers are not. There are many ways by which plagiarism can be detected. A marker may recognize your source, for example. This often happens, for lecturers tend to have read the sources they recommend to their students. Or the marker may be suspicious of the style. It is highly unlikely that you will be able to write convincingly in the same style as the source you have plagiarized – and if you can, then why on earth are you plagiarizing in the first place?

Often plagiarism is a tacit admission by a poor student that they are not able to write good enough text on the subject themselves. But if you do not know enough about media sociology or cultural theory or whatever your topic is to write a reasonable account, you probably don't know enough to judge how to use other writers' work so that it makes sense within your specific essay.

So, I'll say it again: don't do it. If you are found out, you run every academic risk from having to do the assignment again, through failing in that assignment, to being thrown off your course. Academics view plagiarism as a particularly heinous crime because it attacks one of the fundamental components of scholarliness – the probity, the commitment to truth, of the writer.

Because of the difficulties of plagiarism, and because it is generally the resort of the weak, lazy or less able writer, collusion is probably a more common strategy for the cheat. Collusion is where two (or more) students conspire to write an essay or other piece of work together, submitting more or less the same piece under their separate names as the work of individuals.

Collusion, of course, is another unethical practice involving at least one weak student, and should be avoided by anyone truly serious about his or her studies. Its most common form is where the weak student seeks to piggy-back on the strength of another – for example, 'borrowing' a draft essay and stealing its structure and content.

There are many cases, however, where apparent plagiarism or collusion occur, but which are lessened somewhat by the circumstances. For example, a student may have poor study skills, and not have learned that all quotations should be identified as such (by italics, quotation marks or indentation) and all sources attributed [3.2.5]. Few markers will be punitive to a student the first time this problem occurs, but once the correct practice has been pointed out, there will be no excuse.

Collusion can be a difficult area because of the legitimate nature of much group work. Group research, group problem solving, group presentations and group investigations are all good practices which lecturers are likely to encourage. It seems unfair, doesn't it, that you should be encouraged to collaborate in gathering information, but penalized for collaborating in presenting it? In fact, of course, many MCCS courses involve legitimate group assessment.

The key factor is whether the group was supposed to produce the final product, or whether it was supposed to be an individual piece, the sole responsibility of individual students. If the latter, then the tutor's intention is to assess individual skills, knowledge and understanding. These cannot be fairly assessed if a group was responsible for the piece of writing, so each student has to be responsible for his or her own account, giving a personal presentation of the outcomes of the group work.

So, how can you deal with these problems if they arise?

Firstly, as I've already said, you need to be as clear as you can be about the remit of the assignment. What are you being asked to do, and how are you expected to do it? It may be, for example, that the tutor has allowed you some flexibility. Perhaps, for example, you have been given a free choice between group presentation and individual presentation.

Whatever the set-up, be as clear about it as you can. And, if you are not clear, pursue your tutors until they make it clear. Ideally, get a written assignment brief from them, which gives all the details you need. If you can't get this, then write down your understanding of the brief and its constraints, and get your tutor to approve it. Email is a good way to do this, as you'll get a written record of the response as well, and it will be dated. Then, if there is any future question about how you have handled the assignment, at least you'll have a record of what was agreed, including any gaps or ambiguities.

Secondly, if you are tempted to steal someone else's work, whether an established source or a student: don't! Instead, make proper use of that source. I have lost count of the number of times a paragraph thinly disguised from a major authority receives a mark of zero, when, with the addition of quotation marks, a proper reference and an introduction, 'As Stuart Hall [5.15] says, when applying Marxist principles to TV production . . .', it would have attracted at least a couple of ticks, and probably serious credit. After all, if it was a suitable text for plagiarizing, it must be a good choice for citing.

In the case of potential collusion, avoid it by the simple act of writing your own words. Arrange with your group to study together, research together, work together in whatever ways make sense to you. But make your own notes from the group work [2.4.6]. Do not loan them to any of the others. Insist that the group decides when the work is complete, and the individual write-up begins at that moment. You can seek the verbal views of others, because you are unlikely to write down exactly what they say, and they are unlikely to use exactly those thoughts in their own work. But do not use their writings or allow them to use yours. And if, at any point, you do borrow work from another student, treat it in exactly the same way as you would a book or article from a learned source: it is someone else's work to be respected, and only used in an explicit and selective way.

HELPFUL TEXTS RELATED TO CHAPTER 6

The following books will help you improve the quality of your research and writing for assessments:
* Allison, Brian (1997) *The Student's Guide to Preparing Dissertations and Theses*
* Berger, Arthur Asa (2000) *Media and Communication Research Methods*
* Blaxter, Loraine, Hughes, Christina, and Tight, Malcolm (1996) *How to Research*
* Denscombe, Martyn (1998) *The Good Research Guide for Small-scale Social Research Projects*
* Hart, C. (1998) *Doing a Literature Review: Releasing the Social Science Research Imagination*
* Marshall, Peter (1997) *Research Methods: How to Design and Conduct a Successful Project*
* Race, Phil (1999) *How to Get a Good Degree*
* Swetnam, Derek (2000) *Writing your Dissertation: How to Plan, Prepare and Present Your Work Successfully*

7

'How do I . . .?' Trouble-shooting and problem-solving

Throughout this book you will find practical advice on how to tackle different problems that you might encounter in your studies. But one problem you might have is knowing how to find that advice when you need it. So this chapter gives you a solution to this difficulty. It will probably be your main reference tool, once you've an overview of the book, as it can give you both quick solutions to common problems, and entry points to other more detailed material, as you need them.

The chapter can be used as:

- an index of solutions to problems you might have;
- a glossary of quick and dirty definitions for when you need an 'instant' answer to a question, e.g. to jog your memory;
- an index of main topics within the book, as a way in to the rest of the book, for sections you have not yet read;
- an index of topics within the book you have already read, but want to check again, e.g. as a revision aid;
- a list of further readings on topics or problems you want to know more about.

Unlike the other chapters in this book, there are no numbered sections. Instead, the material is arranged as an alphabetical list of topics, each topic having a problem question against it, unless the question is 'what is it?', which is the default question so not given.

So, for example, if you wanted to know how to analyse text, look up 'Analysing text: how do I do it?' but if you want to know what attention is, you'd simply look at the topic 'Attention' On the right hand side of the page you will find one or more of the following:

- a definition;
- a section number or numbers where relevant information can be found;
- one or more references for additional reading, sometimes with a little guidance.

Note that most 'who' questions are not in the list. All the main theorists discussed in this book have an entry in Chapter 5, so if you have a question about a person, you should go straight to the relevant section of Chapter 5, where you will also find at least one item of reading for that person.

Problem	Suggested solution or source
Abstract: how do I write one?	[3.2.4]
Abstraction:	Vague, generalized meaning. [3.1.9]
Academic abbreviations: what are they?	[2.3.6]
Acronym:	A word made from the initial letters of others, like RAM (Random Access Memory).
Active voice:	The normal form of typical sentences, in which the agent or actor comes first, then the action. [3.1.9]
Agent deletion:	Removing the agent or actor from a passive sentence. [3.1.9]
Ambiguity:	The potential for multiple messages in one signal (e.g. many meanings of one word). [4.1]
Analysing exam questions: how do I do it?	[6.4.4]
Analysing text: how do I do it?	[2.3]
Anthropology:	The study of humanity. See Lévi-Strauss [5.24].
Antonymy:	Oppositeness of meaning: a word that has an opposite meaning to another is its antonym. [4.43]
Argument:	The development of a coherent and reasoned case. [2.3.2]
Argument: how do I analyse it?	[2.3.2]
Argument: how do I write it?	[6.3.1]
Assessment: how do I do well?	[6.2.1]
Attention: how does it work?	[2.4.1]
Audience:	The receivers of a message, usually in the context of mass communication. [4.2]
Audience analysis: what should I do?	[3.1.1], [3.1.2], [3.1.3], [3.1.4] Read Stevenson (1997).
Audience attitudes: how	[3.1.3]

Problem	Suggested solution or source
should I handle them?	
Audience effects theory:	Theory that mass media [4.29] messages directly affect audiences. [4.2] Read Stevenson (1997).
Audience expectations: what are they?	[3.1.2]
Audience and talk: how should I handle them?	[3.3.1]
Audio-visual information sources: how do I use them?	[2.2.2]
Authority: how do I test it?	[2.3.2]
Bandwidth:	The amount of information that can be carried by a channel of communication, such as a phone line.
Bibliographies: how do I create one?	[3.2.5]
Bibliographies: how do I use them?	[2.3.5]
Binary opposition:	Structuralist [4.48] idea that meanings are constructed through opposed pairs of signs, which are mutually dependent (e.g. dark/light). [4.16], [4.43], [4.48]
Brainstorming:	Method for generating ideas. [3.2.2]
Broadcasting:	Large-scale dissemination of media messages to mass audiences. [4.3]
Case study: how do I conduct one?	[6.6.7]
Censorship:	Deliberate removal of information from a message, to prevent its dissemination. [4.4] Read Williams (1992).
Choices in language: how do I make them?	[3.1.9] See also Stylistics. Read Halliday (1973) and (1978).
Chunking:	Creating 'bite-sized' blocks of information. [3.1.7]
Clarity of language: how do I get it?	[3.1.9]
Clarity of purpose: how do I get it?	[3.1.5]
Class:	Social stratification: social divisions defined by socio-economic breakdown. [4.5] Read Bernstein (1971).
Clue words: what are they?	Connecting words demonstrate the links between parts of an argument or description. [3.1.7]

Problem	Suggested solution or source
Code:	A system of signs for encoding messages. [4.6]
Cognition:	Thinking, knowledge. Cognitive psychology studies the brain. [4.7]
Coherence:	Consistent connections between a text and the outside world. [3.1.7]
Cohesion:	The internal logic of a text, making all parts fit together in a uniform way. [3.1.7]
Collocation:	The 'co-location' of two words, i.e. words in close physical proximity in a text. [4.10]
Collusion: what should I avoid?	[6.7]
Communication skills: what are they?	[1.5]
Communications technologies: what are they?	Mediated systems for communication, usually thought of as digital technologies, but also including more conventional communications media. [4.8] Read Dutton (1996), Lister et al. (2003), Tannenbaum (1998), Williams and Hartley (1990) and Winston (1998).
Communications technologies: how do I use them?	[2.4.7]
Compare and contrast: how do I do it?	[2.3.3]
Complex audience needs: how do I meet them?	[3.1.2], [3.1.4]
Conclusions: how do I analyse them?	[2.3.2]
Conclusions: how do I write them?	[3.2.2]
Concordance:	Analysis of discourse by examining the text surrounding a keyword. [4.10]
Connectives: what are they?	Connecting words demonstrate the links between parts of an argument or description. [3.1.7]
Connotation:	Associations or non-systematic meanings that may belong to a word or other sign. See Semantics [4.43] and Semiotics [4.44], and Derrida [5.6].
Content analysis:	Analysis of a text by counting instances of particular signs or meanings. [4.9] An example of content analysis is Leiss et al. (1986: 169–74).

Problem	Suggested solution or source
Content analysis: how do I do it?	[4.9] Advice on using it as a method can be found in Berger (1991: 23–33) and Berger (2000: 173–85).
Context:	The situation in which a communication occurs. [4.10] See [3.1.2] for context and expectations.
Conventions: what are they?	Traditional practices established by habitual and customary behaviour. See [3.1.2] for conventions and expectations. See [4.11] for general account.
Conversation analysis:	Analysis of the conventions that enable talk. [4.12] Read Beattie (1983) and Goffman (1981: 5–77).
Cotext:	Words used in close conjunction with a target word or phrase. [4.10]
Creativity: how can I improve it?	[6.2.4]
Creativity: how can I use it in a talk?	[3.3.1]
Critical analysis:	[2.3], especially [2.3.4] Read Ennis (1996).
Critical analysis: how do I do it?	[2.3.2] Read Ennis (1996).
Critical analysis: why do it?	[2.3.1] Read Ennis (1996), Fairbairn and Winch (1997).
Critical audiences: how do I deal with them?	[3.1.3]
Critical linguistics:	The use of linguistics to analyse power structures in discourses. See Critical Linguistics [4.13], Fairclough [5.9] and Kress [5.20]. Read Fairclough (1995a) and (1995b).
Critical linguists: who are they?	See Fairclough [5.9] and Kress [5.20].
Cultural theorists? Who are they?	See Hall [5.15], Hoggart [5.17], Leavis [5.23] and Williams [5.39]. Eighty-seven very useful summaries of key cultural theorists can be found in Edgar and Sedgwick (2002).
Culture:	The practices and values of a social group. [4.14] Read Hall et al. (1980), Hoggart (1981), Leavis and Thompson (1977), Williams (1961).
Cyberculture, cyberspace: what are they?	[4.15] A good contemporary discussion is Chapter 5 of Lister et al. (2003). Also read Gibson (1986).
Deadlines: how do I meet them?	[2.4.2] Read Race (1999).

Problem	Suggested solution or source
Decoding:	Process whereby a receiver of a signal interprets it as a message. [4.32] Read Gill and Adams (1998).
Deconstruction:	An analytical process devised by Derrida [5.6] for exposing the inherent dependencies within binary oppositions. [4.16]
Denotation:	Meaning associated with a word or other sign by virtue of its systematic use in the language (i.e. its 'dictionary definition'). [4.43]
Dewey Decimal system:	A system for classifying books used by most modern libraries. [2.2.2]
Discourse:	A text, form, product or practice with communicative value. See [4.17] and Van Dijk [5.36]. Read Foucault (1999) and Jaworski and Coupland (1999).
Discourse analysis:	The analysis of discourses, conceived from one or many of several disciplinary perspectives. These range from conversation analysis, through various forms of textual analysis, to analysis of the social and cultural interdependencies of particular forms. See [4.17] and Van Dijk [5.36]. Read Fairclough (1995b), Jaworski and Coupland (1999) and Schiffrin et al. (2001).
Dissertation: how do I write one?	[6.5] Read Allison (1997), Hampson (1994), Rudestam and Newton (1992) and Swetnam (2000).
Drafting: how do I do it?	[3.2.2]
Dyad:	A pair of communicators, usually in a conversation. [4.12]
Editing: how do I do it?	[6.2.3]
E-learning tools: how do I use them?	[2.4.7]
Encoding:	Process whereby a sender of a message represents it as a signal. [4.32]
Entailment:	Where one meaning includes another one. [4.43]
Environment and audience: what should I bear in mind?	[3.1.3]
Epistemology:	A branch of philosophy concerned with the nature of knowledge. See Foucault [5.10].
Essays: how do I edit one?	[6.2.3]
Essays: how do I write one?	[3.2.2], [6.3] Read Race (1999).
Evidence:	[2.3.2]
Evidence: how do I analyse it?	[2.3.2]
Examinations: how do I do well?	[6.4] Read Race (1999).

Problem	Suggested solution or source
Expectations of audiences: what are they?	The beliefs of an audience or readership that the communication they will receive is likely to take a particular form. [3.1.2]
Experiment: how do I conduct one?	[6.6.5] Read Berger (2000).
Extensions: when should I get one?	[2.4.2]
Failures in analysis: how do I avoid them?	[2.3.1]
Feedback in a talk: how do I get it?	[3.3.1]
Film:	Visual communication technology, using sequences of photographic images. [4.8]
Focus groups: how do I conduct them?	[6.6.4]
Genre:	A type of cultural product or form, generally historically determined, linked to particular purposes and social contexts. [3.1.1], [4.18]
Getting ideas: how do I do it?	[3.2.2]
Grammar:	See Chomsky [5.5] and Halliday [5.16]. For a specific example, look at the discussion of the passive and active voice [3.1.9]. For introduction to rules of English grammar, and helpful advice on practise, read Crystal (1988).
Group communication:	Communication within groups of different kinds, usually seen from the perspective of social psychology. [4.19] Read Argyle (1994), and Hartley (1997).
Group identity:	[3.3.2]
Group presentation: how do I do it?	[3.3.2] Read Reid and Hammersley (2000).
Group roles: what are they?	According to Belbin (1981): coordinator, team leader, innovator, monitor-evaluator, team worker, completer, implementer, resource investigator. [2.4.6]
Group work: how do I do it?	[2.4.6], [3.3.2]
Harvard convention:	A standard form of academic referencing. [3.2.5]
Hegemony:	The dominance of the ideology of one political group, subordinating others through consent. [4.20]. See also Gramsci [5.13].
Helping readers: how do I do it?	[3.1.7]

Problem	Suggested solution or source
High culture:	Opposed to 'low culture', the elite cultural practices of a privileged social group. [4.21] Read Leavis (1993).
Human information sources: how do I use them?	[2.2.2]
Identity:	For individuals and groups, a sense of self. [4.22] Read Goffman (1971), (1972) and (1982).
Identity: how do we get one in group work?	[3.3.2]
Ideology:	A system of ideas. [4.23]
Idiolect:	Personal habits of language. [4.27]
Information: what is good quality?	[3.1.6]
Information searches: how should I search?	[2.2.4]
Information society:	The postmodernist concept that society is transformed and fragmented by communications technologies. [4.24] Read Dutton (1996) and Lyon (1997).
Information sources: how do I use varied sources?	[2.2.3]
Information sources: which do I use for what?	[2.2.2]
In-group:	Group of which you are a member. [4.19]
Interdisciplinarity:	Treating overlapping links between historically different disciplines as unified. [1.3]
Interpersonal communication:	Communication between individuals or small groups. [4.25]. See also Argyle [5.1]. Read Argyle (1994) and Hartley (1999).
Inter-textuality:	The interdependence of discourses, where one acquires meaning from the other. See Bakhtin [5.2] and postmodernism [4.40]. Read Fairclough (1999).
Interviews: how do I conduct them?	[6.6.3] Read Berger (2000).
Introduction: how do I write one?	[3.2.2]
Invisible writing: how do I do it?	[3.2.2]

Problem	Suggested solution or source
Language:	A complex code, with both spoken and written forms. [4.26] Read Crystal (1971) and (1988), Trask (1995).
Language variation:	Systematic variations in languages according to situation or speaker. [4.27] Read Freeborn et al. (1993), Labov (1972a) and (1972b), Montgomery (1986) and Trudgill (1983).
Large documents: how do I write them?	[6.5.6]
Learning: how can I do it well?	[2.1], [2.4] Read Marshall and Rowland (1993).
Learning tools: how do I use them?	Chapter 2, particularly [2.4.7]. Rowntree (1998) and Race (1999) include much practical advice on being an effective student.
Libraries: how do I use them?	[2.2.2]
Linguistics:	The study of language. See Halliday [5.16], Chomsky [5.5], Saussure [5.32]. Helpful introductory books on linguistics are Crystal (1971) and (1988). Read also Chomsky (1965), Saussure (1974) and Smith and Wilson (1979).
Listening: how do I do it effectively?	[2.4.3]
Literary criticism:	The application of critical analyses of different kinds to the study of written texts, particularly 'high' literary genres [4.18], such as poetry and the novel. See Hoggart [5.17] and Leavis [5.23]. See also [2.3].
Literature review: how do I write one?	[6.5.5] Read Hart (1998).
Logs: how do I write them?	[3.2.6]
Low culture:	Opposed to 'high culture', the popular cultural products of a less privileged social group. [4.21]
Marker psychology: what should I bear in mind?	[3.1.2]
Marks: how do I get good ones?	[3.1.5], [6.1], [6.2] Read Race (1999).
Mass communication:	[4.29] See Williams [5.39]. Read McQuail and Windahl (1993), Stevenson (1995), Williams (1961).
Media: what are they?	The channels through which communication takes place, such as phone, page or TV. [4.30] Read Marris and Thornham (2000).
Media uses and gratifications:	Theory that mass media audiences actively seek mass communications for particular purposes. [4.31]

Problem	Suggested solution or source
Mind maps: how can I use them?	[6.4.3] for main description, [3.2.2] for application.
Mind maps: what are they?	[6.4.3]
Model of communication:	An abstract and figurative account of how communication works. [4.32] See Shannon [5.34]. Read Griffin (2000), McQuail and Windahl (1993) and Shannon and Weaver (1949).
Multidisciplinarity:	Subject area made up of several related disciplines. [1.3]
Multimedia: how do I design it?	[3.4] Read Jacobson (1999) and Tannenbaum (1998).
Myth:	Stories, usually seen as fictional by those who call them 'myths', but often believed in by particular groups. Myths are often stories that encode the 'rules to live by', i.e. complex cultural codes [4.6]. See Lévi-Strauss [5.24], Propp [5.30], Structuralism [4.48]. Read Lévi-Strauss (1968).
Narrowcasting:	Targeted communication through mass media. [4.3]
Noise:	Interference in communication which degrades its quality. [4.32]
Nominalization:	Making a noun from a verb, such as 'communication' from 'communicate'. [3.1.9]
Non-verbal communication:	[4.33]. See also Argyle [5.1]. Read Argyle (1988), (1989) and (1994), Beattie (1983) and Burgoon et al. (1996).
Note-taking: how do I do it?	[2.3.5], [2.4.3]
Note-taking: what conventions should I use?	[2.4.3]
Note-taking: why do it?	[2.3.5], [2.4.3]
Objectivity: how do I judge it?	[2.3.2]
Observation: how do I do it?	[6.6.6]
Online resources: how do I use them?	[2.2.2]
Organizational communication:	Those communications processes particular to organizational structures and processes. [4.34] Also look at Hartley and Bruckmann (2002).
Organizing information: how do I do it in writing?	[3.1.7], [3.2.2]
Organizing notes: how do I do it?	[2.1.3], [2.4.3]

Problem	Suggested solution or source
Out-group:	People who are not members of a group to which you belong to (the in-group). [4.19]
Paradigmatic:	A structural relationship whereby one item in a code [4.6] can be meaningfully substituted for another. [4.35]
Passive voice:	A form of sentence which places the object or thing acted on first in the sentence, making it more important than the actor or agent, which is either placed after the verb, or deleted. [3.1.9]
Patterning:	Structures fundamental to communication, usually thought of either as sequential (syntagmatic) or substitutional (paradigmatic). [4.35]
Perception:	Psychological and cultural process whereby individuals take in and make sense of real-world data. [4.36]
Personal expectations: what are they?	[3.1.2]
Persuasion: how do I do it?	[3.1.8], [4.42] Read Sparks (1999: Chap. 9).
Phenomenology:	Philosophy which argues that we should deal with the world as it appears and not as we assume it to be. [4.38]
Philosophy:	See Foucault [5.10], Russell [5.31], Wittgenstein [5.40].
Plagiarism: what should I avoid?	[6.7]
Plain English: How do I write it?	[3.1.9] Read Collisons et al. (1992), Cutts and Maher (1986).
Planning: how do I do it?	[3.2.2], [6.4.3]
Portfolio: how do I compile one?	[3.2.6]
Positivism:	Philosophy which considers the only worthwhile analyses to be those which are scientifically measureable. [4.39]
Postmodernism:	A view of the world which sees it as consisting of fragmented cultures and inter-connected partial discourses. [4.40]. See also Lyotard [5.25]. Read Lyotard (1979), Storey (1997: 169–200), Strinati (1997).
Post-structuralism:	A reaction against structuralism [4.48] which sees meaning as provisional and explanation based on the deconstruction [4.16] of structuralist models. See Derrida [5.6].
Practical questions in exams: how do I do them?	[6.4.6] Read Race (1999).
Practical skills: how do I use them?	[2.4.4]

Problem	Suggested solution or source
Presentation: how do I give an oral presentation?	[3.3] Read Mandel (1987), and exercises 3.1 to 3.7 in Marshall and Williams (1986).
Presentation: how do I present effectively?	[6.2.2]
Presentation: how do I present using communications technologies?	[3.4]
Print technologies: what are they?	Media and technologies which communicate through typography. [4.8] Read Hall (1996), Jacobson (1999), Lichty (1989) and McLean (1980).
Professional writing: how do I do it?	[3.1.4], [3.1.5] Read Burnett (2000), Crompton (1987), Hartley (1994), Jacobson (1999), St Maur and Butman (1991) and Schriver (1997).
Project work: how do I do it?	[2.4.4]
Project work: how do I report it?	[3.2.3]
Proposal: how do I write one?	[6.5.4] Read Jay (1995).
Psychoanalysis:	The science or art of improving people's mental and emotional well-being through analysing their psychological dispositions. See Freud [5.11], Jung [5.19] and Lacan [5.22]. Read Freud (1975).
Psychology:	Psychology is the study of the mind and human behaviour. See Argyle [5.1] and Piaget [5.29]. Read Ellis and Beattie (1986).
Purpose in communication: what are the considerations?	[3.1.5], [3.3.1]
Pyramid principle:	An approach to constructing argument based on a hierarchical arrangement of questions and answers. [3.1.8] Read Minto (1991).
Questionnaire: how do I design one?	[6.6.1] Read Berger (2000).
Questions: how do I use them in structuring communication?	[3.1.8]
Questions in talks: how do I handle them?	[3.3.1] Read Mandel (1987).
Radio:	Aural broadcast medium. [4.8] Read Barnard (2000).
Reading for seminars: why do it?	[2.4.5]

Problem	Suggested solution or source
Reference:	An aspect of meaning, where a word or phrase is used to indicate a specific entity in a particular context. [4.43]
References: how do I use other people's?	[2.3.5]
References: how do I use them in my own work?	[3.2.5]
Reflection: what is its value?	[3.2.1], [3.2.6]
Register:	Language variation according to situation of use. [4.27]
Reports: how do I write one?	[3.2.3] Read Jay (1995), Sparks (1999: Chap. 10), Sussams (1983) and Turk and Kirkman (1989).
Representation:	Once an event has occurred, any recording or account of that event is a 're-presentation', a partial interpretation of it. [4.41] Read Lacey (1998).
Research results: how do I use them?	[6.6.8]
Researching: how should I do it?	See information gathering [2.2], research audiences [3.1.4], research methods [6.6]. Read Bell (1999), Berger (1991) and (2000), Blaxter et al. (1996), Denscombe (1998) and Marshall (1997).
Reviews of my work: how do I write them?	[3.2.6]
Revision:	[2.4.3]
Revision: how do I do it?	[6.4.2] Read Race (1999).
Rhetoric:	The art of persuasion. See Berger (1991: 67–78) and (2000: 53–68).
Self-analysis: how should I use it?	[2.4.3]
Semantics:	[4.43] See Russell [5.31] and Wittgenstein [5.40]. Read Kearns (2000) and Leech (1974).
Seminar work: how do I do it?	[2.4.5], [3.3.3]
Seminar work: how do I present in a seminar?	[3.3.3]
Semiotic analysis: how do I do it?	An example of semiotic analysis is Leiss et al. (1986: 149–69) and advice on using it in Berger (2000: 35–51). Also see Hawkes (1983) and Lacey (1998).
Semioticians: who are they?	See Barthes [5.3] and Eco [5.8].
Semiotics:	[4.43], [4.44] See Barthes [5.3], Eco [5.8] and Peirce [5.28]. Read Chapters 3, 4 and 5 of Fiske (1990) for an introduction to semiotic analysis, and Eco (1977).

Problem	Suggested solution or source
Social psychology:	See Argyle [5.1]
Socialization	The process by which an individual is made an acceptable member of a particular social group. [4.45] Read Bernstein (1971).
Sociolinguistics:	See Halliday [5.16] and Labov [5.21], and Language Variation [4.27]. Some early seminal papers can be found in Giglio (1972).
Sociology:	See Durkheim [5.7] and Marx [5.27].
Speech:	Oral language. [4.46] Read Beattie (1983), Crystal (1971) and Saussure (1974).
Speech act:	Action performed through speech, e.g. promising, lying. See Searle [5.33]. Read Searle (1969) and (1972).
Stereotype:	Cultural simplification of group characteristics that enables simplified communication, usually with negative connotation. [4.47] Read Perkins and Barker (1997) and Qualter (1997).
Study time: how do I use it?	[2.4.1] Read Race (1999).
Structuralism:	Theory that meaning is a function of structural relationships in codes, typically in the form of a binary opposition. [4.48], Lévi-Strauss [5.24] and Saussure [5.32]. Read Boyne (2000) and Hawkes (1983).
Structure: how do I create a good structure?	[3.1.7], [3.1.8], [3.2.4], [6.5.5]
Structure in talks: how do I create a good structure?	[3.3.1]
Style: of a presentation	Aggregate of linguistic and presentational choices in speech. [3.3.1]
Style: of writing	Aggregate of linguistic and presentational choices in text. [3.1.9]
Stylistics:	Linguistic account of systematic choices in language elements. [4.27], [4.49] See Halliday [5.16]. Read Turner (1973).
Stylistics: how do I make choices?	[3.1.9]
Subculture:	The practices and values of a social group, in relation to a larger social group of which it is part. [4.14]
Summary: how do I write one?	[3.2.4]
Supervisor: how do I choose one?	[6.5.2]
Survey: how do I conduct one?	[6.6.2] Read Berger (2000), Marshall (1997).

Problem	Suggested solution or source
Synonymy:	Sameness of meaning: a word that means the same as another is its synonym. [4.43]
Syntagmatic:	A structural relationship whereby one item in a code [4.6] can be meaningfully placed in sequence with another. [4.35]
Talk: how do I give one?	[3.3.1] Read Mandel (1987) and Race (1999).
Team work: how do we do it?	[2.4.6]
Technological determinism:	The idea that social changes are a direct function of technological changes. [4.50] Read Dutton (1996).
Television:	Visual broadcast technology. [4.8] Read Geraghty and Lusted (1998).
Theory: how do I test it?	[2.3.2]
Time: how do I use it?	[2.4.1], [6.4.5]
Using this book: how do I do it?	[1.6]
Visual aids in a talk: how do I use them?	[3.3.1]
Visual communication:	Use of visual media to convey meaning. Read Kress and van Leeuwen (1996) and van Leeuwen and Jewitt (2001).
Websites: how do I design them?	[3.4] Read Fleming (1998), Neilsen (2000), Price and Price (2002), Rosenfeld and Morville (1998) and Waters (1997). See also Multimedia.
Websites: how do I use them?	[2.2.2]
Word frequency:	Analysis of text by counting frequency of word forms. [4.9]
Working alone: giving a personal talk	[3.3.1] Read Mandel (1987).
Working alone: how do I do it?	[2.4.6]
Working in groups: how do I do it?	[2.4.6], [3.3.2] Read Race (1999).
Writer's block: how do I get over it?	[3.2.2] Read Sharples (1999).
Writing: how do I structure material?	[3.1.7]
Writing: how do I write an essay?	[3.2.2], [6.3] Read Race (1999).

Problem	Suggested solution or source
Writing: how do I write a dissertation?	[6.5] Read Allison (1997), Hampson (1994), Rudestam and Newton (1992) and Swetnam (2000).
Writing: how do I write a report?	[3.2.3] Read Jay (1995), Sparks (1999: Chap. 10), Sussams (1983) and Turk and Kirkman (1989).
Writing: how do I write text for computer screens?	[3.4] Read Jacobson (1999) and Wagner (1988).
Writing process:	Complex series of activities that can combine in different ways to generate text. [3.2.1] Read Kellogg (1994), St Maur and Butman (1991) and Sharples (1999).
Writing technologies: what are they?	Media and technologies which communicate through the written word. [4.8] Read Sharples (1999) and Williams (1991).

READING AND REFERENCES

Adams, Douglas (1979) *Hitchhiker's Guide to the Galaxy*, London: Pan.

Allison, Brian (1997) *The Student's Guide to Preparing Dissertations and Theses*, London: Kogan Page.

Appignanesi, Richard and Zarate, Oscar (1992) *Freud for Beginners*, Cambridge: Icon Books.

Argyle, Michael (1988) *Bodily Communication*, 2nd edn, London: Routledge.

Argyle, Michael (1989) 'Verbal and Non-verbal Communication', in John Corner and Jeremy Hawthorne (eds), *Communication Studies: an Introductory Reader*, London: Edward Arnold, pp.35–44.

Argyle, Michael (1994) *The Psychology of Interpersonal Behaviour*, 5th edn, Harmondsworth: Penguin.

Aubrey, C. (ed.) (1982) *Nukespeak: the Media and the Bomb*, London: Comedia Publishing.

Austin, J.L. (1996) 'Performatives and Connotatives', in P. Cobley (ed.) *The Communication Theory Reader*, London: Routledge, pp. 255–62.

Bakhtin, Mikhail (1999) 'The Problem of Speech Genres', in Jaworski and Coupland (1999) pp. 121–132.

Barker, Chris (2002) *Making Sense of Cultural Studies: Central Problems and Critical Debates*, London: Sage.

Barnard, Stephen (2000) *Studying Radio*, London: Edward Arnold.

Barthes, Roland (1967) *Elements of Semiology*, trans. Annette Lavers and Colin Smith, London: Cape.

Barthes, Roland (1972) *Mythologies*, trans. Annette Lavers, London: Cape.

Barthes, Roland (1975) *S/Z*, trans. Richard Miller, London: Cape.

Barthes, Roland (1984) *Image, Music, Text*, trans. Stephen Heath, reprint of 1977 edn, London: Flamingo.

Beattie, Geoffrey (1983) *Talk: an Analysis of Speech and Non-verbal Behaviour in Conversation*, Milton Keynes: Open University Press.

Belbin, R.M. (1981) *Management Teams: Why they Succeed or Fail*, Oxford: Heinemann.

Bell, Judith (1999) *Doing Your Research Project: a Guide for First-time Researchers in Education and Social Science*, Buckingham: Open University Press.

Belsey, Andrew and Chadwick, Ruth (eds) (1992) *Ethical Issues in Journalism and the Media*, London: Routledge.

Berger, Arthur Asa (1991) *Media Research Techniques*, London: Sage.

Berger, Arthur Asa (2000) *Media and Communication Research Methods*, London: Sage.

Bernstein, Basil (1971) *Class, Codes and Control*, London: Routledge.

Bertens, Hans and Natoli, Joseph (2002) *Postmodernism: the Key Figures*, Oxford: Blackwell.

Blaxter, Loraine, Hughes, Christina and Tight, Malcolm (1996) *How to research*, Buckingham: Open University Press.

Boyne, Roy (2000) 'Structuralism', in Bryan S. Turner (ed.), *The Blackwell Companion to Social Theory*, 2nd edn, Oxford: Blackwell, pp. 160–90.

Burgoon, J.K., Buller, D.B. and Woodall, W.G. (1996) *Non-verbal Communication: the Unspoken Dialogue*, 2nd edn, New York: McGraw-Hill.

Burnett, Rebecca (2000) *Technical Communication*, Boston, MA: Thomson Learning.

Calhoun, Craig, Gerteis, Joseph, Moody, James, Pfaff, Steven and Virk, Indermohan (eds) (2002) *Contemporary Sociology Theory*, Oxford: Blackwell.

Carr, Brian (ed.) (1975) *Betrand Russell: an Introduction*, London: Allen and Unwin.

Cashdan, Asher and Jordin, Martin (eds) (1987) *Studies in Communication*, Oxford: Blackwell.

Chilton, P. (ed.) (1985) *Language and the Nuclear Arms Debate: Nukespeak Today*, London: Frances Pinter.

Chomsky, Noam (1957) *Syntactic Structures*, The Hague: Mouton.

Chomsky, Noam (1965) *Aspects of the Theory of Syntax*, Cambridge, MA: MIT Press.

Cobley, P. (ed.) (1996) *The Communication Theory Reader*, London: Routledge.

Collinsons, D., Kirkup, G., Kyd, R. and Slocombe, L. (1992) *Plain English*, 2nd edn, Buckingham: Open University Press.

Corner, John and Hawthorn, Jeremy (eds) (1989) *Communication Studies: an Introductory Reader*, London: Edward Arnold.

Crompton, A. (1987) *The Craft of Copywriting*, 2nd edn, London: Hutchinson Business.

Crystal, David (1971) *Linguistics*, Harmondsworth: Penguin.

Crystal, David (1988) *Rediscover Grammar*, Harlow: Longman.

Cutts, Martin and Maher, Chrissie (1986) *The Plain English Story*, Stockport: Plain English Campaign.

Danaher, Geoff, Schirato, Tony and Webb, Jen (2002) *Understanding Foucault*, London: Sage.

Denscombe, Martyn (1998) *The Good Research Guide for Small-scale Social Research Projects*, Buckingham: Open University Press.

Docherty, Thomas (ed.) (1993) *Postmodernism: a Reader*, Hemel Hemstead: Harvester Wheatsheaf.

Durham, Meenakshi Gigi and Kellner, Douglas M. (eds) (2001) *Media and Cultural Studies: Keyworks*, Oxford: Blackwell.

Dutton, William H. (ed.) (1996) *Information and Communication Technologies*, Oxford: Oxford University Press.

Eco, Umberto (1977) *A Theory of Semiotics*, London: Macmillan.

Eco, Umberto (1998) *The Name of the Rose*, London: Vintage.

Edgar, A. and Sedgwick, P. (1999) *Key Concepts in Cultural Theory*, London: Routledge.

Edgar, A. and Sedgwick, P. (2002) *Cultural Theory: the Key Thinkers*, London: Routledge.

Elliott, Anthony (ed.) (1999) *The Blackwell Reader in Contemporary Social Theory*, Oxford: Blackwell.

Ellis, Andrew and Beattie, Geoffrey (1986) *The Psychology of Language and Communication*, London: George Weidenfeld and Nicolson.

Ennis, Robert H. (1996) *Critical Thinking*, Upper Saddle River, NJ: Prentice Hall.

Fairbairn G.J. and Winch, C. (1997) *Reading, Writing and Reasoning: a Guide for Students*, Buckingham: Open University Press.

Fairclough, Norman (1995a) *Media Discourse*, London: Edward Arnold.

Fairclough, Norman (1995b) *Critical Discourse Analysis: the Critical Study of Language*, Harlow: Pearson Education.

Fairclough, Norman (1999) 'Linguistic and Intertextual Analysis within Discourse Analysis', in Adam Jaworski and Nikolas Coupland (eds), *The Discourse Reader*, London: Routledge, pp. 183–211.

Fielding, Guy and Hartley, Peter (1987) 'The Telephone: a Neglected Medium', in Asher Cashdan and Martin Jordin (eds), *Studies in Communication*, Oxford: Blackwell, pp. 110–24.

Fiske, John (1990) *Introduction to Communication Studies*, 2nd edn, London: Routledge.

Fleming, J. (1998) *Web Navigation: Designing the User Experience*, Sebastapol, CA: O'Reilly.

Foddy, William (1993) *Constructing Questions for Interviews and Questionnaires*, Cambridge: Cambridge University Press.

Foucault, Michel (1999) 'The Incitement to Discourse', in Jaworski and Coupland (1999) pp. 514–522.

Foucault, Michel (2002) *The Archaeology of Knowledge*, trans. A.M. Sheridan Smith, reissue of 1972 edn, London: Routledge.

Freeborn, D., French, P. and Langford, D. (1993) *Varieties of English*, 2nd edn, London: Macmillan.

Freud, Sigmund (1975) *The Interpretation of Dreams*, trans. James Strachey, Harmondsworth: Penguin.

Geraghty, Christine and Lusted, David (eds) (1998) *The Television Studies Book*, London: Edward Arnold.

Gibson, William (1986) *Neuromancer*, London: HarperCollins.

Giglio, P.P. (ed.) (1972) *Language and Social Context*, Harmondsworth: Penguin.

Gill, David and Adams, Bridget (1998) *ABC of Communication Studies*, 2nd edn, Cheltenham: Nelson Thornes.

Glasgow University Media Group (1976) *Bad News*, London: Routledge and Kegan Paul.

Goffman, Erving (1971) *The Presentation of Self in Everyday Life*, Harmondsworth: Penguin.

Goffman, Erving (1981) *Forms of Talk*, Oxford: Blackwell.

Goffman, Erving (1999) 'On Face-Work: An Analysis of Ritual Elements in Social Interaction', in Jaworski and Coupland (1999) pp. 306–320.

Gramsci, Antonio (1971) *Selections from the Prison Notebooks*, ed. and trans. Quintin Hoare and Geoffrey Nowell Smith, New York: International Publishers.

Griffin, E. (2000) *A First Look at Communication Theory*, 4th edn, Boston, MA: McGraw-Hill.

Gruber, Howard E. and Voneche, J, Jacques (eds) (1977) *The Essential Piaget*, London: Routledge and Kegan Paul.

Habermas, Jürgen (1989) *Critical Theory and Society: A Reader*, ed. Stephen Eric Bronner and Douglas M. Kellner, trans. Sara Lennox and Frank Lennox, New York: Routledge.

Hall, David D. (1996) *Cultures of Print: Essays in the History of the Book*, Amherst, MA: University of Massachusetts Press.

Hall, Stuart (2001) "Encoding/Decoding" in Durham and Kellner (2001) pp. 166–176.

Hall, Stuart, Hobson, Dorothy, Lowe, Andrew and Willis, Paul (eds) (1980) *Culture, Media, Language* London: Hutchinson.

Halliday, M.A.K (1973) *Explorations in the Functions of Language*, London: Edward Arnold.

Halliday, M.A.K (1978) *Language as Social Semiotic: the Social Interpretation of Language and Meaning*, London: Edward Arnold.

Hampson, Liz (1994) *How's Your Dissertation Going? Students Share the Rough Reality of Dissertation and Project Work*, Lancaster: Unit for Innovation in Higher Education, Lancaster University.

Hargie, O. (ed.) (1997) *The Handbook of Communication Skills*, London: Routledge.

Hart, C. (1998) *Doing a Literature Review: Releasing the Social Science Research Imagination*, London: Sage

Hartley, James (1994) *Designing Instructional Text*, 3rd edn, London: Kogan Page.

Hartley, Peter (1997) *Group Communication*, London: Routledge.

Hartley, Peter (1999) *Interpersonal Communication*, 2nd edn, London: Routledge.

Hartley, Peter and Bruckmann, Clive G. (2002) *Business Communication*, London: Routledge.

Hawkes, Terence (1983) *Structuralism and Semiotics*, revised edn, London: Routledge.

Hoare, Quintin and Smith, Geoffrey Nowell (eds and trans.) (1971) *Selections from the Prison Notebooks of Antonio Gramsci*, New York: International Publishers.

Hoggart, Richard (1981) *The Uses of Literacy*, Harmondsworth: Penguin.

Hollows, Joanne, Hutchings, Peter and Jancovich, Mark (eds) (2000) *The Film Studies Reader*, London: Edward Arnold.

Horton, William (1994) *Designing and Writing Online Documentation, Hypermedia for Self-Supporting Products*, 2nd edn, New York: John Wiley.

Jacobson, Robert (ed.) (1999) *Information Design*, Cambridge, MA: MIT Press.

Jakobson, Roman J. (1971) *Selected Writings*, vol. 2, The Hague: Mouton.

Jakobson, R. J. (1999) 'Linguistics and Poetics', in Jaworski and Coupland pp. 54–62.

Jaworski, Adam and Coupland, Nikolas (eds) (1999) *The Discourse Reader*, London: Routledge.

Jay, R. (1995) *How to Write Proposals and Reports that Get Results*, London: Pitman.

Jung, Carl Gustav (1998) *The Essential Jung: Selected Writings*, ed. Anthony Storr, London: Fontana.

Kearns, Kate (2000) *Semantics*, London: Macmillan.

Kellogg, Ronald (1994) *The Psychology of Writing*, Oxford: Oxford University Press.

Kress, Gunther (1985) *Linguistic Processes in Sociocultural Practice*, Geelong: Deakin University Press.

Kress, Gunther (1989) 'The Structures of Speech and Writing', in Corner and Hawthorn (1989) pp. 85–93.

Kress, Gunther and van Leeuwen, T. (1996) *Reading Images: the Grammar of Visual Design*, London: Routledge.

Kress, Gunther and van Leeuwen, T. (1999) 'Representation and Interaction; Designing the Position of the Viewer', in Jaworski and Coupland pp. 377–404.

Labov, William (1972a) 'The Logic of Nonstandard English', in Giglio pp.179–218.

Labov, William (1972b) 'The Study of Language in its Social Context', in Giglio pp.283–307.

Labov, William (1999) 'The Transformation of Experience in Narrative', in Jaworski and Coupland (1999) pp. 221–235.

Lacan, J. (1977) *Ecrits: a Selection*, London: Tavistock.

Lacan, Jacques (1977) *Écrits: a Selection*, trans. Alan Sheridan, London: Tavistock.

Lacey, Nick (1998) *Image and Representation: Key Concepts in Media Studies*, London: Macmillan.

Leach, E. (1985) *Lévi-Strauss*, revised edn. London: Fontana.

Leader, Darian and Groves, Judy (1995), *Lacan for Beginners*, Cambridge: Icon Books.

Leavis, F.R. (1993) *The Great Tradition*, Harmondsworth: Penguin.

Leavis, F.R. and Thompson, Denys (1977) *Culture and Environment*, Westport, CT: Greenwood Press.

Leech, Geoffrey (1974) *Semantics*, Harmondsworth: Penguin.

Leiss, William, Kline, Stephen and Jhally, Sut (1986) *Social Communication in Advertising: Persons, Products and Images of Well-being*, London: Methuen.

Lemert, C. and Branaman, A. (eds) (1997) *The Goffman Reader*, Oxford: Blackwell.

Lévi-Strauss, Claude (1968) *Structural Anthropology*, London: Allen Lane/Penguin.

Lewis, Jeff (2002) *Cultural Studies: the Basics*, London: Sage.

Lichty, T. (1989) *Design Principles for Desktop Publishers*, Glenview, IL: Scott, Foresman.

Lister, Martin, Dovery, Jon, Giddings, Seth, Grant, Iain and Kelly, Kieran (2003) *New Media: a Critical Introduction*, London: Routledge.

Lyon, David (1997) 'The Roots of the Information Society Idea', in Tim O'Sullivan and Yvonne Jewkes (eds), *The Media Studies Reader*, London: Edward Arnold, pp. 384–402.

Lyotard, Jean-François (1979) *The Postmodern Condition: a Report on Knowledge*, trans. Geoff Bennington and Brian Massumi, Manchester: Manchester University Press.

McIntosh, Ian (ed.) (1997) *Classical Sociological Theory: a Reader*, Edinburgh: Edinburgh University Press.

McLean, R. (1980) *The Thames and Hudson Manual of Typography*, London: Thames and Hudson.

McLuhan, Marshall (1962) *The Gutenberg Galaxy*, London: Routledge and Kegan Paul.

McLuhan, Marshall (1964) *Understanding Media*, London: Routledge and Kegan Paul.

McQuail, Denis and Windahl, Sven (1993) *Communication Models for the Study of Mass Communications*, 2nd edn, London: Longman.

Macey, David (ed.) (2002) *The Penguin Dictionary of Critical Theory*, London: Penguin.

MacNealy M.S. (1999) *Strategies for Empirical Research in Writing*, Boston, MA: Allyn and Bacon.

Mandel, S. (1987) *Effective Presentation Skills*, London: Kogan Page.

Marris, Paul and Thornham, Sue (eds) (2000) *Media Studies: a Reader*, 2nd edn New York: New York University Press.

Marshall L. and Rowland, F. (1993) *A Guide to Learning Independently*, Buckingham: Open University Press.

Marshall, Peter (1997) *Research Methods: How to Design and Conduct a Successful Project*, Plymouth: How to Books.

Marshall, Stewart and Williams, Noel (1986) *Exercises in Teaching Communication*, London: Kogan Page.

Merquior, J.G. (1991) *Foucault*, London: Fontana.

Minto, Barbara (1991) *The Pyramid Principle: Logic in Writing and Thinking*, London: Pitman.

Montgomery, Martin (1986) *An Introduction to Language and Society*, London: Routledge.

Morley, David and Chen, Kuan-Hsing (eds) (1996) *Stuart Hall: Critical Dialogues in Cultural Studies*, London: Routledge.

Morris, Pam (ed.) (1994) *The Bakhtin Reader: Selected Writings of Bakhtin, Medvedev and Voloshinov*, London: Edward Arnold.

Neilsen, J. (2000) *Designing Web Usability*, Indianapolis, IN: New Riders.

O'Sullivan, Tim and Jewkes, Yvonne (eds) (1997) *The Media Studies Reader*, London: Edward Arnold.

O'Sullivan, Tim, Hartley, John, Saunders, Danny, Montgomery, Martin and Fiske, John (1994) *Key Concepts in Communication and Cultural Studies*, 2nd ed. London: Routledge.

Peirce, C.S. (1992) *The Essential Peirce: Selected Philosophical Writings*, vol.1, ed. N. Houser and C. Kloesel, Bloomington, IN: Indiana University Press.

Peirce, C.S. (1996) 'A guess at the riddle' in Cobley pp. 48–60.

Perkins, Tessa and Barker, Martin (1997) 'Rethinking Stereotypes' in Tim O'Sullivan and Yvonne Jewkes (eds) *The Media Studies Reader*, London: Edward Arnold.

Piaget, Jean (1932) *The Language and Thought of the Child*, 2nd ed. London: Routledge.

Piaget, Jean (1977) *The Essential Piaget*, ed. Howard E. Gruber and J. Jacques Vonache, London: Routledge and Kegan Paul.

Price, Jonathan and Price, Lisa (2002) *Hot Text: Web Writing That Works*, Indianapolis, IN: New Riders.

Price, Stuart (1993) *Media Studies*, Harlow: Longman.

Price, Stuart (1997) *The Complete A–Z Media and Communication Handbook*, London: Hodder and Stoughton.

Propp, Vladimir (1971) *The Morphology of the Folktale*, trans L. Scott, Austin, TX: University of Texas Press.

Qualter, T.H. (1997) 'The Social Role of Advertising', in Tim O'Sullivan and Yvonne Jewkes (eds) *The Media Studies Reader*, London: Edward Arnold, pp. 154–64.

Race, Phil (1999) *How to Get a Good Degree*, Buckingham: Open University Press.

Reid, M. and Hammersley, R. (2000) *Communicating Successfully in Groups: a Practical Guide for the Workplace*, London: Routledge.

Robinson, Robin (1992) *Beginners Guide to Jungian Psychology*, York Beach, ME: Nicolas-Hays.

Robson, Colin (1993) *Real World Research*, Oxford: Blackwell.

Rosenfeld, L. and Morville, P. (1998) *Information Architecture for the World Wide Web*, Sebastapol, CA: O'Reilly.

Rosengren, K.E. (1999) *Communication: an Introduction*, London: Sage.

Rowntree, D. (1998) *Learn How to Study: A Realistic Approach*, New York: Time Warner.

Rudestam, Kjell Erik and Newton, Rae R. (1992) *Surviving Your Dissertation: a Comprehensive Guide to Content and Process*, London: Sage.

St Maur, S. and Butman, J. (1991) *Writing Words That Sell*, London: Mercury Books.

Saussure, Ferdinand de (1974) *Course in General Linguistics*, trans. Wade Baskin, Glasgow: Fontana/Collins.

Saussure, Ferdinand de (1996a) 'The Object of Linguistics', in Cobley pp. 37–47.

Saussure, Ferdinand de (1996b) 'Linguistic Value', in Cobley pp. 99–114.

Schiffrin, Deborah, Tannen, Deborah and Hamilton, Heidi (2001) *The Handbook of Discourse Analysis*, Oxford: Blackwell.

Schriver, K.A. (1997) *Dynamics in Document Design: Creating Text for Readers*, New York: John Wiley.

Searle, John (1969) *Speech Acts: an Essay in the Philosophy of Language*, Cambridge: Cambridge University Press.

Searle, John (1972) 'What is a Speech Act?' in P.P. Giglio (ed.) *Language and Social Context*, Harmondsworth: Penguin, pp. 136–56.

Shannon, C. and Weaver, W. (1949) *The Mathematical Theory of Communication*, Urbana, IL: University of Illinois Press.

Sharples, M. (1999) *How We Write: Writing as Creative Design*, London: Routledge.

Skinner, B.F. (1974) *About Behaviourism*, London: Cape.

Smith, N. and Wilson, D. (1979) *Modern Linguistics: the Results of Chomsky's Revolution*, Harmondsworth: Penguin.

Sontag, Susan (ed.) (1982) *A Barthes Reader*, London: Cape.

Sparks, Suzanne D. (1999) *The Manager's Guide to Business Writing*, New York: McGraw-Hill.

Stevenson, N. (1995) *Understanding Media Cultures: Social Theory and Mass Communication*, London: Sage.

Stevenson, N. (1997) 'Critical Perspectives within Audience Research', in Tim O'Sullivan and Yvonne Jewkes (eds) *The Media Studies Reader*, London: Edward Arnold, pp. 231–48.

Storey, John (ed.) (1996) *What is Cultural Studies? A Reader*, London: Edward Arnold.

Storey, John (1997) *An Introduction to Cultural Theory and Popular Culture*, 2nd edn, London: Prentice Hall.

Storr, Anthony (1973) *Jung*, London: Fontana.

Storr, Anthony (1998) *The Essential Jung: Selected Writings*, London: Fontana.

Strinati, Dominic (1997) 'Postmodernism and Popular Culture', in Tim O'Sullivan and Yvonne Jewkes (eds) *The Media Studies Reader*, London: Edward Arnold, pp. 421–33.

Sussams, John E. (1983) *How to Write Effective Reports*, Aldershot: Gower.

Swetnam, Derek (2000) *Writing your Dissertation: How to Plan, Prepare and Present Your Work Successfully*, Oxford: How to Books Ltd.

Tannenbaum, R.S. (1998) *Theoretical Foundations of Multimedia*, New York: Freeman.

Trask R.L. (1995) *Language: the Basics*, London: Routledge.

Trudgill, Peter (1983) *Sociolinguistics*, Harmondsworth: Penguin.

Turk, C. and Kirkman, J. (1989) *Effective writing: Improving Scientific, Technical and Business Communication*, London: E and F.N. Spon.

Turner, Bryan S. (2000) *The Blackwell Companion to Social Theory*, 2nd edn, Oxford: Blackwell.

Turner, G.W. (1973) *Stylistics*, Harmondsworth: Penguin.

Van Dijk, Teun A. (1991) *Racism and the Press*, London: Routledge.

Van Dijk, Teun A. (1999) 'Discourse and the Denial of Racism', in Jaworski and Coupland pp. 541–558.

Van Leeuwen, T. and Jewitt, C (2001) *The Handbook of Visual Analysis*, London: Sage.

Vygotsky, Lev Semenovich (1962) *Thought and Language*, trans. Eugenia Hanfmann and Gertrude Vakar, Cambridge, MA: MIT Press.

Wagner, Eric (1988) *The Computer Display Designer's Handbook*, Lund: Chartwell-Bratt Ltd.

Waters, Crystal (1997) *Universal Web Design*, Indianapolis, IN: New Riders.

Watson, James and Hill, Anne (2000) *Dictionary of Media and Communication Studies*, 5th edn, London: Edward Arnold.

Williams, Kevin (1992) 'Something More Important Than Truth: Ethical Issues in War Reporting', in Andrew Belsey and Ruth Chadwick (eds) *Ethical Issues in Journalism and the Media*, London: Routledge, pp. 154–70.

Williams, Noel (1991) *The Computer, the Writer and the Learner*, London: Springer Verlag.

Williams, Noel (1998) 'Educational Multimedia: Where's the Interaction?', in Moira Monteith (ed.) *IT For Learning Enhancement*, Exeter: Intellect.

Williams, Noel and Hartley, Peter (eds) (1990) *Technology in Human Communication*, London: Frances Pinter.

Williams, Raymond (1961) *Culture and society 1780–1950*, Harmondsworth: Penguin.

Williams, Raymond (1962) *Communications*, Harmondsworth: Penguin.

Williams, Raymond (1983) *Keywords: a Vocabulary of Culture and Society*, London: Fontana.

Windahl, S., Signitzer, B. and Olson, J.T. (1992) *Using Communication Theory: an Introduction to Planned Communication*, London: Sage.

Winston, B. (1998) *Media Technology and Society: a History, from the Telegraph to the Internet*, London: Routledge.

Wittgenstein, Ludwig (1969) *Tractatus Logico-Philosophicus*, trans. D.F. Pears and B.F. McGuinness, 2nd impression, London: Routledge and Kegan Paul.

Wittgenstein, Ludwig (1972) *Philosophical Investigations*, Oxford: Blackwell.

Worsley, Peter (ed.) (1991) *The New Modern Sociology Readings*, London: Penguin.

INDEX